THE UNKNOWN MARX

THE UNKNOWN MARX

Reconstructing a Unified Perspective

TAKAHISA OISHI

Foreword by Terrell Carver

LONDON • STERLING, VIRGINIA
in association with Takushoku University, Tokyo

First published 2001
by PLUTO PRESS
345 Archway Road, London N6 5AA
and 22883 Quicksilver Drive,
Sterling, VA 20166–2012, USA

www.plutobooks.com

British Library Cataloguing in Publication Data
A catalogue record for this book is available from
the British Library

Library of Congress Cataloging in Publication Data
Oishi, Takahisa, 1950–
The unknown Marx : reconstructing a unified perspective / Takahisa Oishi; foreword by Terrell Carver.
p. cm.
ISBN 0–7453–1698–0 — ISBN 0–7453–1697–2 (pbk.)
1. Marx, Karl, 1818–1883. 2. Philosophy, Marxist. 3. Capitalism. 4. Communism. I. Title.
HX39.5 .O47 2001
335.4—dc21
00–009581

ISBN 0 7453 1698 0 hardback
ISBN 0 7453 1697 2 paperback

10 09 08 07 06 05 04 03 02 01
10 9 8 7 6 5 4 3 2 1

Designed and produced for Pluto Press by
Chase Publishing Services, Fortescue, Sidmouth EX10 9QG
Typeset from disk by Stanford DTP Services, Northampton
Printed in the European Union by TJ International, Padstow

Communism (a) still of a political nature, democratic or despotic; (b) with the abolition of the state, but still essentially incomplete and influenced by private property, i.e. by the estrangement of man. In both forms communism already knows itself as the reintegration or return of man into himself, the supersession of man's self-estrangement; but since *it has not yet comprehended the positive essence of private property* or understood the human nature of need, it is still held captive and contaminated by private property. True, *it has understood its concept, but not yet its essence*. (EW (*Economic and Philosophical Manuscripts*), pp. 347; emphasis added.)

Relations of personal dependence (entirely spontaneous at the outset) are the first social forms, in which human productive capacity develops only to a slight extent and at isolated points. Personal independence founded on objective [*sachlicher*] dependence is the second great form, in which a system of general social metabolism, of universal relations, of all-round needs and universal capacities is formed for the first time. *Free individuality, based on the universal development of individuals* and on their subordination of their communal, social productivity as their social wealth, *is the third stage*. The second stage creates the conditions for the third. Patriarchal as well as ancient conditions (feudal, also) thus disintegrate with the development of commerce, of luxury, of money, of exchange value, while modern society arises and grows in the same measure. (G, p. 158; emphasis added.)

But in the same measure as it is understood that labour is the sole source of exchange-value and the active source of use-value, 'capital' is likewise conceived by the same economists, in particular by Ricardo . . . , as the regulator of production, the source of wealth and the aim of production, whereas labour is regarded as wage-labour, whose representative and the real instrument is inevitably a pauper . . . , a mere production cost and instrument of production dependent on a minimum wage and forced to drop even below this minimum as soon as the existing quantity of labour is 'superfluous' for capital. In this contradiction, political economy merely expressed *the essence of capitalist production or, if you like, of wage labour, of labour alienated for itself*, which stands confronted by the wealth it has created as alien wealth, by its own productive power as the productive power of its product, by its enrichment as its own impoverishment and by its social power as the power of society. But this definite, specific, historical form of social labour which is exemplified in capitalist production is proclaimed by these economists as the general, eternal form, as a natural phenomenon, and these relations of production as the absolutely (not historically) necessary, natural and reasonable relations of social labour. (Karl Marx, *Theories of Surplus-Value*, Part III, London: Lawrence & Wishart (1972), p. 259; emphasis added.)

In Memory of
Gillian and Barry Dodd

CONTENTS

ABBREVIATIONS

AD	Friedrich Engels, *Anti-Dühring*. (MEC 25, pp. 5–309)
CAP 1	Karl Marx, *Capital*, Vol. 1, trans. B. Fowkes. The Penguin Group, London, 1976.
CAP 3	Karl Marx, *Capital*, Vol. 3, trans. D. Fernbach, The Penguin Group, London, 1981.
EPM	Karl Marx, *Economic and Philosophical Manuscripts*, 1844. (MEC 3, pp. 229–346) FM:FP First Manuscript, Former Part FM:LP First Manuscript, Latter Part
EW	Karl Marx, *Early Writings*, Penguin Books, London, 1975.
G	Karl Marx, *Grundrisse: Foundations of the Critique of Political Economy (Rough Draft)*, trans. M. Nicolaus, Penguin Books, 1973.
GI	Karl Marx, 'I Feuerbach' in *The German Ideology*. (MEC 5, pp. 19–93)
MEC*	Karl Marx and Friedrich Engels, *Collected Works*, Lawrence & Wishart, London , 1975, etc.
MEGA1*	Karl Marx and Friedrich Engels, *Historisch-kritische Gesamtausgabe*, ed. D. Ryazanov et al., Frankfurt and Berlin, 1927, etc. (incomplete)
MEGA2*	Karl Marx and Friedrich Engels, *Gesamtausgabe*, Dietz, Berlin, 1972, etc. (in progress)
MEW*	Karl Marx and Friedrich Engels, *Werke*, Dietz, Berlin, 1956, etc.
OCPE	Friedrich Engels, *Outlines of a Critique of Political Economy*, 1844. (MEC 3, pp. 418–43)
POP	Karl Marx, *The Poverty of Philosophy*, 1847. (MEC 6, pp. 105–212)
SEC	Proudhon, *System of Economic Contradictions, or The Philosophy of Poverty*, 1846.
SW	Karl Marx, *Selected Writings*, ed. D. McLellan, Oxford, 1977.

* multi-volume collections and volumes are indicated thus:
MEC 1, MEW 33, etc.

FOREWORD

Terrell Carver
Professor of Political Theory, University of Bristol

Marx is not only unknown, he is undead. He lies very unquietly in the grave. The more researchers and scholars stalk him with the wooden stake, the more protean will be his spectres. Experiencing Marx is an activity in the present, and in the present there will be an increasing number of Marxes to be experienced. This is so in the usual way with 'great authors', because as we change, so our reading of their texts changes in accord with our concerns; authors who have no contemporary resonance are not read, and cease to be 'great'. This is also true of Marx in another way, again a way he has in common with other 'greats'. Which works to read, what order to read them in, their relative hierarchy of importance, what exactly each is about and how they 'add up' are questions that will be asked again and again. There is no definitive view for all time, not from the author, nor from his family or friends.

Indeed as Paul Thomas has shown in his essay 'Critical Reception: Marx Then and Now',[1] early versions of 'the truth about Marx' were based on what there was available to read at the time, and since then the amount of Marx in print has multiplied by an astronomical figure. Currently the complete *Marx-Engels Gesamtausgabe* (MEGA2) is aiming at 130 double volumes, surely one of the largest scholarly projects ever undertaken. Moreover, as Thomas also shows, 'the truth about Marx' has never been singular or unquestioned, as orthodoxies, revisions and critiques have abounded since his death in 1883. The first 'truth about Marx' is traceable back as far as 1859, to Engels's earliest reviews.[2]

Using a clear and direct logic, Takahisa Oishi ruthlessly blows away some of the most hallowed 'truths' about Marx. Oishi's new book is unusually fresh and timely, and will contribute mightily to the re-evaluation of Marx after the 'fall of the Wall'. In the nature of the exercise it is unlikely that Oishi will succeed in disposing of these familiar 'truths' completely, but it is certain that readers of this remarkable work will experience an intellectual and possibly even physical experience of Pauline proportions. Whether they will continue along the same road as Oishi is another question, but they will certainly feel profoundly shaken. This has to be a productive experience, as even the most hallowed 'truths' need to be tested; otherwise we are left with the deadest of dogmas, as John Stuart Mill – not someone Marx admired, at least as an economist and logician – argued persuasively in *On Liberty* (1859).[3] The reader of Oishi's work will need to be prepared for a very radical and very controversial book.

Takahisa Oishi was promoted to Professor of the History of Economic Theories at Takushoku University, Tokyo, in 1993. This is a distinguished appointment following on from his work at that University, where he started as a lecturing assistant in 1981. Prior to that he completed masters' degrees in economics at Chuo University, Tokyo, and Yokohama National University, Japan. He has published papers in English on Ricardo and Marx in Japanese international journals, and three books on economic history and analysis in Japanese. The Marx–Engels '*Forscher*' (Researchers) is an active group of academics from universities all over Japan, and he is a respected contributor to their debates and conferences.

Oishi positions his revelation of an 'unknown Marx' against a backdrop of Soviet Marxist commentary on Marx and Marxism. This in itself will strike most Anglo-American readers as a fairly unusual perspective, at least since the time of the early Cold War in the 1950s. By the 1960s in 'the West' most Marxists and anti-Marxists were rather more relaxed about the previous linkage between the 'Red Terror Doctor' and the 'World Communist Threat' (or 'Revolution', depending on your political orientation). What comes across at this juncture from Oishi's perspective, however, is the extent to which many of the 'truths' about Marx after the 1950s were shared by orthodox, even Stalinist, Marxists, *and* by Western commentators (both pro- and anti-Marx/Marxism). This happened unbeknownst and unacknowledged, creating a sanitised tradition of 'common knowledge'.

Again, this is something that Thomas notes in his essay on the reception of Marx by readers and followers. Indeed the idea that Marx had a 'reception' is itself productively unsettling, because for those accepting conventional views, 'the truth about Marx' just *is* what it is for anyone to receive at any time. That a history of Marx's 'reception' can be written at all implies a malleability in the story that for many commentators is frankly unwelcome, or at least for them any major contribution or justifiable revision would be almost unthinkable. Paradoxically as the history of this tradition has come down to us, 'revisionists' did not really revise Marx – they were instead said to have created 'revisionism', thus leaving the conventional Marx – of the (singular) 'received wisdom' – in place. Oishi's account is useful in providing an 'outsider's view' of the situation, i.e., someone rather outside the conventions of Anglo-American commentary on Marx. What he says, rightly, is that this tradition shares much more with orthodox, even Stalinist accounts, than is generally admitted.

Oishi also uses Japanese scholarship, as yet little known in Anglo-American or indeed 'Western' circles, notably an edition of *The German Ideology*[4] that is by far the best (the *Marx-Engels Gesamtausgabe* has not yet managed to produce its own complete edition). Oishi also draws on the

Japanese tradition of meticulous attention to textual detail over and above any 'grand narratives' as to what 'the truth' is supposed to be. This allows him to be very sceptical of interpretations of Marx that are filtered through Engels, as it is from Engels that the foundational narratives (or 'truth about Marx') are ultimately derived, saving those left by Marx himself.

Marx, of course, had the advantage of leaving his works to speak in his name, as well as his own bare autobiographical sketch and very sparing reflective commentary on what he said, and what he was doing when he said it. Authorial purpose and contextualised politics play an important role in Oishi's approach to Marx's work, and in his ordering and evaluation of the texts we now have. These, after all, were the ones that Marx had, at least in his own mind – because he himself had written them – and which he is generally known to have had to hand in physical form, anyway.

Oishi's book is not, however, about unravelling Engels from Marx, but rather about putting Marx together in a new way, a way that departs from 'Western' and Stalinist Marxism, and hence from Engels. Oishi's bold claim is that his reading of Marx makes sense of the *oeuvre* as Marx saw it, and in addition makes better sense of his thought and activities for us now, than the traditional interpretative framework derived from Engels and encompassed in the Marxist, anti-Marxist and non-Marxist tradition.

In the first instance this involves a methodological break with almost all previous commentary, which has been organised chronologically as a form of intellectual biography with periodisations or stages along the way. These are teleologically constructed (Marx seems to make the requisite twists and turns in order to get where he needs to go ...) and they typically involve distinct stages (Marx was a liberal, rather than a communist; or a Hegelian rather than a materialist; or a philosopher rather than a social scientist ..., etc.). There are even notable 'breaks' (e.g., between an unscientific and a scientific outlook) or reversals (e.g., accepting and then rejecting Ricardo's theory of value). Rather than tell the Marx story as a periodised intellectual biography riven with hindsight, Oishi radically resets the analytical focus on Marx as *continuity*, albeit developmental. This has the advantage of directing the reader's attention thematically rather than merely chronologically, and it produces a different emphasis on what Marx was saying and which works are most important.

Oishi presents the first genuine re-evaluation of the 1844 'Economic and Philosophical Manuscripts' since the foundational ('Western') commentaries by John Plamenatz and David McLellan in the 1960s and 1970s.[5] These conformed to the tradition of periodisation in intellectual biography, by presenting an 'early Marx', who was rather self-contained in this period. The later story was bracketed off by 'breaks' in outlook, or reversals in content, or at least by a drift from 'philosophy' into 'economics'. This 'early Marx' was a philosopher in the ruminative mode, interested in the classic questions of 'human nature' and its progressive realisation in 'history'. These questions were posed at a high level of generalisation and at a low level of contingency, i.e., the commentary recounted Marx's 'thought' at a level rather above contemporary personalities and events. In this respect 'labour', and particularly 'alienated labour', seemed far more interesting and potent categories than 'wages' or 'value', and much more philosophical in character than economic.

Plamenatz followed a method of explicating the text, without apparently commenting very critically on what he made of it (except for moments of puzzlement), and McLellan rather emphasised the apparently redemptive character of the story as a quasi-religious narrative of faith (after alienation would come emancipation). Neither was particularly concerned to link the 'early Marx' formally and thoroughly with the later 'economic' writings, not least because neither posed as an expert on those works, and neither really wished to become involved in the 'economic' perspective that they assumed this would imply. Mészáros's study[6] of the 'Economic and Philosophical Manuscripts' from the same period is rather closer to Oishi's outlook, but it does not itself follow through on Oishi's hypothesis, namely that a developmental line extends directly from the 1844 manuscript works straight through to *Capital*. Other commentators, while noticing that such a line could be traced, have not done the scholarly job that Oishi has undertaken in *The Unknown Marx*.[7]

Oishi's hypothesis has a number of immediate consequences: Marx's *Poverty of Philosophy* (1846) assumes a new importance, a view not taken by any other commentator that I am aware of; and the *German Ideology* manuscripts (1845–6) and indeed the 'materialist interpretation of history' supposedly inaugurated there, become far less important as landmark events in Marx's intellectual development, and perforce far less interesting in themselves anyway. Oishi suggests that the *German Ideology* be demoted to a 'miscellany', both because it is an insoluble Marx–Engels conundrum textually and because its supposedly empirical thesis about the stages and causes of historical 'developments' is a sideline compared with the real thrust of Marx's over-riding project: the critique of political economy.

Moreover Oishi's work also suggests that 'Marx's theory of history' has been pursued, beginning with Engels, at least partly because its propositions seem to lend themselves to formulations that can be empirically tested, and that this 'scientific' mode of procedure would and could carry over into his 'more difficult' economic studies. Most of all, this hypothesis upsets the status of Marx's 1859 'Preface' to *A Contribution to the Critique of Political Economy*, which contains a restatement of the 'materialist' propositions of the German Ideology.[8] Or rather Oishi presents a new reading of this classic text, one that takes the exact terms of Marx's autobiographical account of his early days much more seriously, and so devalues the empirical and apparently testable propositions about history as a mere sketch or 'thread'. For those whose 'Marx' just *is* the Marx of the 'materialist interpretation of history', starting of course with Engels (in 1859), this view is anathema. Engels would be turning in his grave at this, if he had a grave (his ashes were scattered into the sea off Eastbourne). From Oishi's perspective, the 'materialist interpretation of history' could almost go the same way, and we would be none the worse off.

Oishi's exposition of Marx's method of immanent critique – aimed ultimately at communicating meaning (rather than 'empirical' truth) and at stimulating political action (rather than 'scientific' results) – serves him well in linking the EPM through to the *Poverty of Philosophy* and on to the critical heights of *Capital*. What this trajectory downgrades is the 'empirical science' into which Engels, and Marx's self-styled son-in-law Edward Aveling, sought to fit Marx as the new Darwin.[9] Indeed Engels's further attempts to identify Marx with a 'materialist dialectic' derived from Hegel – the consummate philosophical idealist – look even more strained in this light, and even less relevant to Marx and to his varied political and intellectual relationships with Hegel's works during his career.[10]

Thus EPM emerges from Oishi's account as a reliable if early version of the later Marx – the later Marx of *Capital*. It follows from this view that EPM is not to be bracketed off as unreadably primitive or wrong in the light of Marx's later views on labour or value, nor as intrinsically philosophical or Hegelian, in the light of recent commentators' preferences for the supposedly more discursive and inspiring style of the 'early' Marx as compared with the 'mature' Marx of the 1860s. It follows from this that *Capital* itself is open to a more nuanced reading, one that tries neither to fit it into an 'economic' framework nor into a 'scientific' one demanding empirical proofs. Crucial to this exercise is Oishi's work in establishing a highly nuanced account of Marx's very steady critical encounter with Ricardo, seeing the close fit between Ricardian economics and the operative concepts of commercial society, on the one hand, and the normative and analytical gap, on the other hand, between Ricardo's political economy and Marx's own critique of its categories.

Oishi's perspective usefully disentangles Marx's praise for the early Engels's 'Outlines of a Critique of Political Economy' from his own deeper contemporary perspective on how a communist analysis would differ from that of a 'minor Ricardian', an appellation that fits Engels far better than Marx. Oishi's work thus adds to the growing scepticism concerning the later Engels as editor of Marx's manuscripts for volumes two and three of *Capital*.[11] This scepticism concerns both Engels' competence with the political economy that Marx tackled between 1843 (when Engels wrote his 'Outlines') and the period of his tenure as Marx's legatee and editor (1883–95), and the extent to which Engels was even fully cognisant of the precise character and profound subtlety of an immanent critique such as the one mounted by Marx in *Capital*.

Oishi's work thus deconstructs the grand narrative of Marx as a gifted Hegelian undertaking a materialist transformation of a dialectical method applicable to unified sciences of nature, history and thought, as Engels put it in *Anti-Dühring*.[12] For Oishi, Marx's project was less grandiose and more politically relevant, namely undermining the contemporary science of society (political economy) from an overtly political perspective, challenging its empiricism and its anachronism as an ideology. This is why for Oishi the materialist interpretation of history is not co-equal with the theory of surplus value in terms of contributions to 'science', as the two are for Engels; for Oishi, Marx does not have to be a polymath. Writing a brilliant and influential critique of political economy made him notable as a historian and as a philosopher, but these achievements were in aid of a project that was neither history nor philosophy, not an empirical thesis about social change nor a methodological key or shortcut to knowledge.

The Unknown Marx presents Marx-on-a-mission, and this gives a unique focus to what we think we know about Marx. This reveals the unknown by rearranging 'the known', and it does this by working upwards from the texts to a highly controversial re-write of the grand narratives about Marx. While readers may wish to differ with Oishi at numerous points along the way, they should stick with him as he boldly goes.

PREFACE

THE PURPOSE AND OBJECT OF THIS BOOK

In this book I am concerned with the thought and theories of Karl Marx (1818–83), in particular with his systematic 'Critique of Political Economy'. Marx's critique has been studied all over the world in Philosophy, Politics, Economics, History, Sociology and other disciplines. For that reason, readers may find the title of this book, *The Unknown Marx*, rather strange. However, Marx is not yet fully known, or at least not known well enough. In a sense he is still unknown, but not because the number of studies concerned with him and his work is limited. He is as yet unknown because he has generally been interpreted under the influence of Soviet Marxism, which differs a very great deal from his own perspective. Soviet Marxism, i.e., Stalinism or Marxism-Leninism, modified Marx's thought and theories in order to justify its oppressive political system. Many commentators have been under the political influence of Stalinism, whether they were aware of this or not.

The purpose of this book is to rebuild Marx's original thought and theories by making a thorough investigation of the process through which Marx's thought was formed. I will demonstrate where and how commentators distort Marx's original system. Marx's process of formation shows us that he had only one system: the 'critique of political economy'. Marx's critique of political economy is not a 'Principles of Political Economy', like Ricardo's, but rather Marx's 'human science' or 'real science',[1] superseding the one-sidedness of both the natural and the social sciences.

Marx's critique of political economy is best expressed in his *Economic and Philosophical Manuscripts* (1844), *Grundrisse* (his manuscripts of 1857–58), and *Capital* (1867). As the first and the most primitive representation of his system, EPM displays its principles and structure, and therefore it serves now as an implicit critique of Soviet Marxism. This is the reason why Soviet Marxists have denied the scientific significance of EPM. They have desperately tried to deny that there is anything of significance in EPM, by observing that EPM was subject to 'self-clarification' in *The German Ideology* (1845–46), by claiming that Marx was merely an idealist in EPM, and by arguing that EPM is merely a miscellany of notes made at different times. However, they also think very highly of *The German Ideology*, another miscellany, to which Marx himself did not give much importance.

Thus a proper evaluation of EPM marks a parting of the ways between Marx and Soviet Marxism, which attempted to negate Marx's 'human science' as merely idealist. In the following introductory discussion I summarise and critique two traditional interpretations of Marxism.

TWO TRADITIONAL INTERPRETATIONS OF MARX'S SYSTEM

The Materialist Interpretation of History and Economics

In traditional interpretations of Marx's system there are two main schemes: 'the materialist interpretation of history' and 'the three origins of Marxism'. In the following discussion I examine first one and then the other.

Marx's system was first summarised as 'the materialist interpretation of history and economics'. This scheme originated in Engels's 'Speech at the Graveside of Karl Marx ' in 1883. There Engels compared Marx with Charles Darwin and asserted that:

1. Marx discovered 'the materialist interpretation of history and the theory of surplus-value'.
2. The 'materialist interpretation of history' is 'a universal law in the development of human history'.

It is true that in *A Contribution to the Critique of Political Economy* (1859) and in *Capital* Marx emphasised his concept 'surplus-value' and noted that he was guided by a 'general result'. However, he did not term this 'general result' the 'materialist interpretation of history'. As far as I know, the term 'materialist interpretation of history' was first used by Engels in his 'Book Review: Karl Marx's *A Contribution to the Critique of Political Economy*' (1859). In the 'Book Review' he called the 'general result at which I [Marx] arrived and which, once won, served as a guiding thread for my [Marx's] studies' the 'materialist interpretation of history'. Engels understood it to be Marx's method, and he emphasised the importance of 'applying' it to modern society.

On the other hand, in the 'Postface to the Second Edition' of *Capital* (1873) Marx terms his method of presentation a 'dialectical method', and the 'general result' the 'materialist basis of my method'.[2] According to the Postface, by 'dialectical method' Marx meant an understanding which 'includes in its positive understanding of what exists a simultaneous recognition of its negation, its inevitable destruction'.[3]

It is clear that Engels' 'materialist interpretation of history' differs a great deal from the 'materialist basis' of Marx's 'dialectical method'. The former, in fact, appears to be something *outside* Marx's critique of political economy, whereas the latter is said by Marx to be the 'basis' of his method.

Regarding 'economics', as in 'the materialist interpretation of history and economics', Marx seldom termed his system 'economics'. On the contrary, he termed it 'A Critique of Political Economy', which thus differs from 'economics' and from 'political economy', in objects of inquiry, in method and in viewpoint. Marx's 'Critique of Political Economy' is a critical analysis of capitalist relations of production by means of a critical analysis of economic categories. It presents the formation, development and self-destruction of capitalist relations of production. While it is well known that Marx's system is a critique of political economy, it is nonetheless little understood that Marx criticised the economic categories used by political economists, such as Adam Smith and David Ricardo. Commentators have instead generally understood Marx's concepts, like 'value' and 'surplus-value', to be similar to those of Smith and Ricardo.

This misunderstanding of Marx's method and his system leads commentators to another misunderstanding: the relationship between the 'materialist basis' of Marx's dialectical method and his 'Critique of Political Economy'. As they have misunderstood Marx's 'critique of the economic categories' and the 'materialist basis' of his 'dialectical method' by taking them to be 'economics' and the 'materialist interpretation of history', it is unsurprising that they could not clarify the intrinsic relationship between Marx's 'Critique of Political Economy' and his 'method of presentation'. Rather, they re-mystified the 'rational kernel' of Marx's dialectical method of presentation, which he had revealed in *Capital*. In this book I will elucidate the 'rational kernel' of Marx's dialectical method by investigating his critique of Proudhon's dialectics.

The Three Sources of Marxism

The other scheme, 'the three sources of Marxism', apparently derives from Lenin's 'Karl Marx' (1913). Through this scheme Lenin claimed that 'His [Marx's] doctrine emerged as the direct and immediate continuation of the teaching of the greatest representatives of philosophy, political economy and socialism.' However, this scheme does not make clear the intrinsic connection that Marx makes by critiquing British political economists, German philosophers and French socialists. If Lenin's remark means anything at all, it should really mean more than that Marx criticised the three separately. In other words, it must be demonstrated where and how Marx's three critiques are unified. This will reveal the principles and structure of Marx's system.

As I shall show later, the linking principle between these three objects of critique is Marx's concept of 'estranged labour', or the 'essence of capital'. The core of this concept is that capital is the zenith of private property. Private property develops from landed property and ultimately into capital via many transitory forms. Marx derived the 'general essence of private property' by means of a two-fold analysis of the production process of capital.[4] 'Human anatomy contains a key to the anatomy of the ape', he comments in the *Grundrisse*[5] (1857–58). By analysing the nature of capital Marx is able to comprehend (*begreifen*) these two necessities in human history: the necessity of the formation of capital, and the necessity of its destruction.

THE METHOD AND STRUCTURE OF THIS BOOK

I have argued that Marx's critique of political economy has been misunderstood by Engels and by Lenin. Instead of their misleading schemes, I propose the following formula: 'a critique of economic categories', and a 'dialectical method' of presentation. What needs to be clarified is the intrinsic connection between the two.

Before I start my investigation, I would like to comment here on my method. In order to rebuild Marx's totality as such, the best method to follow is the genetic one. Marx's original thought and theories can be rebuilt only after a thorough investigation of the process of their formation.

This method is not new, as it has been widely accepted in Marxology since World War II. However, it should also be noted that the genetic method does not necessarily guarantee the scientific character of observations. The difference between my genetic methods, and those of Stalinists, must be made clear.

Problems with the Traditional 'Formation of Capital'

Soviet Marxists and their Western followers have asserted that there is a 'rupture' between the Young and the Old Marx. This observation arises partly from their misunderstanding of Marx's system, and also partly from Lenin's claim. As we have seen, traditionalists have misunderstood the 'materialist basis' of Marx's 'dialectical method' as the 'materialist interpretation of history'. Thus they set up a 'rupture' problem between the Young and the Old Marx, marking the division at *The German Ideology*. Lenin, who did not have an opportunity to read Marx's *Economic and Philosophic Manuscripts* (since they were not published until the 1930s), commented once that Marx almost accepted the classical labour theory of value in *The Holy Family* (1845). Consequently, they had no choice but to assert that Marx 'shifted' after *The Holy Family* from the 'negation' to the 'affirmation' of classical value theory, i.e., in *The German Ideology* or in *The Poverty of Philosophy* (1847). Their claim was that Marx shifted from 'negation' (or 'rejection') of the classical labour theory of value to an 'affirmation' (or 'acceptance') of it. They also claim that the formulation of the 'materialist interpretation of history', which is predicated on the importance of labour in human history, led Marx to this conversion.

This view seemed persuasive, mainly because it identifies a development in Marx's thought and theories. He was not born as a 'communist' or a 'socialist'. He was not born as Marx, but *became* Marx at some stage of his life. Part of the reason that the assertion sounds correct is because the shift is explained with dramatic effect, i.e., the formation of the 'materialist interpretation of history' is regarded as a great discovery. However, my view is that this is a fictionalised account.

Marx writes in the Preface to *A Contribution to the Critique of Political Economy* that he arrived at his 'general result' through his 'critical review of the Hegelian philosophy of right'. This indicates that Marx had reached the 'general result' before he wrote EPM and *The Holy Family*. Moreover, the 'rupture' theory is wrong because it is based on a confusion between 'critique' and 'negation'. Negative comments by Marx on Ricardian value theory can be found not only in his early works but also in his later ones. This means that Marx had already been critical of classical value theory from the time of his first encounter with it in 1844 up to the very end of his life in 1883. Indeed, Marx was 'critical' in *his* 'dialectical' sense, that is, affirmative on the one hand and negative on the other.

A careful investigation of *The Poverty of Philosophy*, as we shall see later in this book, does not demonstrate that Marx 'accepted' Ricardian value theory. On the contrary, it reveals that for both Proudhon and Marx the starting-point is a scientific criticism of Ricardian theories. The core of Marx's critique of the Proudhonian method in *The Poverty of Philosophy* is that Proudhon has not superseded classical economists methodologically. In chapter one of *The Poverty of Philosophy*, Marx criticises Ricardian value theory by re-reading and re-casting the Ricardian theory of value.

Both the 'Karl Marx Problem' and the Stalinist 'solution' of it are undialectical. They are examples of a 'poverty of philosophy' in Soviet Marxism. In fact, Marx never 'accepted' or 'affirmed', but rather 'criticised' the classical labour theory of value from his first encounter with it to his death. This is the real reason why Marx titled his book *A Critique of Political Economy* from 1844 onward. The point is that Marx's critique of political economy is a critique of economic categories, including 'value' as such. A 'critique' of the classical labour theory of value includes both a 'negation' and an 'affirmation' of it. Classical value theory is 'accepted' so long as it is a scientific expression of capitalist relations of production, but is then 'negated' because it is insufficient in scientific terms. The generally accepted account of the formation of Marx's *Capital* is a fictional one made up by commentators who do not really understand the actual relationship between Marx and the political economists.

Consequently in this book the examination of Marx's value theory in his works before and after *The German Ideology* makes a central point, not only because it is an important theory, but because it marks a parting of the ways between commentators in understanding the formation of Marx's system: did Marx really 'accept' the Ricardian value theory in *The Poverty of Philosophy*? Did he actually 'negate' classical value theory in its scientific aspects in his critical comments in 1844? I believe that 'to formulate a question is to answer it'.

The Redefinition of the 'Karl Marx Problem'

As I mentioned above, Soviet Marxists and their Western followers schematised the formation of Marx's thought and theories as a movement from a 'negation' to an 'affirmation' of the classical labour theory of value. This sounds persuasive so long as it seems to explain some of the development in Marx's thought and theories. However, as I have suggested, it is based on a misunderstanding. Let us spend some time investigating this matter.

There are three works that represent Marx's systematic critique of political economy: EPM, *Grundrisse* and *Capital*. Among these three, EPM is the first and the most accessible outline of his system. EPM shows very clearly the principles and structure behind Marx's critique of British political economists, German philosophers and French socialists, and it offers the most salient criticism of Soviet Marxism. This is the very reason why Soviet Marxism – which has almost nothing to do with Marx – had been trying to negate the importance of this work by asserting that Marx's works preceding *The German Ideology* were 'clarified' there. This is a life-or-death problem for Soviet Marxism, but Marx's works do not support the Soviet Marxist assertions. In his Preface to *A Contribution to the Critique of Political Economy* Marx writes that:

1. His 'self-clarification' actually began with his 'critical review of the Hegelian philosophy of right'.
2. It is through this 'critical review' that Marx arrived at the 'general result' that served as a 'guiding thread' for his studies.
3. Consequently, works after the 'critical review' are also guided by the 'general result'. This means that the 'rupture' in the development of Marx's thought and theories, if there is any at all, should be before and not after the 'critical review'.

With regard to this, it is completely wrong to assume that Marx's later works are better than any earlier work. Each work has its own authorial purpose. EPM, for example, is Marx's first outline of his system, but *The German Ideology* (1845–46) is not the second, because it is about something else. Thus EPM (1844) is better than *The German Ideology* as a presentation of Marx's critique of political economy. Soviet Marxists have not cared to notice this.

The problem with the Stalinist-Marxist approach is that the genetic method they use is not really genetic. On the contrary, they use a contra-genetic method, which is very imprecise. All Soviet Marxists do is point out limitations in Marx's earlier works. On the one hand, this sounds reasonable, but on the other hand, it is a very superficial method. The 'Karl Marx Problem', a problem of the relationship between the Young and the Old Marx, is the necessary result of this approach.

The 'Adam Smith Problem' has been a subject of much controversy since the end of World War II. It is very helpful to look at this to achieve a breakthrough with the 'Karl Marx Problem'. The 'Adam Smith Problem' concerned the relationship between Smith's thought in *The Theory of Moral Sentiments* and his thought in *The Wealth of Nations*. The problem was that of 'benevolence' in the former work as opposed to 'self-interest' in the latter. Although the understanding that led commentators to set the problem up was not at a very high level, the controversy was a springboard for much more sophisticated scholarly studies. This will probably hold true in the case of the 'Karl Marx Problem'.

The problem was set up by commentators who did not understand Marx's critique of the economic categories, including the category 'value'. They assert that, to begin with, Marx denied the labour theory of value, but then accepted it in *The German Ideology* or in *The Poverty of Philosophy*, and then criticised it again in *Grundrisse* and afterwards. The point I would like to make in this book is that Marx did not 'accept' or 'affirm' the Ricardian value theory even in *The Poverty of Philosophy*. A close look at the structure of *The Poverty of Philosophy*, the relationship between its two chapters, makes it clear that Marx criticised the Ricardian labour theory of value for its ahistorical approach to the concept. In this sense, this new interpretation of *The Poverty of Philosophy* marks a dramatic breakthrough in the 'Karl Marx Problem'. It will change our whole understanding of the process of formation of Marx's thought. Thus there is no methodological 'rupture' but rather a 'development' from the Young to the Old Marx. Here 'development' means that later stages are the developed forms of a 'seed' at an earlier stage. The only difference is the degree of development. I will also investigate Marx's 'guiding thread' for his studies after he completed his 'critical review of the Hegelian philosophy of right'.

The Structure of this Book

As explained above, I will not be using the genetic method in a strict sense. I do not take up Marx's works in a chronological way but rather treat them topically. In my opinion, Marx's critique of political economy consists of the following two aspects: his dialectical method for the presentation of economic categories, and his critique of the economic categories as formulated by political economists.

In Part One I investigate Marx's dialectical method for his presentation of economic categories, a 'genetic presentation', in Marx's phrase. Part Two deals with Marx's first critique of economic categories and is followed by an examination of the principles and structure of Marx's systematic critique of British political economists, German philosophers and French socialists. The whole process of this re-examination represents my critique of the two traditional interpretations of Marx's system: 'the materialist interpretation of history and economics' and 'the three origins of Marxism'. Part One is also my critique of the 'materialist interpretation of history'; Part Two is that of 'economics'; and Part Three is that of the relationship between the 'materialist interpretation of history' and 'economics'.

Part One

Marx's Dialectical Method

1 MARX'S TASK OF HISTORY AND THE NATURE OF HIS CRITIQUE OF POLITICAL ECONOMY

Here I would like to clarify the nature of Marx's critique of political economy by examining his 'road' to it.

It is well known that Marx studied Law at Bonn University from October 1835 to October 1836, and that he only pursued it as a subordinate subject along with philosophy and history. In October 1836, he moved to Berlin to continue law studies at Berlin University till March 1841 and back to Bonn with the intention of taking up a professorship. However, he had to give up the idea because of the reactionary Prussian government, and started writing for the *Rheinische Zeitung* in April 1842. In October 1842, he became one of the editors of the paper. During this time, he studied the French socialists and communists (Fourier, Proudhon, etc.). In January 1843 the Prussian government stepped up its censorship and ordered the suppression of the paper. In March, Marx resigned the editorship and set himself on a critique of Hegel's *Philosophy of Right*. Marx writes in the Preface to *A Contribution to the Critique of Political Economy* (1859):

> 1) In the year 1842–43, as editor of the *Rheinische Zeitung*, I first found myself in the embarrassing position of having to discuss what is known as material interests. 2) The deliberations of the Rhenish Landtag on forest thefts and the division of landed property; the official polemic started by Herr von Schaper, then Oberpräsident of the Rhine Province, against the *Rheinische Zeitung* about the condition of the Moselle peasantry, and finally the debates on free trade and protective tariffs caused me in the first instance to turn my attention to material interests. 3) On the other hand, at that time when good intentions 'to push forward' often took the place of factual knowledge, an echo of French socialism and communism, slightly tinged by philosophy, was noticeable in the *Rheinische Zeitung*. 4) I objected to this dilettantism, 5) but at the same time frankly admitted in a controversy with the *Allgemeine Augsburger Zeitung* that my previous studies did not allow me to express any opinion on the content of the French theories. 6) When the publishers of the *Rheinische Zeitung* conceived the illusion that by a more compliant policy on the part of the paper it might be possible to secure the abrogation of the death sentence passed upon it, I eagerly grasped the opportunity to withdraw from the public stage to my study (Numbers mine).

The 'material interests' and 'an echo of French socialism and communism' have often been quoted as two elements which drove Marx into his study.

However, pointing them out is not enough. The matter is not so simple, because few commentators explain the following two questions.

First, Marx writes in the above quotation that he had criticised 'French socialism and communism' as 'amateurism', but he had already done so in the article of October 16, 1843.

> The Rheinische Zeitung, which cannot concede the theoretical reality of communist ideas even in their present form, and can even less wish their practical realization, or even consider it possible, will submit these ideas to a thorough criticism.[1]

Then what does the phrase 'my previous studies did not permit me even to venture any judgment on the content of the French tendencies' (in 5) really mean?

Second, on 19 June 1843 Marx married Jenny von Westphalen to whom he got engaged in early October 1836. This means that he gave up the editorship when his marriage was drawing near. Why could he 'eagerly' take 'the illusion of the managers' of the newspaper as 'the opportunity to withdraw from the public stage to my study'? Why was 'a thorough criticism' of the French tendencies so important as to quit the editorship? Why was it worth his retirement? Until these questions are answered, the nature of Marx's critique of Hegel's *Philosophy of Right* and of political economy remains unclear.

The point is that Marx writes in the same article of 1842 that he 'will submit these ideas to a thorough criticism'. Although he does not agree with French socialism and communism 'in their present form', he admits the importance of them. The article says:

> If the Augsburg paper demanded and wanted more than slick phrases, it would see that writings such as those of Leroux, Considerant, and above all Proudhon's penetrating work, can be criticized, not through superficial notions of the moment, but only after long and deep study.[2]

In the following sections I will clarify the nature of Marx's critique of political economy and his dialectical method by examining his works preceding the *German Ideology* (1845–46). In the first section I will examine the two elements of Marx's withdrawal more specifically. In the second section I will demonstrate how Marx formulated the two elements into the 'twofold proof of private property'[3] as a major problem of modern times. The next section deals with the relationship between Marx's critique of Hegel's doctrine of the state and his critique of political economy, by investigating two aspects of his former critique with which he restarted his study.

'MATERIAL INTERESTS' AND 'FRENCH SOCIALISM AND COMMUNISM'

Material Interests

The 'material interests' in the Preface of 1859 means:

a) the 'proceedings of the Rhemish Landtag on thefts of wood and parcelling of landed property',

b) 'the official polemic ... on the conditions of the Moselle peasantry',
c) 'debates on free trade and protective tariffs'.

'Parcelling of landed property' means the same process that Marx showed in 'The First Manuscript' of the EPM. Landed property in the feudal period is the monopoly of land, and the 'parcelling of landed property' is the formation of capitalist private property. In the feudal period there was common land where people could collect wood. However, landowners began to privatise those common properties and exclude people from them. Landowners put those who collected timber in the common land on trial and charged them with stealing wood. This is a part of the formation of capitalist private property, that is, of capitalist relations of production. The 'proceedings of the Rhemish Landtag on thefts of wood' mean that the capitalist mode of production was in progress in Germany in the early 1840s.

Here we should also note that the 'proceedings of the Rhemish Landtag' had a special meaning for the Hegelian Marx. *Philosophy of Right* is Hegel's theory of superseding modern civil society. Hegel studied classical political economy and apprehended the nature of modern society in the separation of 'civil society' from the 'political state'. According to Hegel, compared to landed property, capital is very unstable property. The limit of modern society lies in its instability and it is to be transcended by the 'state', which is supposed to mediate between the sovereign and the executive on the one hand, and the people on the other.

However, the investigation of 'Proceedings of the Sixth Rhine Province Assembly' showed Marx that the Assembly is not a mediator between opposing interests but only a representative of the landowners' interests. To the eye of the journalist Marx the deficiency of Hegel's philosophy of the state became clear through the 'Thefts of Wood' problem.

> This logic, which turns the servant of the forest owner into a state authority, also turns the authority of the state into a servant of the forest owner. The state structure, the purpose of the individual administrative authorities, everything must get out of hand so that everything is degraded into an instrument of the forest owner and his interest operates as the soul governing the entire mechanism. All the organs of the state become ears, eyes, arms, legs, by means of which the interest of the forest owner hears, observes, appraises, protects, reaches out, and runs. (MEC 1, p. 245)

> The wood thief has robbed the forest owner of wood, but the forest owner has made use of the wood thief to purloin the state itself. (MEC 1, p. 253)

To sum up, the 'thefts of wood' problem showed Marx that modern capitalist private property is forming before Hegelian Marx's eyes, revealing the fallacies of Hegel's *Philosophy of Right*.

French Socialism and Communism

'French socialism and communism', on the other hand, indicates the abolition of capitalist private property. The capitalist mode of production yields wealth on the one hand and poverty on the other. Classical political economists spoke for the former, and French socialists and communists for the latter. Both parties were one-sided. Most of the French socialists and communists were reformists, and did not intend to supersede modern private property as such. This is the reason why Marx declared himself against its 'amateurism'. However, 'the content of the French tendencies' means that the problem is an important question of modern times.

> That the class that today possesses nothing demands to share in the wealth of the middle class is a fact that, without the Strasbourg speeches and the silence of the Augsburg paper, is clearly recognized in the streets of Manchester, Paris, and Lyons (MEC 1, p. 216).

'The importance of communism', Marx says, 'does not lie in its being a current issue of highest moment for France and England',[4] but in the fact of our 'not having at once prescribed a proven remedy'.[5] He also writes to Ruge that 'our task must be ... not to oppose them [religion and politics in Germany] with any ready-made system such as the *Voyage en Icarie*'.[6] Marx criticises the *Allgemeine Augsburg Zeitung*, which had accused the *Rheinische Zeitung* of communist sympathies.

> Or is the Augsburger angry at our correspondent's expectation that the undeniable collision will be solved in a 'peaceful way'? Or does the Augsburger reproach us for not having given immediately a good prescription and not having put into the surprised reader's pocket a report as clear as daylight on the solution of the enormous problem? *We do not possess the art of mastering problems which two nations are working on with one phrase*. (MEC 1, p. 219; emphasis mine)

The difference between the two newspapers comes from whether they realise the problem set up by socialism. Marx writes:

> If the Augsburg paper demanded and wanted more than slick phrases, it would see that *writings such as those of Leroux, Considerant, and above all Proudhon's penetrating work, can be criticized*, not through superficial notions of the moment, but *only after long and deep study*. (MEC 1, p. 220; emphasis mine)

This is the reason why Marx 'frankly confessed at the same time ... that my previous studies did not permit me even to venture any judgment on the content of the French tendencies'.

To sum up, Marx witnessed, at the same time, both the formation of capitalist private property in Germany and a critique of it in more advanced countries, like England and France. In fact, Marx's two reasons for his quitting the editorship are not two separate reasons but are closely connected. In fact they are two aspects of modern private property in human history: the formation and the decline of capital. Marx could not find any ready-made solution in French socialism or communism, and needed to face it. In other words, Marx's task of history was to comprehend the following 'two-fold proof' of capital in the development of human beings: 'on the one hand that *human* life required *private property* for its realisation, and on the other hand that it now requires the supersession of private property'.[7]

Here I would like to confirm another point on the relationship between Marx and French socialism. It is said that the text of 1842 reveals 'Marx's *initially* hostile reaction to French socialism'. However, his 'hostile reaction' does not change even later. Marx is 'critical' of French socialism in his dialectical sense from beginning to end. For example, in *The Holy Family* (1844) he criticises Proudhon, praising the scientific advance Proudhon has made. Marx writes on the one hand:

> All treatises on political economy take private property for granted … . But *Proudhon makes a critical investigation* – the first resolute, ruthless, and at the same time scientific investigation – *of the basis of political economy, private property. This is the great scientific advance he made, an advance which revolutionizes political economy and for the first time makes a real science of political economy possible.* (MEC 4, p. 32; emphasis mine)

> Herr Edgar [Bauer], who wishes to characterize the standpoint of the treatise *Qu'est-ce que la propriété?*, naturally does not say a word about political economy or *the distinctive character of this book*, which is precisely that *it has made the essence of private property the vital question of political economy and jurisprudence.* (MEC 4, p. 33; emphasis mine)

On the other hand, however, Marx criticises Proudhon for not 'giving this thought appropriate development':

> As the first criticism of any science is necessarily influenced by the premises of the science it is fighting against, so Proudhon's treatise *Qu'est-ce que la propriété?* is *the criticism of political economy from the standpoint of political economy.* (MEC 4, pp. 31f; emphasis mine)

> *Proudhon did not succeed in giving this thought appropriate development.* The idea of 'equal possession' is the economic and therefore itself still estranged expression for the fact that the object as being for man, as the objective being of man, is at the same time the existence of man for other men, his human relation to other men, the social behaviour of man to man. *Proudhon abolishes economic estrangement within economic estrangement.* (MEC 4, p. 43; emphasis mine)

As shown above, Marx is critical of Proudhon's work even in works where Marx is thought to be sympathetic to him. In the dialectical sense Marx is critical of Proudhon from beginning to end. On the one hand, he admits the scientific advance in Proudhon's work, but, on the other, Marx does not completely agree with Proudhon. Marx supports Proudhon against others because Proudhon's work has made 'the essence of private property' the vital question of political economy. On the other hand, Marx criticises Proudhon because Proudhon's critique of political economy is still influenced by the standpoint of political economy. In other words, Proudhon and Marx share the same purpose: a critique of political economy and socialism. The difference between them lies in their methods of its critique. We shall see, later, that is the problem of 'the essence of private property'.

The two reasons for Marx's withdrawal into his study concern the necessity of the birth and decline of capitalist private property in the development of human history. The point is what Proudhon and Marx grasp as 'the essence of private property'. This is the point of crucial importance in understanding the relationship between Proudhon and Marx, and the nature of Marx's critique of political economy.

THE TWO-FOLD PROOF OF PRIVATE PROPERTY

As we have seen in the preceding section, Marx observed the formation of capitalist private property in Germany exactly when it began to be questioned in advanced countries such as England and France. The so-called 'material interests' concern the formation of capital, and the problem of French socialism marks the supersession of it. In this sense the two reasons for Marx's withdrawal into his study are the same, i.e., 'the two-fold proof of private property'.

As I shall demonstrate the relationship between 'private property' and 'capital' in Chapter 6, a few words will be enough here. It is political economists and philosophers, but not Marx, who confuse 'capital' and 'private property' in general. However Marx's description in the so-called 'Estranged Labour', i.e., the latter part of the 'First Manuscripts' of EPM, may be misleading because of its *genetical* method. 'Capital' is first used in the 'Second Manuscript' as the summit of private property. This means that 'private property' in 'Estranged Labour' is not 'capital' as such.

A close investigation of the 'Estranged Labour' and the 'Second Manuscript' reveals:

a) that Marx distinguishes clearly 'capital' from 'private property',
b) that 'capital' is grasped as the zenith of 'private property' which originally formed in the shape of landed property, and
c) Marx's task in the 'Estranged Labour' is to extract 'the essence of private property in general' through the two-fold analysis of the capitalist production process.

Remember Marx's famous phrase: 'The anatomy of man is a key to the anatomy of the ape. On the other hand, rudiments of more advanced forms in the lower species of animals can only be understood when the more advanced forms are already known.'[8]

A Contribution to the Critique of Hegel's Philosophy of Right: Introduction shows well how Marx understands the problems of 'material interests' and 'French socialism'. In fact, Marx understands 'material interest' as 'the relation of industry, of the world of wealth generally, to the political world',[9] or as the relation of civil society to the political state. He writes:

> The relation of industry, of the world of wealth generally, to the political world is one of the major problems of modern times. In what form is this problem beginning to engage the attention of the Germans? In the form of protective duties, of the prohibitive system, or national economy ... People are, therefore, now about to begin, in Germany, what people in France and England are about to end ... Whereas the problem in France and England is: Political economy, or the rule of society over wealth; in Germany, it is: National economy, or the mastery of private property over

nationality. In France and England, then, it is a case of abolishing monopoly that has proceeded to its last consequences; in Germany, it is a case of proceeding to the last consequences of monopoly. (MEC 3, p. 179)

The 'material interests' in Germany are anything other than 'the *German* form of modern problems'. It is the problem of how people should understand capitalism, 'now about to begin, in Germany', but 'about to end' in England and France. In modern Japan, the Government tried hard to catch up with England and France, but Marx does not think it enough.

If we were to begin with the German status quo itself, the result – even if we were to do it in the only appropriate way, i.e., negatively – would still be an anachronism. Even the negation of our present political situation is a dusty fact in the historical junk room of modern nations. If I negate the situation in Germany in 1843, then according to the French calendar I have barely reached 1789, much less the vital centre of our present age. (MEC 3, p. 177)

In Germany, negating private property is just returning to the feudal age and affirming private property is still an anachronism. Germany will be able to become only 'a dusty fact in historical junk room of modern nations'. Then how can Germany reach the point 'of which the present says: This is the question'?[10] Germany can be elevated to the '*height of humanity*', only by facing 'an important problem of the time'.

It is asked: can Germany attain a practice *à la hauteur des principes* – i.e., a revolution which will raises it not only to the *official level* of modern nations, but to the *height of humanity* which will be the near future of those nations? (MEC 3, p. 182)

In order to raise Germany to that level, the theory of human emancipation, which supersedes the present political emancipation of the human being, must be accomplished first. This is the task of history Marx experienced as editor of the *Rheinische Zeitung*, which drove Marx into his study.

THE TWO ASPECTS OF MARX'S CRITIQUE OF HEGEL'S PHILOSOPHY OF RIGHT

As we have seen, Marx's task of history is sublating the political emancipation of human beings, that is, transcending the separation between civil society and the political state. It is grasped as a positive supersession of capitalist private property, and the historical birth of the human being as a real human being.

Here a series of questions arises. The Preface of 1859 says that 'the first work which I [Marx] undertook for a solution of the doubts which assailed me [Marx] was a critical review of the Hegelian philosophy of right'.

a) Why Hegel's doctrine of the state and not political economy?
b) Can a critique of Hegel's *Philosophy of Right* be 'an important problem of the time'?
c) What is the relationship between a critique of it and '*the ruthless criticism of the existing order*'?[11]

It is true that 'once *modern* politico-social reality itself is subjected to criticism, once criticism rises to truly human problems, it finds itself outside the German *status quo*, or else it would reach out for its object *below* its object'.[12] However, Marx replies, 'We are philosophical contemporaries of the present without being its historical contemporaries.'[13] '*German philosophy of right and state* is the only *German history* which is *al pari* [on a level] with the *official* modern present.' (MEC 3, p. 180)

Hegel studied political economy and dealt with modern society. His *Philosophy of Right* is his theory for future society. It is the only German work that deals with the modern politico-social reality and the major problems of modern times. Thus criticising Hegel's philosophy is not an anachronism, but the only way in Germany to criticise the modern society.

However, Hegel's philosophy of state is only a copy, the philosophical reflection of modern conditions, but not 'real politico-social reality itself'. Is the copy worth criticising? Marx claims: 'The only reason for this is that it is concerned with Germany.' (MEC 3, p. 176) Marx's words, 'we are philosophical contemporaries of the present without being its historical contemporaries', has two meanings. On the one hand, it indicates the strong point of German philosophy. Philosophically, Germans are at the level of modern history. On the other hand, however, it is only in philosophy. 'As the ancient peoples went through their pre-history ... in *mythology*, so we Germans have gone through our post-history in thought, in *philosophy*. We are philosophical contemporaries of the present without being its historical contemporaries'.[14] German history is a 'dream-history', but not a real one. To have their own 'real history', it is important for Marx to criticise German 'dream-history' and ask them to have a real one. In this sense, Hegel's philosophy of law is the 'most consistent, richest, and last formulation'[15] of German speculative philosophy. Thus, a critique of Hegel's philosophy of the state has a double meaning: a critique of modern politico-social reality in England and France and of the German way of life.

> The criticism of the *German philosophy of state and right*, ... is both 1) a critical analysis of the modern state and of the reality connected with it, 2) and the resolute negation of the whole *manner of the German consciousness in politics and right* as *practised* hereto, the most distinguished, most universal expression of which, raised to the level of *science*, is the *speculative philosophy of right* itself. (MEC 3, p. 181. Numbers mine)

The point is that a critique of the Hegelian speculative philosophy is not all of Marx's critique of Hegel's *Philosophy of Right*. As you will find in a chapter entitled 'Critique of Hegel's Dialectic and Philosophy in General' in EPM, criticism of Hegel's philosophy is also a criticism of German philosophy as a whole. It is a criticism of the German way of thinking: of the whole German political and legal consciousness as practised hitherto. This is the second aspect of Marx's critique of Hegel's *Philosophy of Right*.

This is not all. Criticism of Hegel's philosophy of the state is, albeit indirectly, a 'critical analysis of the modern state and of the reality connected with it'. Marx repeats the same account in the Preface to EPM. This is the first aspect of Marx's critique of Hegel's doctrine of the state. This aspect is the core of his critique of Hegel's philosophy and is nothing but his critique of political economy. Consequently, for simplicity, we call each of the two aspects 'Marx's critique of political economy' and 'Marx's critique of Hegel's philosophy'. Although both aspects are closely connected, the second one is the basis of the first, because Germans must give up their way of thinking before they can analyse the real politico-social relations.

This explains the following:

a) It is not true that the Young Marx or Philosopher Marx was transformed into the Old Marx or Economist Marx. The truth is that Marx gets to grips with one aspect of his critique of Hegel's philosophy before moving on to the other.
b) Why Marx keeps EPM (his first critique of political economy), until after writing *The German Ideology* (his critique of German philosophy in general). Unfortunately, the latter is also left unpublished in Germany in the 1840s.
c) The nature of Marx's critique of political economy is basically determined by that of his critique of Hegel's philosophy, i.e., the supersession of the separation of civil society and political state.

Let us move on. According to Marx, negating the German *status quo* of the state and law is not enough for him, because the negation has already been there as Hegel's philosophy, i.e., his theory of constitutional monarchy, the bureaucratic state, assembly of the estates. On the other hand, the realisation of Hegel's philosophy cannot resolve the problems of modern times, because such a realisation is the political conditions in England and France, and its supersession is called for now.

Consequently, German philosophers' task of history is to clarify the principle of the future society, i.e., of humanity, and realise it in Germany.

> It is asked: can Germany attain a practice *à la hauteur des principes* – i.e., a *revolution* which will raises it not only to the *official level* of modern nations, but to the *height of humanity* which will be the near future of those nations? (MEC 3, p. 182)

Its task is two-sided. On the one hand, 'you cannot abolish philosophy without making it a reality',[16] on the other, you cannot '*make philosophy a reality without abolishing it*'.[17] A new theory of German revolution is needed first and then its realisation in the real world. A new theory, which transcends Hegel's doctrine of the state and the modern politico-social conditions, is badly needed. However, neither of two German philosophers' parties seems to Marx to deserve this task.

The *practical* political party (Feuerbach), with good reason, 'demands the *negation of philosophy*'. However, 'it believes that it implements that negation by turning its back to philosophy and its head away from it and muttering a few trite and angry phrases about it'.[18]

The '*theoretical* party' (Bauer) 'saw *only the critical struggle of philosophy against the German world*; it did not give a thought to the fact that the *hitherto prevailing philosophy* itself belongs to this world and is its *completion*, although an ideal one'.[19]

Compared to the two parties, Marx emphasises the importance of a critique of religion in Germany. It is noteworthy that 'A Contribution to the Critique of Hegel's Philosophy of Right: Introduction' (1844) opens with words on the meaning of the criticism of religion, such as: 'To abolish religion as the *illusory* happiness of the people is to demand their *real* happiness.' (MEC 3, p. 176) And: 'The criticism of religion ends with the teaching that man is the highest being for man, hence with the categorical imperative to overthrow all relations in which man is a debased, enslaved, forsaken, despicable being... '. (MEC 3, p. 182)

Only a critique of Hegel's philosophy as the positively transcended criticism of religion can supersede German philosophy as a whole.

> The *task of history*, therefore, once the world *beyond the truth* has disappeared, is to establish the *truth of this world*. The immediate *task of philosophy*, which is at the service of history, once the *holy form* of human self-estrangement has been unmasked, is to unmask self-estrangement in its *unholy forms*. Thus the criticism of heaven turns into the criticism of the earth, *the criticism of religion into the criticism of law and the criticism of theology into the criticism of politics*. (MEC 3, p. 176. Emphasis mine)

The point is to face the problems of the times which can be solved by only one means: practice. The new philosophy is the positive element of a radical German revolution. A passive element, a material basis, is the formation of a class of civil society, an estate which is the dissolution of all estates.

Here I would like to note a couple of points. First, Marx finds the basis of the separation of civil society from the political state in the separation of a man into two: 'bourgeois' and 'citoyen'.

> All emancipation is a reduction of the human world and relationships to man himself. Political emancipation is the reduction of man, on the one hand, to a member of civil society, to an egoistic, independent individual, and, on the other hand, to a citizen, a juridical person. (MEC 3, p. 168)

Second, the radical German revolution is defined as an abdication of this separation of each man.

> Only when *the real, individual man re-absorbs in himself the abstract citizen*, and as an individual human being has become a species-being in his everyday life, in his particular work, and in his particular situation, only when man has recognized and organized his 'own powers' as social powers, and, consequently, *no longer separates social power from himself in the shape of political power, only then will human emancipation have been accomplished*. (MEC 3, p. 168)

Third, influenced by Hegel's theory of civil society, Marx finds the basis of civil society in the 'reciprocal complementing and exchange of human activity' and the 'reciprocal exchange of the produce of human activity'.[20] Thus the so-called 'productive forces' are grasped by Marx as the integrating powers of human beings. As I shall demonstrate later, in his works in

1843–44, Marx uses the concept 'social' in his own sense.[21] Here only one quotation would be required to attract the reader's attention: 'Exchange, both of human activity within production itself and of human products against one another, is equivalent to species-activity and species-enjoyment, *the real, conscious and true mode of existence of which is social activity and social enjoyment.*' (MEC 3, p. 216f. Emphasis mine)

There are phrases in which 'exchange' is distinguished from 'mutual integration' in general as its capitalist form. The point I would like to make here is that the 'two-fold proof of private property' is set up in the course of the historical development of man's integrating powers. Please read carefully the closing words of 'On the Jewish Question' (1843):

> Only when *the real, individual man re-absorbs in himself the abstract citizen*, and as an individual human being has *become a species-being* in his everyday life, *in his particular work*, and in his particular situation, only when man *has recognized and organized his 'own powers' as social powers*, and, consequently, *no longer separates social power from himself in the shape of political power*, only then will human emancipation have been accomplished. (MEC 3, p. 168; emphasis mine)

THE NATURE OF MARX'S CRITIQUE OF POLITICAL ECONOMY

As we have seen Marx grasped that the 'relation of industry, ... to the political world'[22] is one of the major problems of modern times. This is the relation of 'civil society' to the 'political state', and is also the central issue in Hegel's *Philosophy of Right*, where the triadic pattern results in 'family', 'civil society' and the 'state'.

Hegel apprehends that the type of sociality found in the market-based 'civil society' is to be understood in contrastive opposition to the more immediate form found in the institution of the 'family'. In *Philosophy of Right* Hegel portrays the state as the sublation (*Aufhebung*) of 'family' and 'civil society', i.e., as the 'ethical universe' and 'inherently rational'. Thus Hegel's doctrine of the state as man's universal interests, in his 'Part 3 Ethical Life Chapter 3 The State A. Municipal Law', marks the central point of Marx's critique of Hegel's *Philosophy of Right*.

According to Hegel, 'family' is a form of sociality mediated by a quasi-natural inter-subjective recognition rooted in sentiment and feeling: love. In the 'family' the particularity of each individual tends to be absorbed into the social unit, giving this manifestation of 'Ethical Life' a one-sidedness. On the other hand, civil society is none other than 'the system of needs'. The member of civil society takes on an intrinsically social and universal dimension through the exchange of labour and commodities. The particularity in civil society is the inverse of that found in the family. In market relations participants grasp themselves in the first instance as separate individuals who enter into relationships that are external to them.

These two opposite but interlocking principles of social existence provide the basic structure in terms of which component parts of the modern state are articulated and understood. As both contribute particular characteristics to the subjects involved in them, part of the problem for the rational state will be to ensure that each of these two principles mediates the one-sidedness of the other. However, the goal of the individual in civil society is not 'wealth' but 'education and recognition'. Hegel argues that the 'Assembly of the Estates' is the sublation of the specificity of civil society.

The problem lies in the mediation. Hegel says that, even within the production and exchange mechanism of civil society, individuals will belong to a particular 'estate', whose internal forms of sociality will show family-like features. The estates are the agricultural estate, that of trade and industry and the 'universal estate' of civil servants.

For Hegel, it is the representation of the estates within the legislative bodies that is to achieve this mediation. Members of the Assembly give voice to those interests within the deliberative processes of legislation, as the estates or civil society groups, according to their common interests, and as the deputies elected from the estates to the legislative bodies.

Hegel's 'republicanism' is here cut short by his invocation of the familial principle: such representative bodies can only provide the content of the legislation to a constitutional monarch who must add to it the form of the royal decree – an individual 'I will ...'. In Hegel's view this unity and synthesis is achieved by means of the sovereign, the bureaucracy as universal class and the 'Assembly of the Estates'. The hereditary sovereign because he is independent of all political groups; the bureaucracy because it is paid by the state and its interests coincide with those of the state; and the Assembly of the Estates because it is a microcosm of political and civil society and can harmonise the conflicting interests of civil society.

Marx copied out Hegel's text paragraph by paragraph and made a detailed internal criticism of Hegel's arguments by means of textual analysis. Marx shows how Hegel's concern to depict the existing state and existing social institutions as 'rational' leads him into internal inconsistencies in his argument. Marx proclaims universal suffrage as the solution to the split between civil society and the political state. The following summarises Marx's critique of Hegel's doctrine of the state:

> It shows Hegel's profundity that he feels the separation of civil from political society as a contradiction. He is wrong, however, to be content with the appearance of this resolution and to pretend it is the substance, whereas the 'so-called theories' he despises demand the 'separation' of the civil from the political estates – and rightly so, for they voice a consequence of modern society, since there the political-estates element is precisely nothing but the factual expression of the actual relationship of state and civil society, namely, their separation. (MEC 3, p. 75)

Hegel starts from the separation of civil society from the state and claims that it can be superseded by the 'Assembly of the Estates'. Marx criticises Hegel, saying that the separation is rooted in 'civil society' itself. This is because modern political emancipation broke up civil society into its simple component parts; 'on the one hand, the individuals; on the other hand, the material and spiritual elements constituting the content of the life and social position of these individuals'.[23] In old civil societies, there was not the separation between civil society and the political state, 'the character of the old civil society was directly political'.[24] The economic relation of the individuals determined their political relation.

The character of the old civil society was directly political, that is to say, the elements of civil life, for example, property, or the family, or the mode of labour, were raised to the level of elements of political life in the form of seigniory, estates and corporations. In this form they determined the relation of the individual to the state as a whole, i.e., his political relation (his relation of separation and exclusion from the other components of society). From this point of view, the scientific insufficiency of Hegel's theory of the state lies in the fact that he cannot comprehend the real contradiction in civil society.

> Hegel's chief error is to conceive the contradiction of appearances as unity in essence, in the idea, while in fact it has something more profound for its essence, namely, an essential contradiction, just as here this contradiction of the legislative authority within itself, for example, is merely the contradiction of the political state, and therefore also of civil society with itself. (MEC 3, p. 91)

Examining the concept of 'human rights' (of 'private property', of 'freedom' and of 'equality'), Marx shows these concepts are none other than the representation of the separation of the individuals into '*bourgeois*' and '*citoyen*'. In civil society the individuals are '*bourgeois*' as the members of civil society, and are independent from the community. On the other hand, the individuals are '*citoyen*', the community-beings in the political sphere.

> None of the so-called rights of man, therefore, go beyond egoistic man, beyond man as a member of civil society, that is, an individual withdrawn into himself, into the confines of his private interests and private caprice, and separated from the community. In the rights of man, he is far from being conceived as a species-being; on the contrary, species-life itself, society, appears as a framework external to the individuals, as a restriction of their original independence. (MEC 3, p. 164)

Here arises a question. Why do the communal character of man and the political community become the means of the sphere of specific-being? Marx explains this in terms of modern political revolution. Economic life is the real life of man but political life is not. The following is Marx's explanation, as he writes:

> The relation of the political state to civil society is just as spiritual as the relation of heaven to earth. The political state stands in the same opposition to civil society, and it prevails over the latter in the same way as religion prevails over the narrowness of the secular world, i.e., by likewise having always to acknowledge it, to restore it, and allow itself to be dominated by it. In his most immediate reality, in civil society, man is a secular being. Here, where he regards himself as a real individual, and is so regarded by others, he is a fictitious phenomenon. In the state, on the other hand, where man is regarded as a species-being, he is the imaginary member of an illusory

sovereignty, is deprived of his real individual life and endowed with an unreal universality. (MEC 3, p. 154)

As the above investigation shows, the modern political revolution is not the real human emancipation. It does not transcend religion nor inequality in real relations. On the contrary, it supersedes religion and inequality in politics. There are religious affiliations and inequalities in real life. The political revolution means that they do not count in politics. What Marx aimed at is the sublation of religion and inequality as such.

Then what kind of supersession is the human emancipation which set man free by transcending religion as such? 'Practical need, egoism, is the principle of civil society, and as such appears in a pure form as soon as civil society has fully given birth to the political state. The god of practical need and self-interest is money.'[25] However, the communicating power of money belongs exclusively to man. The problem is that the communicating power of man has become that of a precious metal outside man. It is the world of fetishism. Thus the point is how man can appropriate his social power back to himself.

Among the Young Hegelians there are philosophers who share Marx's conceptions of money, for example Moses Hess, but it is only Marx who finds out the alienation of labour behind the power of money in civil society.

Selling is the practical aspect of alienation. Just as man, as long as he is in the grip of religion, is able to objectify his essential nature only by turning it into something alien, ... so under the domination of egoistic need he can be active practically, and produce objects in practice, only by putting his products, and his activity, under the domination of an alien being, ... – money –. (MEC 3, p. 174)

To sum up, the fetish character of money lies in capitalist production of commodities, where products are produced to sell. In Marx's words in 'Notes on James Mill' it lies in 'an exchange which in my mind I have already completed'.[26]

Marx apprehends that society is the real sphere of man's species-life, but that political emancipation resolved man into egoistic man. The limitation of civil society lies in that fact that only egoistic and practical need can be the sole bond which connects men, and that men cannot be species-beings only in the political state but not in real life. Consequently, it is natural for Marx to define human emancipation as re-absorbing man's species-power in real life, i.e., in his production activity. Marx writes:

Only when the real, individual man re-absorbs in himself the abstract citizen, and as an individual human being has become a *species-being in his everyday life, in his particular work, and in his particular situation, only when man has recognized and organized his 'own powers' as social powers, and, consequently, no longer separates social power from himself in the shape of political power*, only then will human emancipation have been accomplished. (MEC 3, p. 168; emphasis mine)

From the investigations above, with good reasons, I can summarise the two basic aspects of Marx's critique of Hegel's *Philosophy of Right*, i.e., of private property, in the following two theses:

> All emancipation is a *reduction* of the human world and relationships to *man himself*. Political emancipation is the reduction of man, on the one hand, to a member of civil society, to an *egoistic, independent* individual, and, on the other hand, to a *citizen*, a juridical person. (MEC 3, p. 168)

> Feuerbach resolves the religious essence into the human essence. But the human essence is no abstraction inherent in each single individual. In its reality it is the ensemble of the social relations. (Thesis IV in 'Theses on Feuerbach', 1845)

Marx's critique of Hegel's doctrine of the state is two-fold:

a) a critical analysis of the modern state and of the reality connected with it, and
b) the resolute negation of the whole manner of German consciousness in politics and right.[27]

Thus it cannot be similar to political economy, but is a theory of a future German revolution which is intended to be the positive supersession of the split between civil society and the political state. As we shall expound this basic character more specifically later, we should not forget that the character of Marx's critique of political economy is determined by that of his critique of Hegel's philosophy. It is led and directed by the viewpoint of the separation between civil society and the political state, and of transcending that separation.

THE RELATIONSHIP BETWEEN MARX'S CRITIQUE OF POLITICAL ECONOMY AND FRENCH SOCIALISM

Marx's task of history was to 'develop for the world new principles from the existing principles of the world'. It concerned both religion and politics, that is, 'man's theoretical existence' and 'the reality of the true existence of man'.[28] Since he grasped man as the 'ensemble of the social relations',[29] he began to study the analysis of civil society, i.e., British political economy. This indicates the nature of Marx's relation to political economy: he is 'critical' in his dialectical sense from his first encounter with it. Political economy is read and criticised by Marx from the standpoint of developing new principles.

For Marx modern civil society produces wealth on the one hand and poverty on the other. The mouthpiece of each side is political economy and socialism. Thus Marx in 1844 criticised political economy for its scientific insufficiency, but the reader should not jump to the conclusion made by many commentators that, to begin with, the Young Marx could not understand the scientific aspect of political economy, but that he began to realise it later. This is not true. Marx, on the other hand, characterises it as 'a theoretical reflection of civil society'.

Inversely, the Old Marx does not blindly affirm political economy. As the title of his book says, Marx's work is 'a critique of political economy', i.e., a critique of economic categories of political economy. This does not mean at all that he shares the same standpoint with political economists.

My view of Marx's relation to political economy would be supported by an investigation of Marx's relation to Proudhon, which unfortunately has not been understood correctly. As I will argue on this problem in Chapters 3 and 4, Proudhon and Marx aim to lift political economy to a 'science' by a 'critique' of it. The difference between them lies in the method of the 'critique'. The core of Marx's critique of Proudhon is that Proudhon, in a roundabout way, arrived at the standpoint of political economists, that is, an ahistorical understanding of economic categories.

The point I am making here is that for Marx in 1844 political economy was not scientific because of its methodological and theoretical insufficiencies and was to be criticised. Marx's relation to political economy is a 'critique' in dialectical sense, but not a simple 'negation' or 'affirmation'.

The following remark illustrates Marx's relation to political economy and Proudhon to the full: 'There [in his *The Poverty of Philosophy*] I showed, ... how in this roundabout way *he [Proudhon] arrived once more at the standpoint of bourgeois economy* [of making economic categories eternal].' (Emphasis mine)[30]

CONCLUSIONS

It should be clear by now that the reasons Marx gave for his withdrawal into his study are not two different reasons. They are nothing but the two necessities of modern private property in the development of human history: the 'two-fold proof of private property'. Understanding it thus, it becomes comprehensible why Marx withdrew into his study when his marriage was drawing near. The problem was so enormous that he frankly admitted that 'writings such as those of Leroux, Considérant, and above all Proudhon's penetrating work, can be criticized, ... only after long and deep study'.[31]

The problem meant, for the Hegelian Marx, the revelation of the speculative character of Hegel's doctrine of the state, the only contemporary work in Germany and the final formulation of German philosophy.

Marx's critique of Hegel's philosophy of the state consists of two components:

a) a 'criticism of the whole German political and legal consciousness as practised hitherto', and
b) a 'critical analysis of the modern state and of the reality connected with it'.

Obviously, Marx's papers in the 'Franco-German Year Book' concern the former, and his critique of political economy the latter. Naturally enough, the character of his critique of political economy is determined by that of his critique of Hegel's philosophy, i.e., 'the reduction of man, on the one hand, to a member of civil society, to an egoistic, independent individual, and, on the other hand, to a citizen, a juridical person'.[32] This reduction problem is investigated as the relationship between individual life and species-life, between individual activity and species-activity, as the creation of man through human activity. Marx's critique of political economy investigates capitalist production, but as the historical birth of a 'total man' through his labour. It cannot be his economics on the model of Ricardo's *Principles of Political Economy and Taxation.*

2 'THE MATERIALIST INTERPRETATION OF HISTORY' AND MARX'S DIALECTICAL METHOD

In this chapter, I am concerned with the so-called 'materialist interpretation of history' in 'I Feuerbach' of *The German Ideology* (1845–46) – hereafter GI, and its relation to Marx's critique of political economy (MEC 5, pp. 19–93).

Commentators have asserted that the so-called 'materialist interpretation of history' was formed in GI . However, GI has the editing problems[1] and the so-called 'sharing problem' between Marx and Engels, i.e., Marx's and Engels' hands. Thus I pay special attention to these problems to clarify the identities and differences between the paragraphs written by Marx and Engels.

However, we must always bear in mind that Engels' hand does not necessarily mean his thought. The main body of the text was written in Engels' hand because Marx's hand was unintelligible, written in 'hieroglyphics'. Insertions, supplements and notes can be identified by their hand. Thus, we can sometimes distinguish between their views there.

Based on the edition I give in Appendix I, I will start my investigation by summarising the 'materialist interpretation of history' to specify the identity between Marx's and Engels' thoughts. Then I shall quote the important insertions, supplements and notes in their hands before examining the differences between Marx's and Engels' views. As no English edition reproduces Marx's and Engels' hands, I believe this is helpful for English readers. In the last section, I shall investigate the relationship between the 'materialist interpretation of history' and Marx's critique of political economy. In the following, sheet numbers in Engels' hand and page numbers in Marx's on the manuscripts of GI are indicated by { } and [ ] respectively.

THE SO-CALLED 'MATERIALIST INTERPRETATION OF HISTORY' IN 'I FEUERBACH'

The Structure of 'I Feuerbach'

According to the edition given in Appendix I, the structure of GI is:

1) Introduction: The first volume of *The German Ideology* has the aim of uncloaking these sheep (the Young-Hegelian philosophers) who take themselves and are taken for wolves; of how the boasting of these philosophic

commentators only mirrors the wretchedness of the real condition in Germany.

2) {1}: The Introduction to GI : The purpose of GI is to rate the true value of the German philosophic charlatanry and to bring out clearly the pettiness of the whole Young-Hegelian movement by looking at the whole spectacle from a standpoint beyond the frontiers of Germany.

3) {2}: 'A Philosophy in General, Especially in Germany' : German criticism has, right up to its latest efforts, never quitted the realm of philosophy. The Old-Hegelians had comprehended everything as soon as it was reduced to an Hegelian logical category. The Young-Hegelians criticised everything by attributing to it religious concepts or by pronouncing it a teleological matter. It has not occurred to any one of these philosophers to inquire into the connection between German philosophy and German reality, the relation of their criticism to their own material surroundings.

4) {3} and after: Second Chapter ('B Feuerbach').

i. {3}~{5}: The whole internal structure of a nation itself depends on the stage of development reached by its production and its internal and external intercourse. The structure of the so-called precapitalist societies, i.e., the Asiatic, the ancient and the feudal modes of production, are analysed as examples.

ii. {6}~{8}: The first premise of history: The production of material life itself, which consists of the following five 'elements' or 'aspects': (a) the production of the means of satisfaction, (b) the production of new needs, (c) the production of other men (reproduction), (d) this production of life appears as a natural and social relationship. By social we understand the co-operation of several individuals, no matter under what conditions, in what manner and to what end ([13]). (e) Man possesses 'consciousness'.

iii. {9}~{11}: The second premise of history is the succession of the separate generations, each of which exploits the materials, the capital funds, the productive forces handed down to it by all preceding generations, and thus, on the one hand, continues the traditional activity in radically changed circumstances and, on the other hand, modifies the old circumstances with a completely changed activity.

iv. {20}~{21}: Supplement to this chapter on the materialist basis of the ruling ideas.

v. {84}~{92}: Three stages in the historical development of private property after 'landed property' in the Middle Ages.

The 'Materialist Interpretation of History'

From all the observations above, the so-called 'materialist interpretation of history' can be summarised as follows. The Young-Hegelian philosophers are devoid of premises, but history has its materialist basis, i.e., the production of material life. Thus, we must write history starting from this production of life by social individuals. The relations of production and intercourse form a sum total: civil society. Consequently, we must explain the form of social organisations, the state, laws or consciousness from the form of civil society which underlies them. Marx states:

> Civil society embraces the whole material intercourse of individuals within a definite stage of the development of productive forces … . Civil society as such only develops with the bourgeoisie; the social organization evolving directly out of production and intercourse, which in all ages forms the basis of the state and of the idealistic superstructure, has, however, always been designated by the same name ([68]).

The first point to be noted here is that the object of Marx's investigation is the social production or the co-operation of several individuals. The social production by the social individual has a double relationship: a natural and a social. They represent the productive forces and the relations of production and commerce. The mode of co-operation is itself a productive force and produces the mode of production corresponding to it. Marx thinks that the productive forces and the production relations are the two sides or abilities of social individuals. In other words, the development of social individuals is expressed in their productive forces and production relations. Property is thought to be the sum total of those relations of production and commerce. For Marx, a definite form of production is equivalent to a definite form of 'the division of labour' and of property.

Second, we must understand the above propositions regarding their historical backgrounds. Marx and Engels write that 'to observe this fundamental fact [the production of material life] in all its significance and all its implications and to accord it its due importance' is essential 'in any interpretation of history' ([11]). They do not write that their interpretation is the only interpretation of history. This remark should be understood as a criticism of the German philosophers, who are devoid of premises to history. On the other hand, we should note their two-fold estimation of the French and the English thinkers. According to Marx and Engels, the French and the English 'made the first attempts to give the writing of history a materialistic basis' but 'in an extremely one-sided fashion' ([11]). This implies that mere economic analysis of civil society is not enough, and that a definite form of civil society should be comprehended as a form of production and commerce of individuals. For example, the economic laws must be comprehended from the social activities of individuals. In fact, Marx also says 'there exists a materialistic connection of men with one another' ([13]).

Third, the three forms of common property are ideal types of the mode of existence of social individuals. The development from the Asiatic to the feudal form of property is a result of the development in the form of co-operation of individuals, i.e., from natural to social, or from spontaneous to the 'result of activities of individuals'. In the capitalist mode of production, direct co-operation is mediated by money, the zenith of estrangement of social activity.

Fourth, for the societies in which the capitalist mode of production has developed, the three precapitalist modes of production are in the past and have declined. Thus, in capitalist countries, the mode of production has developed from Asiatic via ancient to feudal. On the other hand, those modes co-existed in Marx's day, and do today. Thus, Marx and Engels have never written that the European is the only or the necessary line of development. They describe the development of the division of labour in the European countries from the Asiatic, the ancient, the feudal, to the capitalist mode of production and an 'association' of free men in the future ({3}, {4}, [42] and thereafter.[2] This is supported by Marx's task, which was how Germany could 'attain a practice *á la hauteur des principes*, i.e., a *revolution* which will raise not only to the official level of the modern nations but to the height of humanity which will be the near future of these nations'. (MEC 3, p. 182).

Last, however, this does not mean that the preceding modes are equal to the capitalist mode of production from the viewpoint of 'the development of the social individual'. As is stated in the Preface to *A Contribution to the Critique of Political Economy* (1859): 'This social formation [the capitalist formation of society] brings, therefore, the prehistory of human society to a close'.[3]

Without doubt, in broad outline, Marx and Engels share a similar interpretation of history. However, a close investigation of their views clarifies the differences between them in detail. Let us examine some of them after reproducing the insertions by Marx's and Engels' hands.

INSERTIONS BY MARX AND ENGELS

Important Insertions in Marx's Hand

In the following, insertions are indicated in single quotation marks and emphases are original.

1) It follows from this that a certain mode of production, or industrial stage, is always combined with a certain mode of co-operation, or social stage, and 'this mode of co-operation is itself a "productive force"' ({7}b=[13]).

2) For as soon as the distribution of labour comes into being, each man has a particular, exclusive sphere of activity, which is forced upon him and from which he cannot escape. He is a hunter, a fisherman, a herdsman, 'or a critical critic', and must remain so if he does not want to lose his means of livelihood; while in communist society, where nobody has one exclusive sphere of activity but each can become accomplished in any branch he wishes, society regulates the general production and thus makes it possible for me to do one thing today and another tomorrow, to hunt in the morning, fish in the afternoon, read in the evening, 'criticise after dinner', just as I have a mind, without ever becoming hunter, fisherman, herdsman 'or critic' ({8}b=[17]).

3) 'Just because individuals seek *only* their particular interest, which for them does not coincide with their communal interest (in fact the general is the illusory form of communal life), the latter will be imposed on them as an interest "alien" to them, and "independent" of them as in its turn a particular, peculiar "general interest"; or they themselves must remain

within this discord, as in democracy. On the other hand, too, the *practical* struggle of these particular interests, which constantly *really* run counter to the communal and illusory communal interest, makes *practical* intervention and control necessary through the illusory "general" interest in the form of the State' (a marginal note on {8}b~c=[17]~[18]).

4) 'Communism is for us not *a state of affairs* which is to be established, an *ideal* to which reality [will] have to adjust itself. We call communism the *real* movement which abolishes the present state of things. The conditions of this movement result from the premises now in existence' (a marginal note on {8}c=[18]).

5) 'This "*alienation*" (to use a term which will be comprehensible to the philosophers) can, of course, only be abolished given two *practical* premises. For it to become an "intolerable" power, i.e., a power against which men make a revolution, it must necessarily have rendered the great mass of humanity "propertyless", and produced, at the same time, the contradiction of an existing world of wealth and culture, both of which conditions presuppose a great increase in productive power, a high degree of its development. And on the other hand, this development of productive forces (which itself implies the actual empirical existence of men in their *world-historical*, instead of local, being) is an absolutely necessary practical premise because without it *want* is merely made general, and with *destitution* the struggle for necessities and all the old filthy business would necessarily be reproduced; and furthermore, because only with this *universal* development of productive forces is a universal intercourse between men established, which produces in all nations simultaneously the phenomenon of the "propertyless" mass (universal competition), makes each nation dependent on the revolutions of the others, and finally has put *world-historical*, empirically universal individuals in place of local ones. Without this, (1) communism could only exist as a local event; (2) the *forces* of intercourse themselves could not have developed as *universal*, hence intolerable powers: they would have remained homebred conditions surrounded by superstition; and (3) each extension of intercourse would abolish local communism. Empirically, communism is only possible as the act of the dominant peoples "all at once" and simultaneously, which presupposes the universal development of productive forces and the world intercourse bound up with communism' (a marginal note on {8}c=[18]).

6) 'Moreover, the mass of *propertyless* workers – the utterly precarious position of labour-power on a mass scale cut off from capital or from even a limited satisfaction and, therefore, no longer merely temporarily deprived of work itself as a secure source of life – presupposes the *world market* through competition. The proletariat can thus only exist *world-historically*, just as communism, its activity, can only have a "*world-historical*" existence. World-historical existence of individuals means existence of individuals which is directly linked up with world history' (a marginal note on {8}d=[19]).

7) 'The historical method which reigned in Germany, and especially the reason why, must be understood from its connection with the illusion of ideologists in general, e.g., the illusions of the jurists, politicians (of the practical statesmen among them, too), from the dogmatic dreamings and distortions of these fellows; this is explained perfectly easily from their practical position in life, their job, and the division of labour' ({21}b=[34]).

8) The relation of the productive forces to the form of intercourse is the relation of the form of intercourse to 'the occupation or activity' of the individuals (a correction of 'self-activity' in Engels' hand on {89}a=[60]).

Important Insertions in Engels' Hand

In the following, Engels' insertions are indicated in single quotation marks and emphases are original, except when otherwise stated.

1) 'It is the communal private property which compels the active citizens to remain in this spontaneously derived form of association over against their slaves' ({3}c).
2) Where speculation ends – in real life – 'there real, positive science begins: the representation of the practical activity, of the practical process of the development of men' ... . 'But they by no means afford a recipe or schema, as does philosophy, for neatly trimming the epochs of history. On the contrary, our difficulties begin only when we set about the observation and the arrangement – the real depiction – of our historical material, whether of a past epoch or of the present. The removal of these difficulties is governed by premises which it is quite impossible to state here, but which only the study of the actual life process and activity of the individuals of each epoch will make evident' ({5}d).
3) 'F[euerbach]'s error is not that he subordinates the flatly obvious, the sensuous appearance to the sensuous reality established by detailed investigation of the sensuous facts, but that he cannot in the last resort cope with the sensuous world except by looking at it with the "eyes", i.e., through the "spectacles", of *the philosopher*' ({6}a=[8]).
4) 'So much is this activity, this unceasing sensuous labour and creation, this production, the basis of the whole sensuous world as it now exists, that, were it interrupted only a year, Feuerbach would not only find an enormous change in the natural world, but would very soon find that the whole world of men and his own perceptive faculty, nay his own existence, were missing. Of course, in all this priority of external nature remains unassailed, and all this has no application to the original men produced by *generatio aequivoca*, but this differentiation has meaning only insofar as man is considered to be distinct from nature. For that matter, nature, the nature that preceded human history, is not by any means that nature in which Feuerbach lives, it is nature which today no longer exists anywhere (except perhaps on a few Australian coral-islands of recent origin) and which, therefore, does not exist for Feuerbach' ({6}b~c= [9]~[10]).
5) 'Division of labour and private property are, moreover, identical expressions: in the one the same thing is affirmed with reference to activity as is affirmed in the other with reference to the product' ({8}b~c=[17]~[18]).

6) 'And out of this very contradiction between the interest of the individual and that of the community the latter takes an independent form of the State, divorced from the real interests of individual and community, and at the same time as an illusory communal life, always based, however, on the real ties existing in every family and tribal conglomeration ... and especially, as we shall enlarge upon later, on the classes, already determined by the division of labour, which in every such mass of men separate out, and of which one dominates all the others. It follows from this that all struggles within the State, the struggle between democracy, aristocracy, and monarchy, the struggle for the franchise, etc., etc., are merely illusory forms – altogether the general interest is the illusory of common interests – in which the real struggles of the different classes are fought out among one another ... . Further, it follows that every class which is struggling for mastery, even when its domination, as is the case with the proletariat, postulates the abolition of the old form of society in its entirety *and of domination itself*, must first conquer for itself political power in order to represent its interest in turn as the general interest, which in the first moment it is forced to do' (a marginal note on {8}b=[17]. Italics are Marx's insertion).
7) This conception of history depends on our ability to expound the real process of production, starting out from the material production of life itself, and to comprehend the form of intercourse connected with this and created by this mode of production (i.e., civil society in its various stages), 'as the basis of all history; describing it in its action as the State', to explain all the different theoretical products and forms of consciousness, religion, philosophy, ethics, etc. etc. *and trace their origins and growth from the basis; by which means, of course, the whole thing can be depicted in its totality (and therefore, too, the reciprocal action of these various sides on one another)* ({10}c=[24]. Italics are Marx's insertion).
8) In the whole conception of history up to the present this real basis of history has either been totally neglected or else considered as a minor matter quite irrelevant to the course of history. 'History must, therefore, always be written according to an extraneous standard; the real production of life seems to be primeval history, while the truly historical appears to be separated from ordinary life, something extra-superterrestrial. With this the relation of man to nature is excluded from history and hence the antithesis of nature and history is created' ({10}c=[25]).
9) This whole conception of history, together with its dissolution and the scruples and qualms resulting from it, is a purely *national* affair of the Germans and has merely *local* interest for Germany, as for instance the important question which has been under discussion in recent times: how exactly one 'passes from the realm of God to the realm of Man' – as if this 'realm of God' had ever existed anywhere save in the imagination, and the learned gentlemen, without being aware of it, were not constantly living in the 'realm of Man' to which they are now seeking the way; 'and as if the learned pastime (for it is nothing more) of explaining the mystery of this theoretical bubble-blowing did not *on the contrary* lie in demonstrating its origin in actual earthy relations ... . The real, practical dissolution of these phrases, the removal of these notions from the consciousness of men, will, as we have already said, be effected by altered circumstances, not by theoretical deductions. For the mass of men, i.e., the proletariat, these theoretical notions do not exist and hence do not require to be dissolved, and if this mass ever had

any theoretical notions, e.g., religion, these have now long been dissolved by circumstances' ({10}d~{11}a= [26]~[27], Italics Marx's insertions).

10) 'It is also clear from these arguments ... , and do not realize that these adverse conditions are spirit of their spirit' (a marginal note on {11}b~c=[28]~[29]. Almost all the text of {11}b=[28] and all that of {11}c=[29] is crossed out).

11) 'Thus money implies that all previous intercourse was only intercourse of individuals under particular conditions, not of individuals as individuals. These conditions are reduced to two: accumulated labour or private property, and actual labour. If both or one of these ceases, then intercourse comes to a standstill. The modern economists themselves, e.g. Sismondi, Cherbuliez, etc., oppose "association of individuals" to "association of capital"' ({90}a~c=[64]~[65]).

12) The division of labour implies from the outset the division of the conditions of labour, of tools and materials, 'and thus the splitting-up of accumulated capital among different owners, and thus, also, the division between capital and labour, and the different forms of property itself' ({90}a~c=[64]~[65]).

13) While in the earlier period self-activity and the production of material life were separated, in that they devolved on different persons, and while, on account of the narrowness of the individuals themselves, the production of material life was considered as a subordinate mode of self-activity, they now diverge to such an extent that altogether material life appears as the end, and that which produces this material life, labour '(which is now the only possible but, as we see, negative form of self-activity)', as the means ({90}c=[66]).

14) 'In the case of the ancient people, since several tribes live together in one town, the tribal property appears as State property, and the right of the individual to it as mere "possession" which, however, like tribal property as a whole, is confined to landed property only. Real private property began with the ancient, as with modern nations, with movable property – (Slavery and Community) (*dominium ex jure Quiritum*)' ({91}b=[69]).

THE DISSIMILARITIES BETWEEN MARX AND ENGELS

The Pre-Capitalist Modes of Production

First, the Asiatic mode of property is considered in {3}b, while it is not in [68] and thereafter.

Second, in {3}b the 'ancient mode of property' is defined with 'State property and private property' while in [69] with 'State property' only. [69] says: 'In the case of the ancient peoples, ... the tribal property appears as State property, and the right of the individuals to it as mere "possession" which ... is confined to landed property only.'

The former definition is almost the same as that in 'formations which precede capitalist societies' in Marx's *Grundrisse* (1857–58) and is undoubtedly Marx's view. Thus the latter, which differs a little from the former, is probably Engels' view. With regard to this, {3}b says that the ancient mode of property 'proceeds especially from the union of several tribes into a city by agreement or by conquest', while [68] says that this property is 'determined ... chiefly by war'. The latter proposition appears at first sight to contradict [62]~[63], a supplement on the role of violence, war and robbery, etc.; but the first proposition itself is an insertion by Engels.

Therefore there is no great difference between Marx and Engels on this point.

Thirdly, in {3}d 'feudal property' is defined as 'landed property' in the country and 'corporative property' in the town, whilst [69] says that the former developed into the latter. According to {3}, country and town are united in the Asiatic and the history of the ancient property is the history of towns, thus the antagonism between country and town begins, necessarily and essentially, from the feudal property.[4] On the other hand, [41] asserts that 'The antagonism between town and country ... runs through the whole history of civilisation to the present day', but lacks the logic to comprehend (*begreifen*) the antagonism.[5]

The Division of Labour and Property

In GI , 'division of labour' is explained four times as being essentially an identical expression of property, but these explanations can be divided into two types:

1) division of labour = the relations of production and intercourse = property relations: {3}b and [52];

2) division of labour = the unequal distribution, both quantitatively and qualitatively, of labour and its products = private property: [16]~[17] and [64]~[65].

In broad outline, both coincide but the division of labour does not necessarily result in private property, as in the Asiatic. The latter interprets private property mainly as the problem of distribution, i.e., to whom the products and the means of production belong. However, the former interprets property as the relations of production. The latter does not contain the Asiatic common property, while the former does. With regard to this, it is also noteworthy that Marx grasped the essence of private property as 'the power to command labour and products'[6] of other men in EPM by re-reading and re-interpreting Smith's concept of 'command'; but the text in [17] incorrectly quotes this definition of private property:

> This latent slavery in the family, though still very crude, is the first property, but even at this stage it corresponds perfectly to the definition of modern economists who call it the power of disposing of the labour-power of others ([17]).

This difference between Marx and Engels,[7] runs through to their last works. The point is that Engels does not appreciate the concept 'the relations of production' and cannot understand Marx's concept of 'property' as the sum total of production relations. It should be noted that the abolition of 'division of labour' or of 'labour' means the abolition of their capitalist form, but does not mean that there is no social division of labour or productive-activity in the future.

The Two Abilities of the Social Individual

In his letter to Annenkov (dated 28 December 1846), Marx remarks that 'the social history of man is never anything else than the history of his individual development, whether he is conscious of this or not'.[8] In

Grundrisse he states that 'Forces of production and social relations [are] – two different sides of the development of the social individual'.[9] Compared to these views, the statement in [61] that the history of the conditions of production is 'the history of the development of the forces of the individuals themselves' seems to be one-sided. Engels does not use the term 'estranged labour' as often as Marx,[10] because he does not comprehend social laws from the social activities of individuals, as his view on economic laws shows.[11] This is not his strong point, but rather his weak point.

Bagaturija distinguishes three formations in the manuscripts of GI and asserts that Marx and Engels gradually gave up the term 'estrangement' as time passed.[12] It is quite true that the first part of the 'large volume' ([8] to [35]) was written first, then the second part of the volume and then the 'small volume'. It is also correct that the term appears less and less in those formations, but, still, Bagaturija's assertion is completely wrong. He did not take authorial purpose, the logical dimensions of the manuscripts, or the differences between Marx's and Engels' views into account. The disappearance of the term is mainly due to Engels' views and the authorial purpose of {1} and {2}, which are the introductions and 'a few general observations' on the Young-Hegelian movement. Bagaturija accepts what he should not, and does not accept that which he should. He is a good example of the best and the brightest of Soviet Marxists.

THE 'MATERIALIST INTERPRETATION OF HISTORY' AND MARX'S CRITIQUE OF POLITICAL ECONOMY

The term 'the materialist interpretation of history', strictly speaking, belongs to Engels. Engels uses the term for the first time in his 'Book Review: Marx's *A Contribution to the Critique of Political Economy*' (1859),[13] indicating Marx's brief formulation of 'The general result at which I [Marx] arrived, which, once won, served as a guiding thread for my studies' in its Preface. Engels used the term again in his *Anti-Dühring* (1877–78).[14] On the other hand, Marx never uses the term the 'materialist interpretation of history'. Instead, as is quoted above, Marx himself called the brief formulation the 'general result', to which he was led by his critical investigation of the Hegelian *Philosophy of Right*, as the 'guiding thread' for his studies. In his 'Postscript to the Second Edition' of *Capital* Marx called the 'general result' the 'materialist basis for my [dialectical] method'.[15]

Let us consider Marx's recollection in the context of its background, that is, as a criticism of Hegelian and Young-Hegelian philosophy. Marx calls the 'general result' 'the materialist basis' for his dialectical method to distinguish 'the material transformation of the economic conditions of production ... , [from] the legal, political, ... , or philosophic – in short, ideological forms'.[16] So far, I do not see any great dissimilarity between Marx and Engels. For both of them, the 'general result' is not the proposition that every political and social antagonism ought to be explained by economic conflict.

However, the term 'the materialist interpretation of history' is very misleading. It has not been understood as 'the materialist basis' for Marx's method, but as the method for doing history as such. For Marx, history is investigated in terms of the process of production and reproduction, through which the economic conditions of production are changed. The term 'history' concerns change, as Marx's 'dialectical method' indicates the method of inquiry which 'regards every historically developed form as being in a fluid state, in motion, and therefore grasps its transient aspect as well'.[17] Thus the 'general result' is equivalent to 'a guiding thread' for his studies and the 'materialist basis' for his method. This means that the terms Marx developed in GI , such as 'productive forces', 'relations of production' and 'economic structure of society', made it possible for him to comprehend the transient aspect of capitalist society as being in motion.

Marx's critique of political economy is a critical system of the economic categories. The economic categories are understood as theoretical expressions of capitalist relations of production and commerce. The historical character and the intrinsic connection between capitalist relations of production and commerce are expressed in the definitions of economic categories. The capitalist formation of society is dialectically comprehended as a transient formation in history through his 'genetic presentation' of economic categories. The term 'materialist interpretation of history', albeit not so irrelevant to the contents of GI, is not very helpful but rather misleading.

What really concerns Marx is the development of the social individual and a revolution which transcends the political emancipation of man in capitalist society. Thus his concepts 'the means of production', 'the relations of production' and 'property' should not be understood, as Marx states in EPM, 'only in the sense of direct, one-sided consumption, of possession, of having'[18] but in the sense of 'the sensuous appropriation of the human essence and human life'.[19]

Last, I will examine the implications of Marx's testimony that he arrived at the 'general result' through his critical inquiry into the Hegelian *Philosophy of Right*. This implies that he had already arrived at the result by the time of EPM, and that EPM, Marx's first critique of political economy, must have been guided by the 'general result', or he could not testify that it 'once won, served as a guiding thread for my studies [critique of political economy]'. On the other hand, GI is the first formulation of the 'general result' but is not at all a critique of political economy. Consequently, for a better understanding of Marx's critique of political economy, we should investigate GI then EPM, even though they were written in reverse order.[20]

CONCLUSIONS

We have examined the so-called 'materialist interpretation of history' in GI and arrived at the following conclusions: first, the 'materialist interpretation of history' is, as a matter of fact, the 'materialist basis' for Marx's dialectical method of inquiry, which enables us to understand a definite form of the state and laws from a certain form of civil society, i.e., the sum total of the relations of production and commerce. The relations of production are the relations of immediate producers to each other: the mode of co-operation. Productive forces are the relationship of producers to nature. Thus, productive forces contain not only the means of production but also the co-operation of individuals itself. Productive forces and the relations of production are the two different sides of the social individual. In other words, the development of the social individual is expressed in the development of productive forces and in the relations of production. A new generation inherits certain conditions of production from all preceding generations. It produces in completely different circumstances and modifies the old circumstances. In this way, a form of property has positive and negative sides.

The relations of production develop from communal to social, that is, the direct unity with other men to the product of social intercourse. In broad outline Asiatic, ancient, feudal and capitalist modes of production can be designated progressive epochs in the economic formation of society. The capitalist mode of production is the mode in which objects (the means of production) subsume the subject (producers). It is the zenith of the estrangement of life-activity but brings, therefore, the prehistory of human society to a close. The capitalist mode of production can be abolished positively only by an association of free men and by appropriating universally developed productive forces which are a result of the estrangement. These insights are expounded through Marx's presentation of economic categories, or his analysis of capitalist relations of production and commerce, but not in GI . Thus, for a better understanding of Marx's thought and theories, we have to investigate EPM, *Grundrisse* and *Capital.*

3 MARX'S METHODOLOGICAL CRITIQUE OF PROUDHONIAN DIALECTICS

Here we are concerned with Marx's dialectical method and its relationship with his critique of economic categories. His *The Poverty of Philosophy* (1847; hereafter POP (MEC 6, pp. 105–212)) offers the key to the problem, as he writes in the Preface to *A Contribution to the Critique of Political Economy* (1859): '*The decisive points of our view were* first *scientifically*, although only polemically, *indicated* in my work published in 1847 and directed against Proudhon: *The Poverty of Philosophy*, etc.' (Emphasis mine)[1]

However, this crucial work has not been fully appreciated by commentators. They have asserted that Marx, to begin with, 'negated' or 'rejected' Ricardian value theory, but began to 'affirm' or 'accept' it in POP. This implies that in POP 'the decisive points' of Marx's view were *not* 'indicated' yet; and that Marx became a Ricardian but was *not* yet Marx.[2] This misunderstanding of POP indicates that Marx has not been appreciated well enough, because the decisive points of his view have not been comprehended. Let me explain the causes of this error.

First, commentators have skipped a necessary, fundamental step, i.e., an investigation of Proudhon's *System of Economic Contradictions, or The Philosophy of Poverty* (1846; hereafter SEC). Marx's POP is his reply to Proudhon's SEC. It follows that, for a full understanding of Marx's POP, it is essential to investigate Proudhon's SEC. However, commentators seem to have skipped this necessary step and misunderstood the relationship between Marx and Proudhon. They have overlooked the similarity and dissimilarity between them.

Modern civil society (capitalist relations of production and commerce) produces wealth on the one hand and poverty on the other. The contradiction between wealth and poverty is represented by the controversy between political economists and socialists. Political economists 'work only to purge economic relations of feudal taints, to increase the productive forces and to give a new upsurge to industry and commerce' (MEC 6, p. 186). 'Poverty is in their eyes merely the pang which accompanies every childbirth, in nature as in industry.' On the other hand, 'the socialists and the communists are the theoreticians of the proletarian class'. (MEC 6, p. 177)

In 1844–45 Marx often visited Proudhon and discussed many problems, in particular the dialectical method.[3] Neither classical political economists nor socialists are methodologically sufficient for either of them. They realise the methodological deficiencies of the political economists fully and 'want to be the synthesis' of the contradiction (MEC 6, p. 178) between political economists and socialists (wealth and poverty) by using the dialectical method. They share the same purpose: a critique of private property. Thus the methodological deficiency of political economists is the starting point for both of them. SEC is Proudhon's methodological and theoretical critique of political economy based on his 'dialectical system'. There Proudhon flatters himself 'on having given a criticism of both political economy and communism'. (MEC 6, p. 178)

Marx and Proudhon diverge from each other on the understanding of dialectics and its relationship to a critique of economic categories, but Proudhon was not aware of it at its publication. Thus, it is Proudhon who invited Marx's criticism of his new book, sending a copy to Marx and asking for 'stern criticism', probably expecting unstinted praise. However, Marx's reply was so severe as to say:

> He [Proudhon] wants to be the synthesis – he is a composite error. He wants to soar as the man of science above the bourgeois and the proletarians; he is merely the petty bourgeois, continually tossed back and forth between capital and labour, political economy and communism. (MEC 6, p. 178)

Faced with this 'stern criticism', Proudhon writes in the margin on a page of Marx's POP, saying: 'The real meaning of Marx's work [POP] is, in particular, his mortification at that I think similarly to him and that I expressed it before he has.'[4] This shows the close relationship between Marx and Proudhon, and their relationship to the political economists.

Second, commentators have read the chapters of Marx's POP separately. Consequently, they have misunderstood Marx's critique of Proudhon. In Chapter One of POP, Marx criticises Proudhonian value theory by contrasting it with the Ricardian. In Chapter Two of POP, Proudhon's dialectics are criticised in contrast with Hegelian. Although Chapter Two includes Marx's methodological critique of political economists, Chapter One has not been understood in its context. By contrasting Ricardo with Proudhon in Chapter One, Marx does not mean that Ricardo is right, but that Proudhon may be ranked below Ricardo (see Marx's above quoted criticism in MEC 6, p. 178).

Consequently, Marx's appreciation of the scientific aspect of Ricardian value theory (in Chapter One) and his methodological critique of it (in Chapter Two) do not contradict each other. On the contrary, a careful investigation of Chapter One reveals that Ricardo's value theory is also criticised indirectly. The Ricardian value theory as opposed to Proudhon is not Ricardian as such, but the one re-read by Marx.[5]

Similarly, Bray is contrasted with Proudhon to show that Proudhon's utopian interpretation of Ricardo's value theory has no originality as such.

In Chapter Two of POP, Marx contrasts Hegel with Proudhon to criticise Proudhon's made-up dialectics. Proudhon's 'dialectic system' has little affiliation with Hegel's dialectics, but with Fourier's 'system'.[6] However, Marx is still right in the following sense: Proudhon, like Hegel, inverts the relationship between categories and economic relations. He understands categories as eternal by deifying them. On the other hand, unlike Hegel, Proudhon's dialectics has a deficiency as speculative dialectics, because his categories do not have life in themselves.[7] Marx's critique of Proudhon's dialectics turns out to be his critique of Hegel's. Readers will see there how Marx re-reads Hegel.

Third, consequently, commentators have completely misunderstood the relationship between Marx and classical political economists. They have asserted that Marx, to begin with, 'negated' or 'rejected' Ricardian value theory, but that in POP he comes to 'affirm' or 'accept' it. Chapter Two of POP expounds how Proudhon failed in transcending the methodological insufficiency of political economists. There Marx criticises Proudhon based on his dialectical method, but not on Ricardo's analytical method. Marx's criticism of Ricardo's method is summarised briefly but decidedly in his letter to J. Schweitzer in 1865, saying:

> For an estimate of his book [Proudhon's SEC], which is in two fat tomes, I must refer you to the work I wrote as a reply [Marx's POP]. *There I showed*, among other things, how little he had penetrated into the secret of scientific dialectics; how, on the other hand, he shares the illusions of speculative philosophy, for instead of conceiving the economic categories as theoretical expressions of historical relations of production, corresponding to a particular stage of development of material production, he garbles them into pre-existing, eternal ideas; and *how in this roundabout way he arrived once more at the standpoint of bourgeois economy.*[8]

Fourth, consequently, commentators have overlooked Marx's criticism of Ricardian value theory in Chapter One. The purpose of POP is to show Proudhon's insufficiency and to make a laughing stock of him, thus Marx's critique of Ricardian method and value theory does not come out into the open. However, the methodological critique in the first chapter necessarily includes a theoretical critique. A close look at Chapter One reveals Marx's indirect critique of Ricardian value theory in his re-reading Ricardo.

Last, commentators have not clarified the *differentia specifica* of Marx's value concept, i.e., the characteristics that distinguish Marx's value concept from others. On the contrary, they seem to have mistaken Marx's value theory as being quite similar to Ricardo's. This is the fundamental deficiency of the assertions made concerning Marx's formation process. It is well known that Marx criticises political economists for their confusion of 'value' and 'price', but this has not been appreciated by many commentators.

Now let us move on to the point of divergence between Marx and Proudhon. Capitalist relations spontaneously emerged from feudal relations and exist now as an historical stage and will evolve into a higher stage. This means that capitalist relations form a sum total by co-existing simultaneously and supporting one another. They form the social structure in which each relation forms a limb. The intrinsic connection between the relations shows the structure and the relative stability in their process: formation, development and resolution.

Naturally, political economists know that capitalist relations are formed historically. However, they virtually understand them to be eternal, because they do not pay any attention to their historical conditions. Theoretically speaking, they understand capitalist relations as eternal by defining economic categories non-historically.

Proudhon wanted to transcend this methodological deficiency by explaining the origin (*genesis*) of each category. Marx rated this attempt very highly.[9] However, Proudhon does not pursue 'the historical movement of production relations, of which the categories are but the theoretical expression'. (MEC 6, p. 162) Proudhon puts economic categories into the order 'which are found alphabetically arranged at the end of every treatise on political economy'. (MEC 6, p. 162) Consequently, Proudhon does not criticise the economic categories of political economists. His critique of political economy is not a critique of economic categories. Proudhon inverted the relationship between economic categories and capitalist relations. Just as in Hegel's dialectics, Proudhon's categories produce real relations. As Marx states: 'he [Proudhon] shares the illusion of speculative philosophy',[10] and makes economic categories eternal. Proudhon made the same mistake as did the political economists, and arrived at their standpoint by a detour, as Marx states: 'in this roundabout way he arrived once more at the standpoint of bourgeois economy'.[11]

In contrast, Marx grasps the economic categories as theoretical expressions of capitalist relations of production in two respects: the historical character and the intrinsic connection.[12] This means that Marx analyses the transitory and historical characters of capitalist relations, and defines each economic category from both sides: historical character and intrinsic connection. Thus POP is crucial for a better understanding of Marx's dialectical method and his critique of political economy.

In short, the following points are the core of a full understanding of POP and consequently Marx's system as such:

1. Proudhon's methodological critique of political economy;
2. Marx's methodological critique of Proudhon;
3. Proudhon's critique of political economy's value theory;
4. Marx's critique of Proudhon's theory of 'constituted value'.

In the next section, Proudhon's dialectics and his presentation of economic categories will be summarised, followed by Marx's critique of Proudhonian dialectics.

PROUDHON'S DIALECTICAL METHOD

Proudhon's Dialectical System

Proudhon's method in SEC is his 'theory of system'. In this section I would like to clarify how Proudhon grasped and presented the economic categories.

According to Proudhon, 'metaphysics' is the modern recognition which emerged from the abolition of 'religion' and 'philosophy', and its content is the 'method of system' or the 'theory of laws of system'. Thus his 'metaphysics' as such is not a 'science', but a 'methodology of science', which provides 'method' and 'accuracy' to 'individual sciences'. It is a methodology to classify 'objects' into 'classes', 'subclasses', 'order', 'family', 'genus', 'species', and to systematise the 'objects' by putting them into order. For Proudhon, 'specific science' is the 'individual science' in which the objects are systematised as well as the nature and regularity by which its system is proved.

In Proudhon's view, political economy is not a 'science', because 'it is nothing but a chaos of a large number of observations and nothing is classified, related or systematised'.[13] Thus Proudhon's SEC is his critique of political economy, i.e., the work to elevate economics to 'economic science', based on his scientific methodology. However, Proudhon's 'system' is not of substance or of causality but an 'order', 'relations' or a 'totality of laws'.[14] His system is the 'collection of the divided', the repetition of the 'similarity' (or 'unit') of the objects. The 'system' is given 'form' by the relationship between units, the 'similarity' and the 'grounds' ('analogy', 'progress' and 'composition') which are variants of the 'similarity'. The only relation of system to economics is the relation of 'equivalence', i.e., the relationship between the two systems in which absolute scope is the same but the number of units differs. Proudhon writes: 'It is by this kind of system [of equivalent relation] that economics will bring a shift from our anarchic, destructive society to a regularly organised society.'[15]

Dialectics in *The System of Economic Contradictions*

Proudhon's 'dialectical system' consists of the following two stages:

1) The first stage in which abstract conception is formed by abstracting (analysing) empirical conception;
2) The second stage in which abstract conceptions are classified, and systematised by further abstraction.

'Systematise' means to classify or assign various abstract conceptions (the dialectical system) to inclusive classification groups by subjects and their contents. The 'abstract conception' is produced by speculation, which is based on experience. Proudhon terms this abstract conception his 'logical system' and the logical system which consists of a unit 'dialectical system'. According to him, 'truth' is a logical system that has reached the state of this 'dialectical system'; and his 'dialectic system' deals with this systematically. In 'dialectics of system', the relation of 'similarity' will be found between various inharmonious abstract conceptions. They will be classified or put into order by a certain 'principle of classification'. Proudhon's method in his SEC, the 'theory of system', is the method to analyse and synthesise abstract conceptions. It is a method to classify economic categories systematically.[16]

Proudhon's View of Economic Categories

As is shown by its title, the purpose of Proudhon's *System of Economic Contradictions* is to show that the present economic system consists of 'many kinds of antagonistic species or powers' and that 'these contradictions, which divide the economic society, bring poverty and subordination to the working class'.[17] In other words, the system of property necessarily causes class struggles, monopoly of wealth and poverty, despotism and robbery and exploitation of human beings by human beings.[18] Political economists analyse capitalist production and deduce abstract concepts and laws, but they do not show their origins. Proudhon tries to explain them; this is rated highly by Marx.

> Economists express the relations of bourgeois production, the division of labour, credit, money, etc., as fixed, immutable, eternal categories. M. Proudhon, who has these ready-made categories before him, wants to explain to us the act of formation, the genesis of these categories, principles, laws, ideas, thoughts. (MEC 6, p. 162)

For example, Proudhon asserts that 'property is theft' and explains its origin by 'miscalculation'. However, we must note here that Proudhon's 'property' includes all kinds of 'unearned income rights', tenant rights to land, rents for houses and furniture, rents for land, interest for money, profits from exchange and so on.[19] This means that his 'property' is not limited to 'capital' in a narrow sense and that he does not distinguish capitalist relations from feudal or other relations. Thus Proudhon does not comprehend the historical character of capitalist relations nor the intrinsic connection between them. In this roundabout way, he arrives at the standpoint of political economists again by making economic categories eternal.

To sum up: Proudhon does not analyse the real movement of capitalist relations but the economic categories. He cannot grasp economic categories as the theoretical expressions of capitalist relations nor explain the origin of those categories. His critique of political economy is not a critique of economic categories.[20] It is not an analysis of capitalist relations, but an abstraction of economic categories.[21] It is merely a moral condemnation of capitalist relations and a proposal for redefining economic categories.

Proudhon's Presentation of Economic Categories

In SEC Proudhon presents (or in his words 'organises') economic categories based on his 'theory of system' (dialectics). 'Class' is followed successively in descending order by some main subordinate categories: genus, species and type. Economic categories (species) are divided into types: 'the good side' and 'the bad side', 'the advantages' and 'the drawbacks', etc. The principle of its classification is 'equality' = 'justice'. In this presentation of economic categories, economic laws and necessities are proved.

The first point to note here is that Proudhon's 'proof of necessity' means discerning 'similarity' – 'equality' or 'poverty' (the negative side of 'equality') – between species.[22] To take a couple of examples, the 'division of labour' is divided into two 'sides', i.e., good side and bad side. On the one hand, the division of labour has a good side 'in which equality of conditions and of intelligence is realised', and a bad side as 'an instrument of poverty'. 'Competition' is divided into the competition for the 'advantage of equality' and the one which 'ruins those whom it drags in its train'. Similarly, each economic category is divided into its positive and negative sides by an outsider, i.e., 'equality'.[23]

As we have seen, Proudhon's system, his presentation of economic categories, is based on 'similarity': the good and bad sides of 'equality'. Thus the basic character of his system is determined by the classificatory criterion ('equality' = 'justice') before the classification. This might be a grouping of categories, but it is not an explanation (or development) of them.

The second point to note is that Proudhon's 'antithesis', 'contradiction', 'synthesis', 'dialectics' and 'necessity' are quite different from those of Marx or Hegel. His 'contradiction' does not mean a co-existence of interdependence and antagonism, but merely a 'distinction' or a 'difference'. His 'antithesis' and 'synthesis' are not the abolition of 'thesis' and 'antithesis'. In his dialectics, the latter are not deduced necessarily from the former. Thus, Proudhon's 'economic progress' is not a 'progress' but a mere 'sequence'. His 'proof of necessity' is by no means a 'necessity'.

Be this as it may, 'equality' as the classificatory criterion is presupposed in the introduction of his SEC, and its 'scientific, or empirical proof' is given through the presentation of economic categories, i.e., through the following 'evolution' of economic categories: division of labour (Chapter 3), machinery (Chapter 4), competition (Chapter 5), monopoly (Chapter 6) and police (Chapter 7). In Chapter 8, the illusion of Providence is negated by the considerations of the 'system of evil' in preceding chapters. From Chapter 9 onward, Proudhon pursues discovery of justice (policies to realise justice): balance of trade (Chapter 9), credit (Chapter 10), property (Chapter 11), common property (Chapter 12) and population (Chapter 13). In Chapter 14 (Summary and Conclusion), he suggests 'mutuality' as the policy to realise justice.

By 'system' Proudhon means 'laws' and 'necessity'. Thus, Proudhon thinks it enough for him to prove that the 'necessity' of categories can be shown successfully by verifying 'similarities' (common characters) between species ('equality' of 'poverty') in the organisation (presentation) of economic categories shown above.[24]

MARX'S CRITIQUE OF PROUDHON'S DIALECTICS

Marx's Critique of Proudhon's View of Categories

Modern civil society (capitalist society) emerged spontaneously from feudal society via many transitional forms, and exists as an historical epoch. It will be superseded by a new society in the future but is relatively stable at the moment, resting on a delicate balance between continuity and transition. Thus, capitalist society is to be grasped from two sides: on the one hand it is historical and transitory; on the other it is a stable whole body. Hereafter I call the two sides the historic and the unifying character of capitalist society. By 'unifying character' I mean the intrinsic connection and mutual support between limbs of the structure.

Marx comprehends 'society' as a product of man's interaction with man', i.e., a certain form of 'organisation, whether of the family, of the estate or of the classes'. (MEC 38, p. 96) He also understands that a definite form of society is determined by the relations of production and commerce that correspond to a certain stage in the development of productive forces. He grasps capitalist relations of production and commerce by defining economic categories in two respects: the historical character of capitalist relations and the intrinsic connection between them. Thus categories are defined as theoretical expressions of those relations.

In short the transitory and unifying characters of capitalist society are comprehended theoretically through the historical character and the intrinsic connection between categories. Up to now we have explored only the method of investigation. However, the method of presentation cannot be the same as that of investigation. In science, presentation of categories must be made in sequence by explaining the unknown based on the known. Marx calls this method 'genetical presentation'[25] because the genesis of each category shall be demonstrated by its process. Our main concern in this section is on the method of investigation, and the next section will focus on its method of presentation.

Political economists analyse capitalist relations of production and formulate laws of them. They were methodologically unclear, but grasped economic categories, virtually as theoretical reflections of the capitalist relations of production and commerce. They analyse historical capitalist relations but fail to define their categories as historic ones, e.g., 'capital' is a certain amount of 'accumulated labour', tools or machines. It is well known that Ricardo criticised Smith by referring to 'the weapon necessary to kill the beaver and the deer' in 'that early state to which Smith refers' as 'capital'.[26]

Even Ricardo, however, fails to understand the *differentia specifica* of capital. He cannot tell 'machinery as capital' from 'machinery as machinery'.

The reduction of 'capital' into 'accumulated labour' makes it possible for Smith and Ricardo to develop a labour theory of value: to grasp capitalist society as a form of mutual interrelations of human beings with labour and the products of labour. On the other hand, their reduction shows the insufficiency of their 'analytical method',[27] i.e., deleting the historic character from each economic category. Their strong point is at the same time their weak point. This insufficiency comes from the fact that 'they do not explain how these relations themselves are produced, that is the historical movement[28] that gave them birth.' (MEC 6, p. 162)

Political economists do not pay any attention to the 'origin' of 'profit' and 'rent', for example. They take the 'origin' of 'profit' as 'natural', and reduce that of 'rent' into natural, unhistorical factors, i.e., 'the differentiation of the land in location and fertility'.[29] Consequently, their concern is only with the quantitative laws, that is, with 'the average rate', 'the highest rate' and the 'lowest rate'. As a result of their reduction of 'capital' into 'accumulated labour' and of 'rent' into 'the differentiation of the land in location and fertility', the political 'economists express the relations of production ... as fixed, immutable, eternal categories'. (MEC 6, p. 162) Here is Marx and Proudhon's criticism of economists. Their first concern is with the 'origin' or the 'genesis' of economic categories. Proudhon writes in SEC: 'How does use value become exchange value? ... The genesis of the idea of (exchange) value has not been noted by economists with sufficient care. It is necessary, therefore, for us to dwell upon it.' (quoted in MEC 6, p. 111)

It is true that Proudhon dwells upon the origin of economic categories which have been ignored by economists, but he does not 'pursue the historical movement of production relations, of which the categories are but the theoretical expression'. (MEC 6, p. 162) Furthermore, he does not distinguish capitalist relations from other forms of economic relations which transform into them. Thus, Proudhon does not grasp economic categories as the reflection of capitalist relations, much less the transitory character of the categories. Having ready-made categories before him, he merely puts those into his framework by the classificatory criterion 'equality' or 'justice'. Thus, in his dialectical system, just as in Hegelian dialectics, categories produce the real social relations. Although Marx's criticism that Proudhon inverts the relationship between the social relations of production and economic categories is not accurate, the criticism is still true and effective. Let me demonstrate Marx's critique of Proudhon's explanation of the genesis of exchange value.

As will be shown in the next section, Proudhon's dialectics has no contradiction in a Hegelian sense and his categories cannot develop by themselves. To solve this problem Proudhon makes 'a man' intervene, who proposes to other men that they establish exchange and make a distinction between use value and exchange value. He does not explain the genesis of exchange value from the history of exchange.

Marx criticises Proudhon's above explanation and makes a laughing stock of it by calling the 'man' a '*deus ex machina*'. A *deus ex machina* is a 'person who appears unexpectedly to save a situation'[30] in a drama. Admitting the proposal of the man in Proudhon's explanation, the reasons why the man made the proposal and why other men accepted it are not explained at all. The real problem stays unsolved. Instead Marx explains the genesis of exchange value from the three stages in the development of exchange:

1) 'There was a time, as in the Middle Ages, when only the superfluous, the excess of production over consumption, was exchanged.' (MEC 6, p. 113)

2) 'There was again a time, when not only the superfluous, but all products, all industrial existence, had passed into commerce, when the whole of production depended on exchange.' (MEC 6, p. 113)

3) 'Finally, there came a time when everything that men had considered as inalienable became an object of exchange, of traffic and could be alienated. This is the time when the very things that till then had been communicated, but never exchanged; given, but never sold; acquired, but never bought – virtue, love, conviction, knowledge, conscience, etc. – when everything finally passed into commerce.' (MEC 6, p. 113)

After the second stage, the product obtains not only a use value but also an exchange value.

> The product supplied is not useful in itself ... . In the course of production, it has been exchanged for all the costs of production, such as raw materials, wages of workers, etc., all of which are marketable values. The product, therefore, represents, in the eyes of the producer, a sum total of marketable values. What he supplies is not only a useful object, but also and above all a marketable value.' (MEC 6, p. 118)

As to demand, on the other hand, 'it will only be effective on condition that it has means of exchange at its disposal. These means are themselves products, marketable values'. (MEC 6, p. 118) Consequently, the concept of 'exchange value' is the result of supply and demand.

> But in the real world [based on division of labour and private exchange], ... [t]he competition among the suppliers and the competition among the demanders form a necessary part of the struggle between buyers and sellers, of which marketable value is the result. (MEC 6, p. 119)

In other words '(exchange) value' distinguished from 'price' can be conceptualised only under an advanced division of labour and private exchange, that is, only in the age of large-scale industry and free competition, in which products are produced as commodities. Only in such an age is abstracting 'value' from 'prices' possible and a 'truth', because the relation it expresses continues to exist.[31]

That which Marx illustrates, in similar criticisms all through POP, is the real economic relations that are to be expressed by economic categories but not history as such. We can witness there the dissimilarity between Marx's and Proudhon's critique of political economy, i.e., between a critique of economic categories with analysis of the real economic movement (of production and consumption) and a critique without them. Since 'critique' means clarifying the grounds and the limitations, a critique of economic categories means comprehending the grounds and the limitations of economic categories as reflections of capitalist relations of production and commerce, which correspond to a certain stage in the development of productive forces. Proudhon, on the other hand, does not have such a critique of economic categories and fails to understand the historical character of capitalist society. 'Proudhon does not directly assert that to him bourgeois life is an eternal truth: he says so indirectly, by deifying the categories which express bourgeois relations in the form of thought.' (MEC 38, p. 102)

To sum up, Proudhon wants to 'rise above the bourgeois horizon' (MEC 38, p. 102) but 'in this roundabout way he arrived once more at the standpoint of bourgeois economy' mainly because he does not pursue the real movement of capitalist relations.

Marx's Critique of Proudhon's Presentation of Economic Categories

The Intrinsic Connection between Economic Categories

Here I would like to investigate the intrinsic connection between categories, i.e., Marx's presentation of economic categories.

In POP Marx criticises Proudhon's artificial presentation of categories by analysing some of them, by clarifying the real economic relations that they express: 'exchange', 'money' (Chapter One), 'division of labour and machinery', 'competition and monopoly' and 'landed property or rent' (Chapter Two). Written in this polemic form, Marx's own presentation is not clear as such. However, when we read between the lines, the outline of it breaks the surface: 'logical development' (MEC 6, p. 193) on the basis of the intrinsic relations of the economic categories. Here I would like to demonstrate this by following Marx's critique of Proudhon's 'division of labour and machinery' and 'rent'.

Needless to say, 'property' developed in many epochs under wholly different sets of social relations. Thus, a definite form of 'property' comprises all the social relations of production of that time. With Proudhon the issue is modern bourgeois property as it exists today. However, Proudhon does not understand that bourgeois property is the whole of capitalist relations of production, or that it is the capitalist form of the division of labour. Consequently he investigates 'property' and 'division of labour' separately and does not clarify their historical features at all. He thinks of 'modern bourgeois property' as an independent economic category and a phase of his 'economic evolution'.[32] That is to say, Proudhon cannot grasp the intrinsic connection between capitalist relations of production, and thus between economic categories.

The Historical Character of Categories

Division of Labour and Machinery

In the real world, the 'division of labour' develops in many epochs and under many different relations of production. For Proudhon, however, the division of labour is 'an eternal law, a simple, abstract category'. (MEC 6, p. 179). He is only concerned with the 'division of labour' in general, thus 'caste, corporations, manufacture, and large-scale industry' must be explained by the single word 'divide' (MEC 6, p. 179), instead of analysing its capitalist form. According to him, 'division of labour' is the 'thesis' of labour and a method to realise 'equality'. It consists of the good and the bad sides: the manner in which equality of conditions and of intelligence is realised: an instrument of poverty. To derive the drawbacks from the division of labour, Proudhon considers 'modern factory' as the 'antithesis' and moves into 'machinery' as the 'synthesis'.

As Marx criticises, 'He [Proudhon] opposes the division of labour of one historical epoch to the division of labour of another historical epoch.' (MEC 6, p. 182) Consequently, in Proudhon's paradialectics each following category is given artificially as an antidote for the preceding one without any connection with the real world, i.e., with the order in which categories produce each other.[33] To illustrate this let us compare Proudhon's investigation into 'machinery' and Marx's critique of it.

According to Proudhon, the 'machine' or the modern 'workshop' is a method to combine small parts divided by the 'division of labour', which introduces the principle of authority in society, and theoretically results in the 'wage system'. 'Machinery', on the one hand, restores the workers divided by the 'division of labour', reduces the pains of workers and the price of products, increases the general welfare and brings equality with intelligence. On the other hand, it reduces wages, produces overproduction, degrades the social position of workers and brings poverty.

From the 'historical and economic point of view' (MEC 6, p. 184), Marx examines the two kinds of division of labour, i.e., in the workshop and inside society, 'whether it [the workshop] rehabilitated the worker on the one hand, while submitting him to authority on the other; whether the machine [or the workshop] is the recomposition of divided labour, the synthesis of labour as opposed to its analysis'. (MEC 6, p. 184) After pointing out the similarity of 'society as a whole' and the 'workshop', Marx points out the dissimilarity between them:

> While inside the modern workshop the division of labour is meticulously regulated by the authority of the employer, modern society has no other rule, no other authority for the distribution of labour than free competition.
>
> ... It can even be laid down as a general rule that the less authority presides over the division of labour inside society, the more the division of labour develops inside the workshop, and the more it is subjected there to the authority of a single person.

> Thus authority in the workshop and authority in society, in relation to the division of labour, are in *reverse ratio* to each other. (MEC 6, pp. 184f)

Then Marx examines the kind of workshop 'in which the occupations are very much separated, where each person's task is reduced to a very simple operation, and where the authority, capital, groups and directs the work', (MEC 6, p. 185) i.e., the developing process of 'manufacturing industry' without machinery. After pointing out that the 'division of labour' is generally regulated by the extent and the form of the market, Marx counts the following as indispensable conditions for the formation of manufacturing industry:

1) The accumulation of capital, facilitated by the discovery of America and the import of its precious metals (the depreciation of wages and land rents, and the growth of industrial profits) (MEC 6, p. 185).

2) The so-called primitive accumulation of capital – e.g., 'the increase of commodities put into circulation from the moment trade penetrated to the East Indies by way of the Cape of Good Hope; the colonial system; the development of maritime trade' (MEC 6, p. 185) – on the one hand, and the proletariat on the other. In short:

> The growth of the market, the accumulation of capital, the modification in the social position of the classes, a large number of persons being deprived of their sources of income, all these are historical preconditions for the formation of manufacture. (MEC 6, p. 186)

Marx shows that manufacture:

> ...consisted much more in the bringing together of many workers and many crafts in one place, in one room, under the command of one capital, than in the analysis of labour and the adaptation of a special worker to a very simple task. (MEC 6, p. 186)

For Proudhon, who sees things upside down, the division of labour precedes the workshop, which is a condition of its existence. In reality, however, 'once the men and the instruments had been brought together, the division of labour, such as it existed in the form of the guilds, was reproduced, necessarily reflected inside the workshop'. (MEC 6, p. 186)

Furthermore, Marx clarifies that the 'machine is a uniting of the instruments of labour, and by no means a combination of different operations for the worker himself' and that the 'machine, properly so-called, dates from the end of the eighteenth century'. (MEC 6, p. 186) Through this developing process of the 'machine', the following propositions are shown:

1) for Proudhon the concentration of the instruments of production is the negation of the division of labour. In reality, however, as 'the concentration of instruments develops, the division develops also, and vice versa' (MEC 6, p. 187);

2) the 'invention of machinery brought about the separation of manufacturing industry from agricultural industry' and 'to the application of machinery and of steam, the division of labour was able to assume such

dimensions that large-scale industry, detached from the national soil, depends entirely on the world market, on international exchange, on an international division of labour' (MEC 6, p. 187);

3) the 'machine has so great an influence on the division of labour, that when, in the manufacture of some object, a means has been found to produce parts of it mechanically, the manufacture splits up immediately into two branches independent of each other' (MEC 6, p. 187);

4) '[F]rom 1825 onwards, almost all the new inventions were the result of collisions between the worker and the employer who sought at all costs to depreciate the worker's specialised ability' (MEC 6, p. 188);

5) consequently, we need not speak of 'the providential and philanthropic aim that M. Proudhon discovers in the invention and the first application of machinery'. (MEC 6, p. 188)

To sum up, in the real historical movement, 'with the introduction of machinery the division of labour inside society has increased, the task of the worker inside the workshop has been simplified, capital has been concentrated, the human being has been further dismembered'. (MEC 6, p. 188) This means Proudhon's presentation of economic categories – economic evolution – is not scientific but utopian.

Incidentally, the division of labour in the automatic workshop is characterised by the fact that 'labour there has completely lost its specialised character' (MEC 6, p. 190), which Proudhon overlooks. Marx sees the revolutionary side of the modern automatic workshop in the following fact. 'However the moment every special development stops, the need for universality, the tendency towards an integral development of the individual begins to be felt.' (MEC 6, p. 190)

Landed Property or Rent

As has already been stated, Proudhon cannot comprehend 'property'. In spite of his claim to clarify the origin of 'property', he 'declares himself incapable of understanding the economic origin of rent and of property' (MEC 6, p. 197), because he abandons the clarification of its economic origin by affirming 'that there is something mystical and mysterious about the origin of property'. (MEC 6, p. 197) As a matter of fact, he says on the average amount of rent:

> Ricardo's theory answers this question. In the beginnings of society, ... , rent must have been nil ... . Little by little, the multiplication of families and the progress of agriculture caused the price of land to make itself felt. Labour came to give the soil its worth: from this, rent came into being. The more fruit a field yielded with the same amount of labour, the higher it was valued; hence the tendency of proprietors was always to arrogate to themselves the whole amount of the fruits of the soil, less the wages of the farmer – that is, less the costs of production. Thus property followed on the heels of labour to take from it all the product that exceeded the actual expenses ... . In essence and by destination, then, rent is an instrument of distribu-

tive justice, one of the thousand means that the genius of economy employs to attain to equality. (MEC 6, p. 198)

This is Ricardo's theory of rent itself. Proudhon does better by making the 'proprietor' intervene, like a *deus ex machina*, to explain 'property' or 'rent'. Here again, Proudhon avoids his original task to explain the economic origin of rent by making use of the intervention of the proprietor to explain property, by using the intervention of the rent-receiver to explain rent. That is why he cannot get beyond the phrase: 'property is theft'.

The main cause lies in his views on economic categories. Without pursuing the historical movement of the real relations of production, understanding those relations as 'principles, categories, abstract thoughts', instead understanding economic categories as the 'scientific expression' of those relations, he has no choice but to develop economic categories from the movement of a 'pure reason', i.e., from the classificatory criterion 'equality' brought from outside.

To explain historically means to explain from its historical conditions by starting from the 'praxis' – productive activity – of real individuals. This is possible only on the basis of a minute examination of the following points: 'their respective needs, their productive forces, their mode of production, the raw materials of their production – in short – ... the relations between man and man that result from all these conditions of existence'. (MEC 6, p. 170). As to the origin of 'rent', Marx writes as follows:

1) the 'origin of property' is 'the relation between production itself and the distribution of the instrument of production' (MEC 6, p. 197) and is reproduced every day before our eyes;

2) Ricardo explains 'rent' from the difference in the location and the fertility of lands on two conditions. He asserts that in 'manufacturing industry, the price of the product obtained by the minimum of labour regulates the price of all other commodities of the same kind' (MEC 6, p. 199), and that in 'agricultural industry, on the contrary, it is the price of the product obtained by the greatest amount of labour that regulates the price of all products of the same kind' (MEC 6, p. 199);

3) the historical conditions for the Ricardian doctrine to be generally true, or the historical conditions 'rent' should express, are the original accumulation, the development of capitalist mode of agriculture and the transformation of landowners to capitalists:

The abasement of the labourer, reduced to the role of a simple worker, day labourer, wage-earner, working for the industrial capitalist; the intervention of the industrial capitalist, exploiting the land like any other factory; the transformation of the landed proprietor from a petty sovereign into a vulgar usurer: these are the different relations expressed by rent. (MEC 6, p. 201)

4) land, insofar as it yields interest, is land capital, and as land capital it yields no rent. Consequently, land does not constitute landed property

anymore. 'Rent ... is industrial capital applied to land' (MEC 6, p. 201) and is a 'result of society and not of the soil'. (MEC 6, p. 205)

As is shown in the above account, it is safe to say that Marx's 'historical', 'genetical' presentation of economic categories means the clarification of the real historical, economic relations expressed by the categories. On the other hand, Proudhon tries to explain the origin of the economic categories, about which political economists were not concerned, but he cannot finish it properly 'chiefly because he does not know history'. (MEC 38, p. 100)

Proudhon is certainly an Hegelian insofar as he grasps the economic categories as principles, not as the expression of the relations of production. In fact, he does not pursue the real movement of relations of production. In theory, Proudhon, like Hegel, explains the origin of economic categories from the movement of a pure reason: 'equality'. On the other hand, unlike Hegel, Proudhon's categories do not have life in themselves because there are no real 'contradictions' in them. Proudhon's dialectics is not Hegelian dialectics but mere paradialectics. That is why he needs a *deus ex machina* to explain the origin of economic categories.

Marx views economic categories as the theoretical expressions of the relations of production and of the mutual interactions between individuals. In other words, Marx sees what the individuals are through their relations of production, or their expressions of their mutual activities. Consequently, Marx's critique of political economy is not another political economy but the only one 'human science', the science of man incorporated into 'natural science'.[34]

CONCLUSIONS

Capitalist society produces wealth on the capitalist side and poverty on the worker side. Wealth and poverty are both sides of the same coin and two necessary results of capitalist relations of production. However, political economists represent wealth and socialists poverty exclusively. Political economists start from the principle that labour is the sole source of wealth, but they do not care about the poverty of labourers. On the other hand, socialists do not investigate the structure and the movement of capitalist production that yields poverty. Thus socialists do little other than implore the mercy of the rich for the poor.

Marx and Proudhon want to transcend the contradiction by using the dialectical method. Thus, the methodological and theoretical deficiencies of political economists and socialists are their starting point. They share not only the same purpose (a critique of political economy), but also the method (the dialectical method). Their works appear quite similar. However, their critiques of political economy are quite divergent.

Political economists understand that capitalist society is natural and eternal, because they make economic categories non-historical. Both Proudhon and Marx start from this methodological insufficiency of political economists.

However, Proudhon does not pursue the real movement of capitalist production, and cannot clarify the origin of each economic category successfully. He does not criticise the economic categories of political economists, but accepts them as 'ready-made catgories'. Thus, he is concerned with only rearranging their order. He systematises the order of economic categories by outside standards which are irrelevant to the economic categories: the good sides and the bad sides, the advantages and the drawbacks. His dialectics has no intrinsic connection with any economic analysis. His critique of political economy is not a critique of economic categories, but nothing more than a moral condemnation of capitalist relations. 'Proudhon does not directly assert that to him *bourgeois life* is an *eternal truth*; he says so indirectly, by deifying the categories which express bourgeois relations in the form of thought.' (38 MEC, p. 102)

By a detour Proudhon arrived at the starting point, i.e., the standpoint of political economists who assert capitalist relations are natural and eternal. On the other hand, Marx's dialectics is his method to comprehend the capitalist relations of production as historical relations in two respects: the historical character of capitalist relations and the intrinsic connection between them.

Marx analyses the real movement of capitalist relations, and redefines economic categories as the scientific expressions of capitalist relations. Marx's critique of economic categories means comprehending the grounds and the limitations of economic categories as scientific expression of capitalist relations, which correspond to a certain stage in the development of productive forces. He demonstrates that capitalist relations are transitory by clarifying the origin (*genesis*) of economic categories. Proudhon, on the other hand, lacking such a critique of economic categories, fails in understanding capitalist society as historical. He wants to 'rise above the bourgeois horizon', but 'in this roundabout way he arrived once more at the standpoint of bourgeois economy'.

As we have clarified here, 'the decisive points' of Marx's dialectical method are scientifically indicated in POP. Unfortunately, this scientific method has been misunderstood as the so-called 'materialist interpretation of history', which has no direct connection with a critique of economic categories. Consequently, Marx has been misunderstood. However, I believe that we have now arrived at the core of Marx's method and his system.

4 MARX'S METHODOLOGICAL CRITIQUE OF CLASSICAL POLITICAL ECONOMISTS

Marx's POP is a methodological and theoretical critique of political economy and socialism. It is a demonstration of Marx's dialectical method. It is a critique of economic categories in order to explain the genesis – or the origin – of economic categories. The point we would like to make here concerns Marx's dialectical method in Chapter Two of POP, with special reference to his methodological critique of political economy. Marx's theoretical critique of political economy in POP will be expounded in Chapter 8.

Capitalist society, the sum total of capitalist relations of production and commerce, yields wealth on the one hand and poverty on the other, each of which is represented by political economists and socialists. Thus Proudhon declared in his SEC that he established 'a revolutionary theory' in order to abolish capitalist society by transcending both political economists and socialists. SEC is a critique of political economy.

Thus Marx's POP, directed against SEC, is not only a critique of Proudhon but also a critique of political economy and socialism. The methodological insufficiency of political economy, i.e., the unhistorical understanding of economic categories, is a premise for both Proudhon and Marx. The core of the controversy between Proudhon and Marx is how to transcend the insufficiency of political economy, i.e., the method used in a critique of economic categories. The core of Marx's critique of Proudhon is that Proudhon, in a roundabout way, arrived at the standpoint of political economists, i.e., the ahistorical understanding of economic categories. The quotation from *On Proudhon* below demonstrates this to the full: 'There [in POP] I showed, ... how in this roundabout way he [Proudhon] arrived once more at the standpoint of bourgeois economy [of making economic categories eternal].'[1]

The point here is that political economists, as well as Proudhon and Hegel, are methodologically and theoretically criticised by Marx for their unhistorical understanding of economic categories, and thus of capitalist society. This is the reason why Marx states as follows: 'The decisive points of our view [of his critique of political economy] were first scientifically, although only polemically, indicated in my work [POP] published in 1847 and directed against Proudhon.'[2]

Marx's POP is not the work in which Marx defended political economy from Proudhon's attack but the work in which he expounded how political economy is to be criticised. Thus, in this sense, Marx's methodological critique of Proudhon in Chapter Two of his POP is also directed against political economy, including Ricardo.[3] Added to this, a careful investigation of Chapter One of POP will reveal that the Ricardian value theory is also criticised, albeit indirectly, with regard to the historical understanding of economic categories.

Methodologically speaking, 'the decisive points' indicated in POP can be summarised as follows:

a) Capitalist relations of production and commerce are historical, transitory.
b) They form a sum total by co-existing simultaneously and supporting one another.
c) Economic categories are only the theoretical expressions of capitalist relations. Thus each economic category must represent the historical character of capitalist relations which it expresses and the intrinsic connection with other relations.
d) Understanding economic categories via this dual focus is a means of explaining the genesis, or the origin, of each economic category, i.e., what, how and by what means each category is yielded. This is the crux of Proudhon's and Marx's methodological critiques of political economy, i.e., of ahistorical understanding of categories.
e) Economic categories should be presented in accordance with their genesis, i.e., in 'the order in which they engender one another' (MEC 6, p. 169) which was later termed the 'genetical presentation' of economic categories.[4]

In the first section we examine the general character and limitations of both political economists' and Marx's methods. The second and third sections expound the historical character and the intrinsic connection between economic categories. The last section investigates Marx's genetical presentation of economic categories.

RICARDO V. MARX ON METHOD

The Character and Limitations of Ricardo's and Marx's Method

The methodology of classical political economy is termed the 'analytical method'. Political economists analysed capitalist relations of production and commerce, and abstracted their essences. For example, they reduced capital and commodity to labour. Also they analysed fluctuations in prices and abstracted central price from it. They called it the 'natural price' (Smith) or the 'cost of production' (Ricardo) and defined the value of a commodity accordingly. It is this analytical method which made their economics scientific and led them to the formation of the labour theory of value.

This analytical method, however, is inadequate to comprehend historical organisms which pass through the process of formation, development and resolution. On the one hand, the method cannot clarify the historical character of capitalist relations. It reduces the substance of commodity, capital, rent, etc., but does not demonstrate historical conditions which transform the substance, i.e., labour, into capital or commodity. The 'First Observation' of POP says: 'Economists explain how production takes place in the above-mentioned relations, but what they do not explain how these relations themselves are produced, that is, the historical movement which gave them birth.' (MEC 6, p. 162)

On the other hand, the method is inadequate to grasp the intrinsic connection between capitalist relations of production and commerce. Capitalist relations form a sum total by co-existing simultaneously and supporting one another. They form the social structure in which each relation forms a limb. The intrinsic connection between the relations shows the structure and the relative stability in their process of formation, development, and resolution: capitalist relations spontaneously emerged from feudal relations and exist now as an historical stage and will evolve into higher levels. In the 'Third Observation', Marx emphasises the interrelation of capitalist relations:

> The different limbs of society are converted into so many separate societies [by Proudhon], following one upon the other. How, indeed, could the single logical formula of movement, of sequence, of time, explain the structure of society, in which all relations co-exist simultaneously and support one another. (MEC 6, p. 167)

In short, the analytical method is inadequate to comprehend the following two aspects of capitalist relations: the historical character and the intrinsic connection.

Both Proudhon and Marx attempt to explain the origin of economic categories in order to transcend those insufficiencies of political economy by using a dialectical method.[5] Although Proudhon does not analyse the real movement – process – of capitalist production, Marx's dialectical method is a means of comprehending capitalist relations from the two aspects based on an anlysis of the real capitalist relations. In this sense, the analytical method of political economy provides the basis for Marx's critical analysis of economic categories. The general character and limitations of the analytical method, thus of political economists, is observed in Marx's *Manuscripts of 1861–1863* as follows:

> Classical economy is not interested in elaborating how the various forms come into being, but seeks to reduce them to their unity by means of analysis, because it starts from them as given premises. But analysis is the necessary prerequisite of genetical presentation, and of the understanding of the real, formative process in its different phases.[6]

Because he was once an Hegelian, Marx is critical of the analytical method from his first encounter with political economy in 1843.[7] For example, Marx writes in EPM as follows:

> Political economy proceeds from the fact of private property [the right of ownership]; it does not explain it to us. It grasps the material process of private property, the process through which it actually passes, in general and abstract formulae which it

then takes as laws. It does not comprehend these laws, i.e., it does not show how they arise from the nature of private property. (MEC 3, pp. 270f)

As a matter of fact, in the passage which follows the quotation above, Marx sets himself the task of comprehending economic laws of political economists from the 'general nature of private property'[8] with the help of the two concepts: 'private property' and 'estranged labour' (MEC 3, p. 281). This reminds us of Marx's *Manuscripts of 1861–1863*[9] and should be understood as his first plan of the genetical presentation of economic categories, but this has been interpreted as evidence of immaturity of the 'early Marx'.

It is also noteworthy that Marx's 'On Proudhon' quoted partly above is preceded by a critique of the Hegelian speculative dialectics, a method of understanding organisms from two aspects: the historical character and the intrinsic connection. Here this can be mentioned only briefly but the point is that in Hegelian dialectics categories and abstract ideas produce real social relations, as Marx writes in his 'Postface' to the second edition of *Capital*.[10]

Marx's dialectical method, however, is only the dialectic of description, no more and no less than that. It is said to be a systematic description for comprehending capitalist relations from the two aspects: the historical character and the intrinsic connection.

Therefore, his dialectic is, unlike Hegel's, not the self-development or self-creation of concepts themselves. The movement of categories in Marx's dialectical presentation is not 'the real act of production' of categories but, in fact, 'a product of thinking and comprehending'.[11] In short, the limitation of Marx's dialectical method is that it is nothing but 'the working-up of observation and conception into concepts'.[12] This can be observed in Marx's critique of Proudhon's made-up dialectics. In the 'Fifth Observation' Marx states: ' ... now we have M. Proudhon reduced to saying that the order in which he gives the economic categories is no longer the order in which they engender one another'. (MEC 6, p. 169) Marx presents categories in the order in which they do engender one another.

Ricardo v. Marx on View of Economic Categories

Political economists reduce the various forms of wealth to their inner unity, but they do not explain the real formative process in its different phases. This is a necessary result of their method. The idea of explaining the genesis of economic categories never came into their minds. As Marx states in the 'First Observation' : 'what they ... do not explain is how these relations themselves are produced'. (MEC 6, p. 162)

To take a couple of examples, they reduce 'commodity' to 'labour', but they are not concerned with why, how and by what means the 'labour' appears in the 'value' of a product under capitalist conditions. Similarly, they do not explain 'natural price' or 'production cost' from 'value' nor the possibility and necessity for the historical abolition of commodities. They concentrate instead on the quantitative analysis of economic relations, i.e., average, highest and lowest rates. The deficiency of political economists in this respect is a necessary result of their analytical method. Consequently, Ricardo is not an exception.

It should be clear from these examples that political economists do not understand capitalist relations, or economic categories, as historical, because their method necessarily abstracts all characteristics distinctive of capitalist relations. At least in theory, political economists do not understand economic categories as theoretical reflections of capitalist relations of production and commerce. They do not directly assert that capitalist relations are eternal, but they say so indirectly. In the 'First Observation' Marx remarks: 'Economists express the relations of bourgeois production, the division of labour, credit, money, etc., as fixed, immutable, eternal categories.' (MEC 6, p. 162)

On the other hand, Marx understands: 'Economic categories are only the theoretical expressions, the abstractions of the social relations of production'. (MEC 6, p. 165) What concerns Marx is the historical conditions which transform 'labour' into the 'value' of a commodity, or into 'capital'. In other words, the genesis of economic categories is explained, as Marx states in the 'First Observation' as follows: 'Economists explain how production takes place in the above-mentioned relations, but what they do not explain is how these relations themselves are produced, that is, the historical movement which gives them birth.' (MEC 6, p. 162) By 'the historical movement' in the quotation, we should not understand history qua history. Once capitalist relations are established, they are produced every day before our eyes. Furthermore, by 'movement' Marx means 'process'. The point here is that economic laws are grasped from the 'very nature of private property' through this genetical presentation of economic categories. Comprehending economic laws as necessary laws of private property is the other side of explaining the genesis of economic categories. This requires a critical analysis of capitalist relations which even Ricardo had never thought of. Thus for Marx's genetical presentation of economic categories, the arrival-point of political economists serves, at best, only as the starting-point.

For example, Marx points out that the following must be examined minutely: what are men's 'respective needs, their productive forces, their mode of production, the raw materials of their production, in short, what [are] the relations between man and man which resulted from all these conditions of existence?' (MEC 6, p. 170)

This leads us to the definition of economic categories from the two aspects. As the theoretical expression of capitalist relations, each category must express the stage in the development of productive forces to which it corresponds. In the 'Second Observation' Marx writes that 'Social relations are closely bound up with productive forces' (MEC 6, p. 166); each category, on the other hand, must reflect the interconnection with other relations, which co-exist simultaneously and support one another.

There are a couple of points worth mentioning in regard to Marx's dialectical method. First, economic categories 'are truths only insofar as those relations continue to exist'. (MEC 38, p. 100) Marx specifies that Proudhon's and Hegel's dialectics has to be speculative because they do not 'pursue the historical movement of production relations, of which the categories are but the theoretical expression'. (MEC 6, p. 162) As we shall see later, this concerns the order in which economic categories should be presented.

Second, capitalist relations must be separated from feudal or mere transitional relations through critical analyses of the movement of capitalist production and consumption. The term 'capital, ' for example, has been used from ancient times. It is, however, careless to jump from this simple suggestion to the conclusion that capitalism is as old as the term. As Marx points out in 'Chapter 2 §4. Property or Rent' 'property has developed differently and under a set of entirely different social relations'. (MEC 6, p. 197) Confusing modern capital with that in ancient times, e.g., cattle, will lead us to a complete misunderstanding of our modern society based on large-scale industry.

In the following two sections, let us examine further the point we have been considering with special reference to the Ricardian rent theory.

RICARDO V. MARX ON THE 'HISTORICAL CHARACTER'

Let us take up Marx's critical analysis of rent in POP and demonstrate how the historical character of rent is grasped by Marx. Proudhon declares himself incapable of understanding the economic origin of rent by saying that it is 'so to speak, extra-economic'; though he refers to the Ricardian rent theory as the average rent. To begin with, Marx summarises Ricardo's rent theory as follows:

a) 'In agricultural industry, ... it is the price of the product obtained by the greatest amount of labour which regulates the price of all products of the same kind.' (MEC 6, p. 199)

b) 'Then, as population increases, land of an inferior quality begins to be exploited, or new outlays of capital, proportionately less productive than before, are made upon the same plot of land. In both cases a greater amount of labour is expended to obtain a proportionately smaller product.' (MEC 6, p. 199)

c) 'As competition levels the market price, the product of the better soil will be paid for as dearly as that of the inferior. It is the excess of the price of the products of the better soil over the cost of their production that constitutes rent.' (MEC 6, p. 200)

After this summary, Marx points out that the Ricardian rent theory partly shows the economic origin of rent: 'Rent, in the Ricardian sense, is property in land in its bourgeois state, that is, feudal property which has become subject to the conditions of bourgeois production.' (MEC 6, p. 199)

In contrast with Proudhon, Marx rates the Ricardian rent theory as a scientific analysis of real production relations. However, it should also be noted that Marx points out the insufficiency of Ricardo's analysis of rent as an historical relation, or a production relation.

For example, Marx names the following as the historical conditions of the Ricardian doctrine:

a) that 'capital should be freely applicable to different branches of industry';

b) that 'a strongly developed competition among capitalists should have brought profits to an equal level';

c) that 'the farmer should be no more than an industrial capitalist claiming for the use of his capital on inferior land, a profit equal to that which he would draw from his capital, if it were applied in any kind of manufacture';

d) that 'agricultural exploitation should be subjected to the regime of large-scale industry'; and finally,

e) that 'the landowner himself should aim at nothing beyond the money return'. (MEC 6, p. 200)

In a succeeding paragraph, with regard to the subjective essence of rent, Marx counts the following as 'the different relations expressed by rent':

a) 'The abasement of the labourer, reduced to the role of a simple worker, day labourer, wage-earner, working for the industrial capitalist';

b) 'the intervention of the industrial capitalist, exploiting the land like any other factory';

c) 'the transformation of the landed proprietor from a petty sovereign into a vulgar usurer'. (MEC 6, p. 201)

It should be clear from this critical analysis that Marx grasps rent as a capitalist production relation by analysing historical conditions which rent expresses. This analysis, however, separates the rent relation from other feudal, transitional or untypical relations. The following serves as an example: 'Farm rent can imply again, apart from rent proper, the interest on the capital incorporated in the land. In this instance the landowner receives this part of the farm rent, not as a landowner but as a capitalist ...'. (MEC 6, p. 205)

It is well-known that Ricardo determines rent by the following two factors:

a) the different 'situation' of land to market; and

b) the different 'degrees of fertility of soil'.

Marx argues against this determination. Since the two factors are unhistorical, this determination makes his rent unhistorical and unsocial. In this sense, his rent theory illustrates the insufficiency as well as the scientific aspect of the Ricardian economics. Marx writes:

> Ricardo, after postulating bourgeois production as necessary for determining rent, applies it [the conception of rent: in the German ed.], nevertheless, to the landed property of all ages and all countries. This is an old trick [error: in the German ed.]

common to all the economists, who represent the bourgeois relations of production as eternal categories [relations: in the German ed.]. (MEC 6, p. 202)

Although he had not yet completed his own rent theory in POP, basic points of Marx's view have already become clear. For example, he asserts: 'Rent results from the social relations in which the exploitation of the land takes place.' (MEC 6, p. 205) Rent should express those social relations. However, this is beyond the scope of the analytical method.

RICARDO V. MARX ON THE 'INTRINSIC CONNECTION'

Capitalist relations of production co-exist simultaneously, support one another and form a whole. They are all interconnected, so economic categories accordingly must express the intrinsic connection between capitalist relations. To 'give an exposition of all the social relations of bourgeois production' is 'to define bourgeois property' (MEC 6, p. 197). On the other hand, unless the 'bonds' are shown, each capitalist relation is understood as independent of the others.

In his SEC, Proudhon gives property an independent chapter (Chapter 11). Furthermore, as a matter of fact, there he investigates only rent. In the opening paragraph of 'Chapter 2 §4 Property or Rent', Marx criticises this: 'To try to give a definition of property as of an independent relation, a category apart, an abstract and eternal idea, can be nothing but an illusion of metaphysics or jurisprudence.' (MEC 6, p. 197)

However, this criticism can be applied to political economy too. The Ricardian rent theory provides an example. He deals with rent in relation to 'value' (Chapter 2 On Rent), but his point of view is limited to whether rent is a component of natural price or a result of it. Rent, especially average rent, is already presupposed in his determination of value (Chapter 1). Rent is not explained as a 'particular and developed expression' (MEC 3, p. 281) of value. Similarly, the intrinsic connection between value, profit, rent or cost of production (including profit) are neither grasped nor developed from value by Ricardo.

Thus, from Marx's point of view or from the standpoint of the genetical presentation of economic categories, Ricardo does not grasp the connection between the categories. He explains nothing. His presentation of economic categories is nothing but a tautology. This is also an inevitable result of his analytical method.

Another notable example occurs in Chapter One of POP. Marx investigates money as 'a social relation' (MEC 6, p. 145) closely connected with a whole chain of other economic relations. Although the criticism is directed against Proudhon, it should also be understood as a critique of the Ricardian money theory because he does not differ much from Proudhon in this respect. This is the reason why Ricardo is no longer contrasted with Proudhon. Thus Marx's critique of Proudhon's money theory can be equally applied to Ricardo's.

Marx's critique can be summarised as follows: Proudhon does not distinguish money itself from its functions and grasps money only in its concrete roles, i.e., only as a means of exchange. He presupposes the necessity for money as a special agent of exchange rather than explaining its wider significance. He explains only a secondary question, i.e., 'why this particular function [a special agent of exchange] has developed upon gold and silver rather than upon any other commodity'. (MEC 6, p. 146) He does not realise that 'this [the money] relation corresponds to a definite mode of production neither more nor less than does individual exchange'. (MEC 6, p. 146) Gold and silver are commodities and also have the capacity of being the universal agent of exchange. Thus the first question to be asked is, 'why, in exchanges as they [the values] are actually constituted, it has been necessary to individualize exchangeable-value, so to speak, by the creation of a special agent of exchange'. (MEC 6, p. 145) Commodity production and commodity exchange require and perpetually produce money. The necessity for the creation of money is in the determination of value itself. This is, however, beyond Ricardo's comprehension. Marx specifies this in his *Manuscripts of 1861–63* by saying:

> But Ricardo does not examine the form of the peculiar characteristic of labour that creates exchange-value or manifests itself in exchange-value as the nature of this labour. Hence he does not grasp the connection of this labour with money or that it must assume the form of money. Hence he completely fails to grasp the connection between the determination of the exchange-value of the commodity by labour time and the fact that the devlopment of commodities necessarily leads to the formation of money.[13]

As we have examined above, the Ricardian theory of rent and money does not comprehend the intrinsic connection with other capitalist relations, or economic categories. Understanding money as a means of exchange does not necessarily mean comprehending it as 'a production relation'. (MEC 6, p. 145) Marx, on the other hand, comprehends the connection between commodities and money in terms of the social substance of value.[14]

So far we have examined the inadequacy of the Ricardian method from three points of view: the view on economic categories, the historical character of capitalist relations and the connections between them. Those limitations are necessary results of his analytical method. They are not three different things, but three aspects of the same: the analytical method. In the next section we will give readers the full particulars of Marx's methodological confrontation with Ricardo in POP by unifying those three aspects.

MARX'S PRESENTATION OF ECONOMIC CATEGORIES

The 'First Observation' in Chapter Two of POP specifies that the crux of the Proudhonian and Marxian methodological critique of political economy is the historical understanding of economic categories by explaining the genesis of them, i.e., a dialectical method. Their point of divergence is whether they pursue the real movement of capitalist production and commerce or not, or whether their critique of political economy is a critique of economic categories or not.

Proudhon does not analyse the real movement. He does not examine the historical conditions or the interrelation of capitalist relations which the categories express. He explains their origins by introducing a person, just like a *deus ex machina*,[15] who makes the proposition to other persons to establish the relation in question. Thus for Proudhon, economic categories do not express their historical conditions or their interrelation. He presents economic categories in the order classified by an outside principle, i.e., 'equality'. In this sense, Proudhon's critique of political economy is not a critique of economic categories.

Marx, on the other hand, analyses the movement of capitalist production from the following two aspects in order to explain their genesis: the historical character and the intrinsic connection. Economic categories are presented accordingly in the order which is shown by the intrinsic connection between the categories. Marx later calls this method of presenting economic categories the 'genetical presentation', because it explains the genesis of economic categories, and thus of the capitalist relations they express.

It is through this presentation that the logical necessity for capitalist society, i.e., of formation – development – resolution, is grasped by the two-fold determination of economic categories:[16] the historical character of capitalist relations corresponding to a certain stage in the development of productive forces; and the intrinsic connection between capitalist relations co-existing simultaneously and supporting one another. In this sense Marx's critique of political economy is a critique of economic categories.

With regard to this, it should be noted that Proudhon's attempt at explaining the genesis of economic categories as such is rated highly by Marx in the 'First Observation'.[17] Unfortunately, not all economic categories are presented in POP because of its polemical nature, but the outline of Marx's genetical presentation can be read between the lines, for example: 'The same men who establish their social relations in conformity with their material productivity, produce also principles, ideas and categories, in conformity with their social relations.' (MEC 6, p. 166) And:

> Now that he has to put this dialectics into practice, his reason is in default. M. Proudhon's dialectics runs counter to Hegel's dialectics, and now we have M. Proudhon reduced to saying that *the order in which he gives the economic categories is no longer the order in which they engender one another. Economic evolutions are no longer the evolutions of reason itself.* (MEC 6, p. 169; italics added)

Here we should note that the so-called 'return journey' from abstract to concrete[18] is suggested by the sentence in italics. Taking into account his critical analysis of rent in POP and his plans in the works preceding POP,[19] it would be safe to say that Marx plans to develop economic categories in the following order: from the abstract to the concrete; from the simple to the aggregate; from those of the production process to those of the circulation process. For example, commodities and money before capital, profit and average profit before rent. The term 'engender' in the above quotation indicates the 'premise – development' relation between the categories.

It is worth mentioning the 'spontaneity' of economic categories. The following passage in POP may mislead us unless we keep it within context.

> Indeed, from the moment the process of the dialectic movement is reduced to the simple process of opposing good to bad, of posing problems tending to eliminate the bad, and of administering one category as an antidote to another, the categories are deprived of all spontaneity; the idea 'no longer functions'; there is no life left in it. It is no longer posed or decomposed into categories. (MEC 6, p. 169)

It is careless to jump from this to the interpretation that Marx's categories have spontaneity or life in themselves. On the contrary, the quotation above indicates the inadequacy of Proudhon's made-up dialectics even as speculative dialectics.

First, Proudhon does not 'pursue the historical movement of production relations, of which the categories are but the theoretical expression'. (MEC 6, p. 162) He inverts the relationship between economic categories, just as in Hegel's speculative dialectics.

Second, however, Proudhon's dialectics differs from Hegel's. Contradictions produce other categories in Hegel's dialectics, but not in Proudhon's, because, for Proudhon, 'the dialectic movement is the dogmatic distinctions between good and bad'. (MEC 6, p. 168) His contradictions are not real contradictions but mere distinctions.

Third, consequently, in Proudhon's speculative dialectics, unlike Hegel's, categories have to be developed through the power of other categories, i.e., other categories must be presupposed. For example, 'to arrive at the constitution of value, which for him is the basis of all economic evolutions, he could not do without division of labour, competition, etc'. (MEC 6, p. 166) Thus the quotation above is followed by: 'The sequence of categories has become a sort of scaffolding. Dialectics has ceased to be the movement of absolute reason. There is no longer any dialectics but only, at the most, absolutely pure morality.' (MEC 6, p. 169)

In contrast to that, Marx's genetical presentation is the dialectic of description and merely 'the working-up observation and conception into concept'. It must be based on the analysis of 'the historical movement of production relations'. (MEC 6, p. 162) Consequently, however his presentation of economic categories may appear as the self-development or self-creation of the 'concept', it is not a dogma. As Marx warns us, 'the subject, society, must constantly be kept in mind as the premise from which we start'[20] in the whole process of his presentation.

From all the observations above, we may conclude that Marx suggests the 'genetical presentation of economic categories' in POP.

CONCLUSIONS

In the early 1840s Marx faced the so-called 'material interest' and the problem of the abolition of capital. At the time when capital was establishing itself and causing friction with feudal property in Germany, the abolition of capital was acclaimed by socialists and communists in England and France. Thus it was an anachronism for Marx to deal with German domestic problems, because they had already been solved in England and France. The first step he took to solve the problem was a critical investigation of Hegel's *Philosophy of Right* which is an exceptional critique of capitalist society in England.

Through that work, Marx realised that the separation of civil society and political state has its root in civil society, i.e., in the separation of individuals into citizen (*citoyen*) and bourgeois. Consequently, he formulates the thesis that human emancipation will be accomplished only when 'the real, individual man ... in his particular work ... has reorganised and organised his "*forces propres*" as social forces, and consequently no longer separates social powers from himself'. (MEC 3, p. 168) In this way, Marx comes to the conclusion that a critical analysis of capitalist relations of production is necessary for him to clarify material conditions for it.

For Marx the real question is: Can 'Germany attain a practice *à la hauteur des principes*, i.e., a revolution which will raise Germany not only to the official level of the modern nations but to the height of humanity which will be the near future of these nations' (MEC 3, p. 182)? Marx tackles this question by separating out the general essence (*Wesen*) of private property through a two-fold analysis of the capitalist production process in EPM.

Capitalist society, i.e., the sum total of capitalist relations, develops antagonistically by producing wealth on one hand and poverty on the other. A controversy between political economists and socialists follows. 'Political economists are a fatalist school and represent a bourgeoisie which works only ... to increase the productive forces and to give a new upsurge to industry and commerce.' (MEC 6, p. 176)

They understand capitalist society as eternal by conceptualising capitalist relations into unhistorical categories. They do not comprehend how economic laws arise from the very nature (*Wesen*) of capital nor demonstrate economic laws as necessary laws of capital. This is a necessary result of their analytical method. Socialists, on the other hand, are on the workers' side and try to reform society, especially distribution relations,without abolishing capitalist production relations. Neither economists nor socialists comprehend capitalist society as an historical, transitory society corresponding to a certain stage in the development of productive forces.

Proudhon claimed in his SEC that he had transcended both political economy and socialism.Therefore, Marx in POP is directly concerned with Proudhon, but indirectly concerned with political economy and socialism. The methodological inadequacy of Ricardo's analysis was understood by Proudhon and Marx in 1846. The core of the problem is the new method required to transcend the inadequacy of the analytical method of political economy, including Ricardo's.

As we have seen, the point is how to understand economic categories by explaining the genesis of them. Marx's critique of Proudhon's flawed dialectics is only his methodological critique of Ricardo from the following two aspects: the historical character of economic categories; and the intrinsic connection between those categories.[21]

5 MARX'S CRITIQUE OF RICARDIAN VALUE THEORY

Modern civil society, or capitalist society, produces wealth on the one hand and poverty on the other. Both were represented by political economists and socialists. In his SEC Proudhon declared that he had transcended both political economy and the socialist critique, by using a dialectical method. He wrote to Marx asking for a 'stern criticism', probably expecting praise. Marx answered him in his POP by expounding the following three propositions, contrasting Ricardo, Bray and Hegel:

1. Political economists understand capitalist society as eternal by defining economic categories ahistorically.
2. Proudhon attempted to transcend this methodological insufficiency of the economists, including Ricardo.
3. However, Proudhon made the same mistake as the economists and made economic categories eternal ideas. This quotation summarises POP: 'I showed there [in POP] ... how in this roundabout way he [Proudhon] arrived once more at the standpoint of bourgeois economy.'[1]

The point here is that in POP the political economists are criticised by Marx. The methodological inadequacy of the political economists, i.e., the ahistorical understanding of economic categories, is only the starting-point for both Proudhon and Marx. Marx's methodological and theoretical critique of Proudhon is nothing but his methodological and theoretical critique of the political economists, including Ricardo. This is the reason why Marx states: 'The decisive points of our view [his critique of political economy] were first scientifically, although only polemically, indicated in my work published in 1847 and directed against Proudhon [POP].'[2] Consequently, POP represents Marx's methodological and theoretical critique of Ricardo.

In Chapter 3, I examined Marx's methodological critique of Ricardo in POP, which is best summarised in his phrase: 'Economic categories are only the theoretical expressions, the abstractions of the social relations of production'. (MEC 6, p. 165) To put it more concretely, he explained 'the genesis' of the economic categories by deriving them from the following: the historical character of the capitalist relations which they express, and the intrinsic connection between the capitalist relations themselves.

This chapter is devoted to investigating two respects of Marx's methodological critique of political economy in POP: the historical character and the intrinsic connection. In other words, we examine here Marx's critique of Ricardo's value and price theory in Chapter One of POP as a notable instance of his methodological critique of the political economists.

Over the past decades a considerable number of studies have focused on the formation of Marx's thought, including POP. Surprisingly, however, few have clarified what is meant by the 'decisive points of our view' in POP, or of Marx's methodological and substantive critique of Ricardo's value theory,[3] for the following reasons:

1. Marx's dialectical method in his 'critique of political economy' has been misunderstood as the so-called 'materialist conception of history';
2. little attention has been paid to authorial purpose in Proudhon's SEC and Marx's POP;
3. the two chapters of POP have been read separately;
4. Marx's value theory has been misunderstood as being very similar to Ricardo's.

It is true that Marx stresses the scientific aspect of Ricardo's value theory, and his own value theory is in the Ricardian line. For example, in his *Manuscripts of 1861–63* Marx writes:

> He [Ricardo] begins with the determination of the magnitude of the value of the commodity by labour time and then examines whether the other economic relations and categories contradict this determination of value or to what extent they modify it. The historical justification of this method of procedure, its scientific necessity in the history of economics, are evident at first sight, … .[4]

However, it should not be overlooked that the sentence is followed by: 'but so is, at the same time, its scientific insufficiency'. For Marx, pointing out the scientific aspect of Ricardo's analysis does not contradict his criticising its insufficiency. In fact, these are both sides of Marx's 'critique'.

A careful investigation of POP reveals that this work is not an exception but a good example of his critique. In POP Marx, on the one hand, contrasts the scientific aspect of Ricardo's value theory favourably with Proudhon's. On the other hand, Marx also criticises the scientific inadequacy of Ricardo's value theory only implicitly, as the work is not directed against Ricardo but Proudhon.

First, Ricardo's value theory is criticised through Marx's explanation of the genesis of exchange-value. The political economists, including Ricardo, were concerned solely with the quantitative analysis of exchange-value but not with the genesis of the category. Consequently, they did not fully grasp the historical character of exchange-value and the intrinsic connection between value and price. Proudhon understood this methodological inadequacy of Ricardo's analysis very well and attempted to transcend it in his SEC by explaining the genesis of economic categories, which was rated highly by Marx in his POP (see, for example, MEC 6, p. 111).

However, Proudhon's 'historical and descriptive method' (MEC 6, p. 113) did not pursue the real movement of capitalist production. He explained the genesis of the economic categories only by inventing a person who proposed to establish the relation in question to 'other men, his collaborators in various functions' (MEC 6, p. 112), a '*deus ex machina*'. (MEC 6, p. 198) Proudhon, as Marx said, 'answers the problem by formulating the same problem and adding an extra syllable' (MEC 6, p. 199), therefore explaining nothing. In this sense, Marx's explanation of the genesis of exchange-value represents his critique of Ricardo's value theory in the following two respects: the historical character of capitalist relations, and the intrinsic connection between them.

Second, Ricardo's value theory is criticised through Marx's re-reading or re-interpretation. Ricardo's value theory, summarised and contrasted by Marx with Proudhon's, is not Ricardo's original theory but one re-read and re-interpreted by Marx. To overlook this re-reading or re-interpretation is to miss the *differentia specifica* of Marx's value theory, i.e., of Marx's critical analysis of commodities as a (social) production relation.

Consequently, it is very important for us to separate Marx's value theory presented by Marx as Ricardo's, from Ricardo's value theory as such. The *differentia specifica* of Marx's critical analysis of the commodity must be kept in mind. For this purpose, the next section summarises Ricardo's original value theory. The third and fourth sections analyse Marx's indirect critique of Ricardo's value in POP in two respects: the historical character and the intrinsic connection.

RICARDO'S VALUE THEORY

Ricardo's Concept of 'Value'

First, we note that Marx's 'critique of political economy' is a critique of the economic categories used by political economists. Thus it follows that Marx criticised Ricardo's 'value' in *Capital*. In this chapter we summarise Ricardo's value theory before we examine Marx's indirect critique of it in Chapter One of POP.

Second, we note that Ricardo's subject for analysis is 'value' – as his first chapter is 'On Value' – while Marx opens *Capital* with 'The Commodity'. For Marx economic categories are theoretical expressions of capitalist relations of production and commerce and are to be presented genetically. The commodity was chosen by Marx as the starting-point of his 'genetic presentation', because it is the simplest 'social form in which the labour-product is presented in contemporary society'.[5] On the other hand, Ricardo's presentation reveals that he did not share 'genetic presentation' with Marx.

Third, Ricardo distinguishes 'relative value' from 'absolute value', i.e., the value of a commodity measured by 'an invariable measure'.[6] In fact, he was in search of such a measure in vain until he died.[7] Thus, by value he meant 'relative value' or 'exchangeable value', i.e., 'the quantity of any other commodity for which it will exchange', while Marx distinguishes between value and exchange-value. The former (value) is 'something common to them [commodities] which is wholly independent "of their use-value",'[8] while the latter (exchange-value) is the 'necessary mode of expression or form of appearance of value'.[9]

Fourth, the relationship between 'natural price' and 'market price' in Ricardo's value theory should be noted. He admits that there is nothing which is not subject to the fluctuation of prices and that 'it is only in consequence of such variations that capital is apportioned precisely, in the requisite abundance and no more, to the production of the different commodities which happen to be in demand'.[10] Philosophically, this indicates that Ricardo understood the exchange of commodities as the capitalist form of the social distribution of labour.

However, on the other hand, he says that 'the deviations of the actual or market price of commodities from ... The natural price'[11] are 'accidental and temporary'. In other words, only the market price is subject to the accidental and temporary variations of price, and natural price is not affected by competition, i.e., supply and demand. This means, theoretically speaking, that he failed to grasp the historical character of the capitalist form of the social distribution of labour.

Ricardo's Concept of 'Cost of Production'

Fifth, we note that Ricardo's 'value' includes 'profits', in particular 'average profit'. As his 'value' is 'relative value' or 'exchangeable value', Ricardo determines 'value' through 'natural price' or 'cost, including profits'. Ricardo asserts: 'Mr. Malthus appears to think that it is a part of my doctrine that the cost and value of a thing should be the same; it is, if he means by cost, 'cost of production' including profits.'[12]

The point here is that Ricardo does not share Marx's genetic presentation of economic categories. In Ricardo's presentation, 'price' – 'cost of production' – is not developed or distinguished from 'value'. On the contrary, his 'value' is a sort of 'price', i.e., 'natural price' or 'central price'. This means that in the determination of 'value', the very starting-point of his presentation, Ricardo already presupposes 'average profit', which has not been explained yet. This makes Ricardo's presentation a tautology.

Last, we should note the relationship between 'value', 'quantity of labour' and 'cost of production' in Ricardo's theory. According to him, there are two causes or laws which determine 'how much of one shall be given in exchange for another':[13] the comparative quantity of labour expended, and an alteration of wages without any variation in the quantity of labour, although the latter he said 'could not exceed 6 or 7 per cent'.[14] Ricardo never said that his 'cost, including profits' was equal to the 'labour' employed in production. Confusing value with price, Ricardo said that the 'labour' employed was almost in proportion to the 'cost, including profits'. In his words in the *Notes on Malthus* (1820):

> Mr. Malthus accuses me of confounding the very important distinction between cost and value. If by cost, Mr.Malthus means the wages paid for labour, I do not confound cost and value, because I do not say that a commodity the labour on which cost £1,000, will therefore sell for £1,000; it may sell for £1,000, £1,200, or £1,500, – but I say it will sell for the same as another commodity the labour on which also cost £1,000; that is to say, that commodities will be valuable *in proportion to the quantity of labour expended on them* (italics added).[15]

As is shown by this quotation, Ricardo does not equate 'labour' with 'cost, including profits'. For Ricardo, average profit affects all commodities equally and does not cause any change in the exchange-value of the commodities. On the other hand, by 'the quantity of labour' Ricardo means the sum total of wages. According to Ricardo's value theory, 'in proportion to "cost, including profits" is almost equivalent to 'in proportion to wages'. He prefers 'the quantity of labour bestowed on them' to 'the sum total of wages' for the following two reasons:

1. Labour is the original purchase money.
2. In order to distinguish 'the sum total of wages' from 'the alteration in wages' 'without any variation in the quantity of labour'.[16]

Consequently, Ricardo's value theory can be schematised as follows: 'Value' is equivalent to 'exchange-value' and 'relative value'. 'Value' is in proportion to 'cost of production' and 'the average wage and profit'. 'Value' is not equivalent to the comparative quantity of labour bestowed on the product but is 'almost in proportion' to it.

In the following two chapters, I clarify Marx's implicit criticism of Ricardo's value theory in Chapter One of his POP, i.e., historical character and intrinsic connections.

VALUE AS A CAPITALIST RELATION

The Genesis of Exchange-Value

In POP Marx explains the genesis of exchange-value from the 'historical and economic point of view'. (MEC 6, p. 184) He explains 'the process by which use-value is transformed into exchange-value' (MEC 6, p. 111) by pursuing 'the historical movement of production relations'. (MEC 6, p. 162) Initially, Marx distinguishes three stages in the history of exchange:

1. 'There was a time, as in the Middle Ages, when only the superfluous, the excess of production over consumption, was exchanged';
2. 'There was again a time, when not only the superfluous, but all products, all industrial existence, had passed into commerce, when the whole of production depends on exchange';

3. 'Finally, there came a time when everything that men had considered as inalienable became an object of exchange, of traffic and could be alienable.' (MEC 6, p. 113) At this stage, 'the very things which till then had been communicated, but never exchanged; given, but never sold; acquired, but never bought – virtue, love, conviction, knowledge, conscience, etc ... finally passed into commerce'. (MEC 6, p. 113)

According to Marx, it is only after stage 2) that, on the one hand, supply and demand meet only through exchange – competition – after the fact, and that, on the other, the concept of 'cost of production' begins to function as the regulator of the exchange-value of commodities.

Competition among suppliers and among consumers forms a necessary part of the struggle between buyers and sellers, of which marketable value is the result. (MEC 6, p. 119)

In supply and demand, then, we find, on the one hand, a product which has cost marketable values, and the need to sell; on the other, means which have cost marketable values, and the desire to buy. (MEC 6, p. 118)

'As a category, ... exchange-value leads an antediluvian existence',[17] but it has been similar to price in stage 1). However, value, as it is distinguished from price, can be conceptualised only under capitalist conditions, in which products are produced as commodities. Thus the category 'makes a historic appearance in its full intensity only in the most developed condition of society'.[18] In his phrase in POP, exchange-value corresponds to 'large-scale industry' and 'free competition'.

After all, the determination of value by labour time – the formula M. Proudhon gives us as the regenerating formula of the future – is therefore merely the scientific expression of the economic relations of present-day society, as was clearly and precisely demonstrated by Ricardo long before M. Proudhon. (MEC 6, p. 138)

As is shown by the quotation above, Ricardo understands exchange value as an historical category; but Marx outdoes him. As we have seen in the above section, Ricardo asserts that the deviation of the market price from the natural price is only 'accidental and temporary'. For Marx it is these deviations which determine the exchange-value of commodities as cost of production measured by labour time.

It is not the sale of a given product at the price of its cost of production that constitutes the 'proportional relation' of supply to demand, or the proportional quota of this product relative to the sum total of production; it is the variations in demand and supply that show the producer what amount of a given commodity he must produce in order to receive at least the cost of production in exchange. And as these variations are continually occurring, there is also a continual movement of withdrawal and application of capital in the different branches of industry. (MEC 6, p. 134)

Competition implements the law according to which the relative value of a product is determined by the labour time needed to produce it. (MEC 6, p. 135)

Only those who missed Marx's critique of Ricardo's value theory in Chapter 1 of *Capital* can neglect the meaning of these quotations. Marx's cost of production in POP will be investigated in the third section of this chapter. Before we move on, let us quote a passage from Marx's *Grundrisse*, the manuscripts of 1857–58, in order to confirm that for Marx determining value by 'cost of production' is the same as supply and demand:

> The value (the real exchange-value) of all commodities (labour power included) is determined by their cost of production, in other words by the labour time required to produce them.[19]

> Similarly, the labour which the worker sells as a use-value to capital is, for the worker, his exchange value, which he wants to realize, but which is already determined prior to this act of exchange and presupposed to it as a condition, and is determined like the value of every other commodity by supply and demand; or, in general, which is our concern here, by the cost of production.[20]

To comprehend the historical character of the commodity is to clarify the historical conditions which make products commodities by comparing them with articles of tribute, gifts and simple commodities. Marx emphasises that after the second stage of exchange, fluctuation is a necessary element in the social distribution of labour in capitalist conditions. For example:

> *Fuit Troja* (Troy is no more). This correct proportion between supply and demand, which is beginning once more to be the object of so many wishes, ceased long ago to exist. It has passed into the stage of senility. It was possible only at a time when the means of production were limited, when exchange took place within very restricted bounds. With the birth of large-scale industry this correct proportion had to come to an end, and production is inevitably compelled to pass in continuous succession through vicissitudes of prosperity, depression, crisis, stagnation, renewed prosperity, and so on. (MEC 6, p. 137)

Capitalist Society as a Caricature of the True Community

It seems clear to me that in POP Marx understands the exchange of commodities as the capitalist form of social metabolism. This is supported by Marx's view of the social division of labour.

Neither Proudhon nor Ricardo distinguishes the division of labour inside society from that in the modern workshop. It is Marx who, for the first time, distinguishes between two kinds of division of labour. However, the reason for this distinction has still not been appreciated. It concerns Marx's method for understanding capitalist relations as an historical form of metabolism between men, and between men and nature. Let us devote a little space to discussing the matter. In Chapter Two of POP Marx writes: 'While inside the modern workshop the division of labour is meticulously regulated by the authority of the employer, *modern society has no other rule, no other authority for the distribution of labour than free competition.*' (MEC 6, p. 184; italics added) By contrasting the two authorities, Marx shows that it is free competition that distributes labour socially.

Moreover, it is Marx who calls 'the process of exchange' 'a process of social metabolism'.[21] The core of Chapter 1 §4 'The Fetishism of the Commodity and its Secret' of *Capital* is to clarify that 'the labour of the private individual manifests itself as an element of the total labour of society only through the relations which the act of exchange establishes between the products, and, through their mediation, between the producers'.

All these show that the exchange-value of products is the capitalist form of social metabolism, i.e., of the social distribution of labour. The movement or process through which exchange-value is regulated is the capitalist form of the social distribution of labour. Value, as a content distinguishable from exchange-value, is only the capitalist form of social labour, i.e., of the social character of human labour. His letter to Kugelmann dated 11 July 1868 clarifies this point:

> And the form in which this proportional distribution of labour asserts itself in a state of society in which the interconnection of social labour expresses itself as the private exchange of the individual products of labour, is precisely the exchange-value of these products. (MEC 43, p. 68)[22]

Let us now return to the main point. Marx, like Ricardo and Smith, understands that labour, products and capital are socially distributed through fluctuations in price. In other words, all three understand exchange as the capitalist form of the social distribution of labour. Smith knew very well that natural price – average wage, profit and rent – is the central price in the fluctuation, but he did not explain it in terms of labour. On the other hand, theoretically speaking Ricardo was inferior to Smith in making fluctuation accidental for natural price. He wrote that 'the variation of the actual or market price of commodities from ... natural price' is 'accidental and temporary'. However, Marx understands that it is these variations which make the cost of production the regulator of exchange value. Thus Marx makes fluctuating movement an element of the law of value: labour time and free competition. In this sense, it is only Marx who comprehends this law as a necessary law of capital.

> If M. Proudhon admits that the value of products is determined by labour time, he should equally admit that it is the fluctuating movement alone that makes labour time the measure of value. There is no ready-constituted 'proportional relation' [between supply and demand], but only a constituting movement. Competition implements the law according to which the relative value of a product is determined by the labour time needed to produce it. (MEC 6, p. 135)

Theoretically speaking, Ricardo determines exchange-value by a single element: cost of production. On the other hand, Marx grasps exchange value as a capitalist production relation consisting of the following two elements: cost of production and free competition. In order to demonstrate that Proudhon has not transcended political economy, Marx supports the scientific character of Ricardo's value theory against Proudhon by saying:

'Ricardo shows us the real movement of bourgeois production which constitutes value.' (MEC 6, p. 123) We should note that this is not true as a summary of Ricardo's theory. To overlook this is to miss Marx's critique of Ricardo's value theory in POP, or 'the decisive points' of his critique of the economic categories in POP.

The most important point to be made here is that each level of analysis of the economic categories clarifies the position of the capitalist relations which they express in the history of social individuals, i.e., in regard to preceding societies and to a higher society.[23] For example, the social distribution of labour through exchange-value indicates, on the one hand, that it is the most developed form that history has ever known, and on the other, that men still have not obtained control over their mutual interactions. It is not producers but their movements that control men. In this two-fold sense, capitalist society is 'a caricature of the true community',[24] of 'the manifestation of the nature of men, their mutual complementing the result of which is species-life',[25] of truly human relations of production and commerce. Marx's critical analysis of commodities offers insights such as:

> *Fuit Troja.* This correct proportion between supply and demand, ... was possible only at a time when the means of production were limited. (MEC 6, p. 137)

> Thus relative value, measured by labour time, is inevitably the formula of the modern enslavement of the worker, instead of being, as M. Proudhon would have it, the 'revolutionary theory' of the emancipation of the proletariat. (MEC 6, p. 125)

> In a future society, in which class antagonism will have ceased, in which there will no longer be any classes, use will no longer be determined by the minimum time of production; but the time of production devoted to an article will be determined by the degree of its social utility. (MEC 6, p. 134)

'Cost of Production' as 'Labour Time'

As we have already seen, Ricardo determines exchange-value by 'cost, including profits' which consists of average wages and profits. In other words, his cost is 'production cost' in *Capital*, Volume 3.[26] Concerned with relative value only, Ricardo asserts that commodities are exchanged in proportion to their comparative 'cost' and almost in proportion to their comparative quantity of labour – wages – expended on them. He states in the *Notes on Malthus* (1820):

> If I had said that the value of commodities was the same thing as the value of the labour expended on them, the remark [Malthus' remark] would have been well founded, but I have said the relative value of commodities is in proportion to the quantity of labour bestowed on them. That value may be double what the labour cost.[27]

On the other hand, Ricardo's theory of value summarised and praised by Marx as 'the scientific interpretation of actual economic life' (MEC 6, p. 124) is 'the determination of value by labour time'. The point here is that Marx equates cost with labour time. 'The determination of value by labour time is, for Ricardo, the law of exchange-value; for M. Proudhon, it is the synthesis of use value and exchange-value.' (MEC 6, p. 124) And: ' ... it is the variations in demand and supply that show the producer what amount of a given commodity he must produce in order to receive at least the cost of production in exchange.' (MEC 6, p. 134)

There are two points to be made here: Marx's 'cost of production' and 'labour time' differ from Ricardo's 'cost' and 'labour'. First, Marx's cost of production is determined in the production process before the exchange of commodities, as he writes:

> In the course of production, it has been exchanged for all the costs of production, such as raw materials, wages of workers, etc., all of which are marketable values. The product, therefore, represents, in the eyes of the producer, a sum total of marketable values. What he supplies is not only a useful object, but also and above all a marketable value.
>
> As to demand, it will only be effective on condition that it has means of exchange at its disposal. These means are themselves products, marketable values. (MEC 6, p. 118)

It is clear that Marx's 'cost of production' in POP differs from Ricardo's 'cost, including profits'. This means that Marx distinguished his value theory from Proudhon's by identifying it as Ricardo's.[28]

Second, as far as I know, Ricardo does not use the term 'labour time'. Even if he had, it is not the term itself but the method we should note here. As we have already seen, Ricardo's 'quantity of labour' is equal to 'a sum total of wages' which the labour costs. It is by no means 'labour time' nor 'the minimum time it could possibly be produced in'. (MEC 6, p. 136)

Historically speaking, it is Hegel who measured labour by time when he distinguished wage labour from slave labour.[29] However, this is more noteworthy from the following methodological point of view.

Ricardo's determination of value is nothing but a *petitio principi* (begging the question), because it presupposes those which are to be explained, i.e., the average wage and profit, at the very starting-point of his presentation of the economic categories. However, Marx's determination of value makes a good starting-point, because labour time does not presuppose any other category which is to be explained. This leads us to the other aspect of Marx's critique of Ricardo's value theory in POP. Before we move on, let us summarise this chapter. Although Marx identifies his value theory with Ricardo's, which he supported against Proudhon's, he also re-interpreted Ricardo's value theory historically to grasp the commodity as a capitalist production relation.

VALUE AS A CAPITALIST PROCESS

Value Determination as the Beginning

In this section we are concerned with Marx's critique of Ricardo's value theory from the other aspect, i.e., the intrinsic connection between capitalist relations, or economic categories. Since I have already examined briefly the intrinsic connection between value and rent, and between value and money, in Chapter 3, I would like to concentrate on the connection between value and price.

First, we should remember that the real problem for Marx is to explain the origin of exchange-value, that is, 'the process by which use-value is transformed into exchange-value'. (MEC 6, p. 111) In other words, why the amount of labour realised in products cannot directly appear as such but has to take the form of the value of the products. It was already clear for Marx in POP that economic categories are to be presented genetically or dialectically, when we read and invert the following criticism of Proudhon's presentation:

> Now that he [Proudhon] has to put this dialectics into practice, his reason is in default. M. Proudhon's dialectics runs counter to Hegel's dialectics, and now we have M. Proudhon reduced to saying that the order in which he gives the economic categories is no longer the order in which they engender one another. (MEC 6, p. 169)

Without doubt the scientific aspect of Ricardo's analysis is that he abstracted natural price or cost of production from market price. However, it should also be noted that Ricardo does not share Marx's dialectical method of presentation, i.e., the genetical presentation of economic categories. Therefore it follows that Ricardo and Marx differ on the determination of value.

For Marx, the determination of value is the starting-point of his genetic presentation of economic categories. Therefore value should not be determined by other categories which are to be explained later, e.g., wage, profit or rent. Furthermore, following Hegel, Marx measures the quantity of labour by labour time too.

However, this does not necessarily hold true in Ricardo. His labour is not labour time but the sum total of wages. He presupposes average wage and profit, as his illustrations show, in the determination of value, i.e., the very starting-point of his presentation. He does not and cannot logically distinguish the determination of value by labour from that by 'cost, including profits', so his presentation is a tautology. This explains Ricardo's confusion of value with price in his 'modification' problem.

Transformation of Value into Price

Ricardo assumes an average wage and average profit in the determination of value. Thus he creates a problem in that labour time does not directly regulate the price of commodities except as a modification of his principle. He says that the following three conditions 'introduce another cause, besides the greater or less quantity of labour necessary to produce commodities, for the variations in the relative value – and this cause is the rise or fall in the value of labour':[30]

1. the unequal composition of 'fixed capital' and 'circulating capital' between capitals;
2. the unequal durability of 'fixed capital'; and
3. the unequal rapidity with which it is returned to its employer.

Ricardo asserts that under these conditions 'a rise in the wages of labour would not equally affect commodities produced' and change their relative value. In other words, he says there are two causes of change in the relative value of commodities: the comparative amount of labour and an alteration in wages without any variation in the quantity of labour. His real assertion is that the former is the foundation and the latter is 'comparatively slight in its efffects'.[31] The point is that Ricardo creates this problem (principle+modification) in the determination of value.

On the other hand, Marx formulates the problem in another way. For Marx the point to be explained – but not the starting-point – is that the price of commodities is determined by the average wage and average profit in the long run in the course of fluctuations in prices, so in his view average wage and profit must be explained first.[32] In the genetic presentation of economic categories, or in order to comprehend capitalist relations scientifically, this problem has no direct relation to value determination, the very starting-point of the presentation. This means that the determination of value as the *Anfang* (beginning) for Marx's presentation differs considerably from that of Ricardo. In his *Results of the Immediate Process of Production* (1863–66), Marx repeats that the commodity analysed in Chapter 1 of *Capital* is 'the individual commodity viewed as an autonomous article'[33] but not the 'commodity as the product of capital' which is to be explained later. This means that in Marx's system commodities are logically determined step by step. Thus value, as his *Anfang*, is the simplest and most abstract category which does not comprise any of the more complicated and concrete categories.

The most important point to be made here is that exchange-value in POP consists of the following elements: cost of production and free competition. 'If M. Proudhon admits the value of products is determined by labour time, he should equally admit that is is the fluctuating movement alone that makes labour time the measure of value.' (MEC 6, p. 135) Ricardo negates the effect of the fluctuation in prices on natural price, while J.B. Say negates the cost of production in the determination of exchange-value. Marx criticises both of them and determines value by cost of production – labour time – and competition. As a matter of fact, this two-fold critique can be found in his works from 1844 and has been interpreted as an example of the immaturity of the 'early Marx';[34] but this judgment is quite wrong. On the contrary, this early critique illustrates the maturity of the Young Marx, as the quotations from *Grundrisse* show.

The nub is that individual private labour is not directly but only potentially social. It must become social through universal exchange or the fluctuation in prices, or it will be wasted. Added to this 'The continual depreciation of labour is only one side, one consequence of the evaluation of commodities by labour time.' (MEC 6, p. 136) If exchange-value is defined by labour time only, it lacks the element which transforms value into price or Ricardo's cost of production. It cannot be overemphasised that it is 'Competition [which] implements the law according to which the relative value of a product is determined by the labour time needed to produce it.' (MEC 6, p. 135): 'It is important to emphasize the point that what determines value is not the time taken to produce a thing, but the minimum time it could possibly be produced in, and this minimum is ascertained by competition.' (MEC 6, p. 136)[35]

We should not overlook that in *Capital*, where value is not defined directly by the two elements noted above. Value is defined by 'the labour time which is necessary on an average, or in other words is socially necessary',[36] which presupposes this context – cost of production and competition. We have been discussing how Ricardo's 'cost' – average wage and average profit – differs from Marx's 'cost of production' – minimum labour time – and have explained that this is a necessary result of the difference between their methods. Ricardo's cost of production is re-read or re-cast by Marx into value as *Anfang*: the principle and starting point of his genetic presentation.

Consequently, we should no longer interpret Marx's value theories as similar to Ricardo's. Ricardo's *Principle of Political Economy and Taxation* (first published in 1817) opens with: 'The value of a commodity, or the quantity of any other commodity for which it will exchange, depends on the relative quantity of labour which is necessary for its production ...'.[37] However similar it sounds to that of Marx, they have in fact little in common.

CONCLUSIONS

Ricardo's political economy is the best of the classical political economy. It is scientific, but scientifically still insufficient. This is because of his analytical method. He analyses capitalist relations of production and commerce, and discovers determinant and abstract categories such as value, wage, profit and rent. However, Ricardo's method is inadequate for comprehending historical entities, such as capitalist society as the sum total of capitalist relations of production. First of all, Ricardo does not grasp the historical character of capitalist relations. His analytical method cannot clarify the historical conditions which give capitalist form to the relations of production and commerce. Second, Ricardo cannot comprehend the intrinsic connections amongst capitalist relations. Capitalist relations, co-existing and supporting one another, form the structure of capitalist society, but Ricardo's method cannot display the structure.

Marx uses a dialectical method to transcend these inadequacies in his presentation of economic categories. He pursues the real movement of production and consumption and defines these categories as theoretical reflections of the historical character of capitalist relations. In other words, he explains the genesis of economic categories one by one. Marx's explanation of exchange value represents a radical critique of Ricardo's value theory.

From Marx's point of view expressed in POP, Ricardo the political economist is to be criticised because he makes capitalist society eternal and the only possible form of the metabolism between men and nature. Ricardo does not assert this directly, rather he says so by understanding economic categories as ahistorical. Thus he does not grasp the historical character of capitalist relations nor the intrinsic connections between them. My investigation of Marx's critique of Ricardo's value theory in POP leads to the following conclusions.

First, the category 'exchange-value' expresses the capitalist form of the social distribution of products, and thus of labour. Irrespective of its form, society is the product of man's interaction with man and the organisation of the metabolism between men, and between men and nature.

Second, Ricardo, like Smith, understands that exchange-value is the capitalist form of the social distribution of capital, commodities and labour. However, theoretically speaking, Ricardo, like Smith, does not sufficiently grasp the historical character. On the one hand, Ricardo deals relative (exchange) value and asserts that commodities are exchanged in proportion to their comparative cost of production – average wage and profit – or cost of labour (wages). On the other hand, he excludes the fluctuations in price from the elements of value. Nevertheless, his analysis provides the starting-point for Marx's critical analysis of commodities. Marx gets to the bottom of the historical character of exchange value. According to him, 'value' corresponds to the stage of large-scale industry and free competition in which supply and demand meet only through the fluctuation in prices in the long run. Thus Marx understands that labour time and free competition are the necessary elements of exchange value. In short, he defines value by 'the minimum (labour) time it could possibly be produced in' (MEC 6, p. 136), i.e., 'the labour time ... socially necessary' as outlined in Chapter 1 of *Capital*, Volume 1.

Third, Ricardo's value theory is nothing but a tautology. He presupposes average wage and profit in the definition of value: the very starting-point of his presentation. Furthermore, he excludes the fluctuation in prices from his value determination. As a result, his 'value' is not the concept from which other categories are developed. Since prices are to be explained from value, it is inevitable that his 'modification problem' follows.

On the other hand, Marx re-casts Ricardo's determination of value by cost of production into the *Anfang* of his presentation: Ricardo's cost of production becomes 'the minimum (labour) time it [a product] could possibly be produced in' (MEC 6, p. 136), i.e., labour time and free competition. Thus, Ricardo's modification problem is also re-cast into the transformation of value into price, the terminal-point – but not the starting-point – of his presentation of economic categories.

As POP is directed against Proudhon, Marx's critique of Ricardo as expounded here is not explicit. However, a careful and thorough investigation of the two chapters of POP makes it clear.

Part Two

Marx's First Critique of Political Economy

6 DEFINING CAPITALIST LAWS OF STRUCTURE AND MOVEMENT

The Economic and Philosophical Manuscripts, *Grundrisse* (1857–58) and *Capital* represent Marx's system, that is, the trinity of a critique of English political economy, French socialism and German philosophy, in the 1840s,[1] 1850s and 1860s. Among these three works, EPM expressly reveals the principle and structure of the trinity. This principle is, without doubt, the concept of 'estranged labour'.[2]

Unfortunately, however, the role of 'estranged labour' in Marx's system has been negated by Soviet Marxists and their Western followers for two reasons: (1) 'Estranged labour' belongs to thought but not to theory and was given up as Marx formed his economic theories; (2) the concept contradicts the labour theory of value and led Marx to the negation of the Ricardian labour theory of value.

This is due to their methodological inadequacy. They have investigated the manuscripts of EPM separately. Philosophers have read solely 'Estranged Labour' and Marx's critique of Hegel in the 'Third Manuscript', separately from other parts, as if these were the only philosophical parts. Economists, on the other hand, have read mainly the preceding part of 'Estranged Labour', the former part of the 'First Manuscript', as if it were the only economic part. Few commentators have attempted to understand the structure of EPM.[3] From the outset, it is inevitable that they will not understand the structure of EPM and will fail to appreciate it.

Thus, in the following chapters, I argue against these propositions by clarifying the structure of EPM and the role of 'estranged labour' in EPM, and thus in Marx's system. The component parts[4] of EPM resolve into:

1) The 'First manuscript: Former Part' (hereafter 'FM: FP') in which Marx conceptualises economic laws of capitalist society through the words of political economists and socialists.

2) The 'First Manuscript: Latter Part' (hereafter 'FM: LP') and the 'Second Manuscript', in which, as the first result of the working-up of observation and conception into concepts, Marx analyses the two sides of the process of capitalist production.[5]

3) The 'Third Manuscript', an Appendix to the 'Second Manuscript', in which Marx comprehends the intrinsic connections between things as

aspects of estranged labour. In the following sections, we examine the 'FM:FP', i.e., its position in EPM and its contents.

THE POSITION OF THE 'FIRST MANUSCRIPT: FORMER PART'

The Merits of Bibliographical Studies

Marx's 'Paris Manuscripts' consists of many notes and a draft of his book, i.e., *Notes on Say, Notes on Smith, Notes on Ricardo, Notes on James Mill*, etc., and EPM. Although bibliographical studies are the basis, or the premise, of the investigation of the texts, it was not until 1969 that a serious bibliographical study was made by N.I. Lapin.[6] He revealed, for the first time, that some facts can be brought to light only by those who have access to the originals or the facsimiles of them.

For example, he revealed that each page of the 'FM: FP' is divided into three columns and 'Wages of Labour', 'Profit of Capital' and 'Rent of Land' were written in a comparative way, but not separately as they had been published. He asserted that the 'FM: FP' consists of three stages. Lapin presumed that Marx encounters Engels' *Outlines of a Critique of Political Economy* (1844) twice, concluding that Marx's brief summary of it was made on the second encounter. From the fact that Ricardo's name can be found in the 'Second Manuscript' and 'Third Manuscript' but not in the 'FM: FP', Lapin inferred that the writing order of the 'Paris Manuscripts' was not so simple as it was supposed to be at that time. He assumes that Marx wrote the 'FM: FP' first, then *Notes on Ricardo*, and the 'Second and Third Manuscript'. All these were sensational and eye-opening at the time.

The Demerits of Bibliographical Studies

However, not all of these assertions are supported by his bibliographical investigation. Some of them are not persuasive but misleading. For example, the simple fact of whether Ricardo's name appears or not does not necessarily mean that Marx had or had not read Ricardo by that time.[7] Although Smith is often quoted while Ricardo's name does not appear in the 'FM: FP', Marx's rent theory there is in line with Ricardo rather than Smith. Furthermore, Marx's understanding of political economy seems to be deeper in the 'Second and Third Manuscripts' than in the 'FM: FP'. However, this does not mean at all that Marx read Ricardo between the two, simply that their position in EPM differs.

The point is to distinguish between facts and the interpretations of them. Facts are objective, but the interpretations of them necessarily include subjective factors and are always controversial. Lapin's bibliographical study should be appreciated as a critique of the texts, i.e., insofar as it brought out some facts which had not as yet become known. However, it is controversial as an interpretation of the texts, that is, it should be criticised insofar as it asserts his personal interpretations as if they were the only possible conclusions. As a matter of fact, Lapin is not a specialist on Marx's economics, politics or philosophy. In this sense, he lacks the ability to appreciate and interpret the facts properly.

A careful examination of the manuscripts of EPM, as I am going to demonstrate in this chapter, reveals that EPM has a structure. Whatever the writing order in the 'Paris Manuscripts' may be,[8] the manuscripts of EPM have an intrinsic connection between themselves and have their own position in EPM, forming a unit. However, Lapin's study does not accelerate but obstructs the further studies of EPM, by dividing EPM into separate pieces and opening the way to deal with the draft (EPM) as pieces, like other notes in the 'Paris Manuscripts'.

The Position of the 'First Manuscript: Former Part'

The authorial purpose of the 'FM: FP' differs from the 'FM: LP'. As Marx's summary of the 'FM: FP' in the opening paragraph of the 'FM: LP' shows, the purpose of the 'FM: FP' is to conceptualise the economic laws of capitalist society through the words of political economists and socialists. In his phrase, Marx confines himself 'to the propositions of political economy itself'. (MEC 3, p. 247, EW, p. 295) However, in the 'FM: LP', as is shown in the succeeding paragraphs, Marx criticises the methodological inadequacy of political economy and sets out to comprehend the economic laws as necessary laws of capital.

> Political economy proceeds from the fact of the right of private property. It does not explain it. It grasps the material process of private property, the process through which it actually passes, in general and abstract formulae which it then takes as laws. It does not comprehend these laws, i.e., it does not show how they arise from the essence [*Wesen*] of private property ... .
>
> We now have to grasp the essential connection between the right of private property, greed, the separation of labour, capital and landed property, exchange and competition, value and the devaluation of man,[9] monopoly and competition, etc., – the connection between this entire system of estrangement and the money system. (MEC 3, pp. 270f, EW, p. 323; italics original)

Thus, we can say that the position of the 'FM: FP' in EPM is the conceptualisation or idealisation of economic laws of capitalist society which are to be formulated into the central concept from the 'FM: LP' onward. To overlook this difference in the logical distinction between the 'FM: FP' and its following parts is to fail to understand EPM, Marx's relation to political economists, and thus Marx's critique of political economy in 1844. This means:

1. that the 'FM: FP' is not the part where Marx expounds his own views, and
2. that the conclusions there are not fully developed because political economists did not and could not do so. This is not Marx's fault at all. On the contrary, he shows that this is their basic scientific inadequacy.
3. In the 'FM: LP' and after, Marx attempts to comprehend the laws of capital, starting by analysing the 'essence of private property in general'.

Two Stages in the 'First Manuscript: Former Part'

Theoretically, each column of the 'FM: FP' consists of two stages:

WAGES OF LABOUR	PROFIT OF CAPITAL	RENT OF LAND
MEC 3, pp. 235–41, l. 10 from the bottom EW, pp. 282–9, l. 11 from the bottom	MEC 3, pp. 246–50, l. 20 from the bottom EW, pp. 295–9, l. 10 from the bottom	MEC 3, pp. 259–64, l. 6 EW, pp. 309–15, l. 10
MEC 3, pp. 241–6 EW, pp. 289–95	MEC 3, pp. 250(sect. 4) –258 EW, pp. 299–309	MEC 3, pp. 264–70, l.14 EW, pp. 315–22

The first stage of each column is the analysis of the structure of capitalist society. The second stage is the analysis of its movement. And the two stages are connected by the 'two questions' set up in the column of 'Wages of Labour' which concerns the meaning of wage-labour in history:

> What is the meaning, in the development of mankind, of this reduction of the greater part of mankind to abstract labour?
>
> What mistakes are made by the piecemeal reformers, who either want to raise wages and thereby improve the situation of the working class, or – like Proudhon – see equality of wages as the goal of social revolution? (MEC 3, p. 241, EW, p. 289)

MARX'S ANALYSIS OF THE STRUCTURE OF CAPITALIST SOCIETY

The Column 'Profit of Capital'

The column entitled 'Profit of Capital' consists of four numbered sections. The first section ('1. Capital') opens with the following question: 'What is the basis of capital, i.e., of private property in the products of another's labour?' (MEC 3, p. 247, EW, p. 295)

Marx leads us from the sphere of jurisprudence to economics by answering the question with quotations from J.B. Say and Adam Smith. As Say asserts, capital cannot be reduced to 'simple theft or fraud' but to 'inheritance', which is sanctified by the assistance of legislation. However, 'What does one acquire with capital, with the inheritance of a large fortune, for example?' Marx answers with quotations from Smith that it is not 'any political power' but 'the power of purchasing' which the person gains who acquires a great fortune through what Say call the 'positive law'. Thus Marx defines capital as 'a certain command over all the labour, or over all the produce of labour, which is then in the market'. 'Capital is therefore the power to command labour and its products.' (MEC 3, p. 247; EW, p. 295)

It should be noted that Marx re-reads and re-interprets Smith's conception of 'command' here. In the third edition of *The Wealth of Nations*, Adam Smith added a paragraph to criticise and redefine Hobbes' concept of 'command' from political power to the power of purchasing.[10] However, by 'wealth' Smith means commodities but not 'capital'.[11] Later we will see further what Marx really means by this definition of capital, but here we should note that

Marx, like Smith, reduces capital to a certain amount of (accumulated) labour.

As Smith writes, a certain quantity of accumulated labour is 'only called capital when it yields its owner a revenue or profit'. However, Smith does not explain from where, why and how profit is yielded. Thus in section 2 'The Profit of Capital' Marx examines Smith's profit theory by investigating the following points in the *The Wealth of Nations*:

1. The profits of capital are regulated altogether by the value of the stock employed, although the labour of inspection and direction for different capitals may be the same.
2. Why does the capitalist demand this proportion between profit and capital?
3. The average, lowest and highest rate of ordinary profit on capitals.

It is quite interesting and noteworthy that Marx criticises political economists on 2. Adam Smith explains the proportion as follows:

> He [a capitalist] could have no interest in employing these workers, unless he expected from the sale of their work something more than was sufficient to replace the stock advanced by him as wages; and he could have no interest to employ a great stock rather than a small one, unless his profits were to bear some proportion to the extent of his stock. (MEC 3, p. 248; EW, p. 296)

As Marx criticises in the 'FM: LP', Smith and Ricardo 'take the interest of the capitalists as the basis of its analysis; i.e., it assumes what it is supposed to explain'. (MEC 3, p. 271; EW, p. 323) Neither Smith nor Ricardo explains the capitalist's economic entitlement.[12] However, Marx explains the two origins of profit through quotations from the *The Wealth of Nations.* 'He [the capitalist] profits in two ways: firstly from the division of labour and secondly, and more generally, from the growing role played by human labour in fashioning the natural product.' (MEC 3, p. 249; EW, p. 298)

Here Marx distinguishes the two ways the capitalist profits. Moreover, he knew Proudhon's exploitation theory of 'collective forces' very well by this time. However, here he does not look at the division of labour in detail, saying 'More later about the profit which the capitalist derives from the division of labour.' (MEC 3, p. 249; EW, p. 298) Instead he concentrates his analysis on the growing role played by human labour and analyses the production process of capital: '3. The Rule of Capital over Labour and the Motives of the Capitalist', in which Marx sees 'how the capitalist, by means of capital, exercises his power to command labour'. (MEC 3, p. 247; EW, p. 295)

This section only consists of three quotations from Smith and Say. No comments by Marx can be found. Consequently, some commentators assert that Marx did not investigate 'the rule of capital over labour' at all. However, Marx, especially in the first stage of each column, is just demonstrating economic laws in political economists' words, as he writes 'From political economy itself, using its own words, we have shown ...' (MEC 3, p. 270; EW, p. 322) in the 'FM: LP'. On the other hand, in the second stage, Marx writes

'Let us now rise above the level of political economy.' Thus we should look at and understand Marx's quotations from economists in the context of his text, rather than in their original context. A close look at the quotations shows what Marx has in mind by 'command over labour'. The third quotation says: 'The plans and projects of the employers of stock regulate and direct all the most important operations of labour, and profit is the end proposed by all those plans and projects ...' (MEC 3, p. 250; EW, p. 299)

Taking into account the context, Marx expounds through the quotations that the capitalist employs the worker and derives profit through the command over labour in the production process, not to mention of the profits from the division of labour. The most important thing to note here is that Marx's re-reading and redefinition of the concept of 'command' has become clearer than before. Adam Smith re-read Hobbes' 'command' re-interpreting his political power in terms of the power of purchase in the circulation process. Marx re-reads Smith's and redefines 'the power of purchase' in the production process.

From EPM onward, Marx defines capital as 'command over labour', usually with the phrase 'as political economy defines'.[13] The importance of this re-reading and redefinition is best expressed in his *Grundrisse* (the manuscripts of 1857–58), in which he expounds how he succeeds in understanding the origin of surplus-value using 'command' , and why Smith fails in it even with the concept. 'Capital becomes command over labour in the sense that labourers enter under command of the capitalist, but not in Smith's sense in which wealth is command over labour.' (MEGA2· II–3; p. 83)

> Capital, on the other hand, appears to him – because, although he defines labour as productive of value, he conceives it as use-value, ... as human natural force in general, ... but as wage labour, not in its specific character as form in antithesis to capital – not as that which contains wage labour as its internal contradiction from its origin, but rather in the form in which it emerges from circulation, as money, and is therefore created out of circulation, by saving.Thus capital does not originally realize itself – precisely because the appropriation of alien labour [*fremde Arbeit*] is not itself included in its concept. Capital appears only afterwards, after already having been presupposed as capital – a vicious circle – as command over alien labour. (G, p. 330)

In short, Smith grasps 'command over labour' only in the circulation process but not in the production process. The above quotation also explains Smith's confusion in his labour theory of value. Smith has two types of value theory: the so-called 'dissolving' and the 'composing'. As long as Smith fails to comprehend the creation of surplus value in the production process of capital, he has to limit the dissolving type so that it regulates only in his 'early and rude state of society'. However, Marx expounds that money-holders become capitalists through positive law, i.e., human rights.[14] Comprehending capital as command over alien labour in the production process leads Marx to understand the unity of capital and wage-labour, capital as 'self-increasing value'.

Now let us return to our main subject. Marx ends the column with the paragraphs which indicate that capitalists' interests are not identical with those of society, because they decide which branches of production to invest in only from the standpoint of profit.

The Column 'Rent of Land'

Quoting J.B. Say, Marx remarks on the origin of rent that 'The right of the landlords can be traced back to robbery' and backs up his argument with evidence. Then he criticises Smith's rent theory. According to Smith, as well as Ricardo, the volume of rent depends upon the location and the degree of fertility of the land. If this proposition was right, rent would be an eternal category, i.e., it would exist in all historical societies. In short, Smith failed to grasp rent as a capitalist relation of production.

> These propositions of Smith are important, because they reduce the rent of land, where costs of production and size are equal, to the degree of fertility of the soil. This clearly demonstrates the perversion of concepts in political economy, which turns the fertility of the soil into an attribute of the landlord. (MEC 3, p. 260; EW, p. 311)

Just like 'profit', political economy cannot grasp 'rent' as an historical production relation. Economic categories are not understood by political economists as theoretical expressions of historical production relations. Marx clarifies that rent is nothing but the capitalist form of landed property by asserting that 'The rent of land is established through the struggle between tenant [read as capitalist] and landlord.' (MEC 3, p. 260; EW, p. 311) He also states through quotations from Smith that 'Rent, considered as the price paid for the use of land, is naturally the highest which the tenant can afford to pay' and that 'high or low rent is the result of it [the high or low price]'. (MEC 3, p. 261; EW, p. 312)[15] In accordance with the definition in the column 'profit of capital', rent is clarified as being derived from profit; for example, 'The highest rate to which ordinary profits can rise may be such that the price of the greater part of commodities, eats up the whole of the rent of the land ...'.

It is obvious that Marx remains consistent with the 'dissolving' value theory from beginning to end.[16] Based on this theory, Marx demonstrates that landlords are parasites on capitalists (tenants), that landlords fall into the category of capitalists and that the modern civil society consists of two main classes: capitalists and workers. The 'abolition of the distinction between capitalist and landowner' (MEC 3, p. 266; EW, p. 317) is explicitly stated for the first time in the second stage of this column, but it can be implicitly observed here.[17]

Last, Marx shows through quotations from Smith how the landlord exploits everything which is of benefit to society. He concludes that 'it is foolish to conclude, as Smith does, that since the landlord exploits everything which is of benefit to society, the interest of the landlord is always identical with that of society.' (MEC 3, p. 263; EW, p. 314) On the contrary 'In the economic system, under the rule of private property, the interest which any individual has in society is in inverse proportion to the interest which society has in him.' (MEC 3, p. 263; EW, p. 314) Marx, confining himself to the propositions of political economists, proves that the interest of the landowner is 'fiercely opposed to the interests of society – the tenants, the farm labourers, the factory workers and the capitalists – '. (MEC 3, p. 264; EW, p. 315)

The Column 'Wages of Labour'

Marx begins this column with a summary of Smith's proposition that 'Wages are determined by the fierce struggle between capitalist and worker.' (MEC 3, p. 235; EW, p. 282) He understands that the nature of wages is the price of the commodity (labour-power) which the worker sells. 'The worker has become a commodity, and he is lucky if he can find a buyer.' (MEC 3, p. 234; EW, p. 283) '[B]ecause of his subordinate relationship to the capitalist, he is the first to suffer' (MEC 3, p. 236; EW, p. 283) in the struggle. He continues later, 'In theory, ground rent and profit on capital are deductions made from wages. However, in reality wages are a deduction which land and capital grant the worker, an allowance made from the product of labour to the worker, to labour.' (MEC 3, pp. 240f; EW, p. 288) With regard to and based on the propositions in the other two columns, he concludes: 'It is therefore only for the worker that the separation of capital, landed property and labour is a necessary, essential and pernicious separation.' (MEC 3, p. 235; EW, p. 282)

On the volume of wages he summarises the propositions of political economists in that 'According to Smith, the normal wage is the lowest which is compatible with common humanity, i.e., with a bestial existence.' (MEC 3, p. 235; EW, p. 283) Obviously Marx accepts Smith's proposition that 'The natural price, or the price of free competition, ... is the lowest which can be taken, not upon every occasion indeed, but for any considerable time together'.[18] And it is through the worker's loss that the market price gravitates towards the natural price.

Second, considering 'the three main conditions which can occur in society and their effect on the worker' (MEC 3, p. 237; EW, p. 284), Marx expounds that 'The worker has not only to struggle for his physical means of subsistence; he must also struggle for work, i.e., for the possibility and the means of realising his activity.' (MEC 3, p. 237; EW, p. 284) There is space here only for the second condition of society which differs most from that of Adam Smith: a society in which wealth is increasing.[19] This is the only favourable condition to the worker, but is only possible:

1) 'as a result of the accumulation of a large quantity of labour, for capital is accumulated labour; that is to say, when more and more of the worker's products are being taken from him, when his own labour increasingly confronts him as alien property and the means of his existence and of his activity are increasingly concentrated in the hands of the capitalist'. (MEC 3, p. 237; EW, pp. 284f)

2) The accumulation of capital leads to the increase of the division of labour and of the number of workers in factories. This results in the worker

becoming more and more uniformly dependent on labour, and on a particular, very one-sided and machine-like type of labour.

3) The accumulation of capital leads to the fall of the profit rate. This then leads to the reduction of the moneyed class to the capitalist class, leading to an increase in the competition which causes the ruin of the small capitalist who sinks into the working class.

In short, Marx states that:

> ... even in the state of society most favourable to him, the inevitable consequence for the worker is overwork and early death, reduction to a machine, enslavement to capital which piles up in threatening opposition to him, fresh competition and starvation or beggary for a section of the workers'. (MEC 3, p. 238; EW, pp. 285f)

The point to observe is not only the fate of the worker himself but also its root cause:

> But when society is in a state of progress the decline and impoverishment of the worker is the product of his labour and the wealth produced by him. This misery therefore proceeds from the very essence of present-day labour. (MEC 3, p. 241; EW, p. 288)

The worker, i.e., the majority in society, expresses the dissolution of the principle of modern civil society, i.e., 'private property, as founded on the labour of its proprietor'. Smith tells us that a society in which the greater part suffers is not happy. Thus 'it follows', Marx concludes, 'that society's distress is the goal of the economic system.' (MEC 3, p. 239; EW, p. 286) The next questions for Marx are: can the worker be the subject of future emancipation? Can the worker liberate the whole of society? Are the claims and rights of this class truly the rights and claims of society itself? Is this class in reality the heart and head of society? Marx answers this question by examining the theoretical and practical claims of the worker.

Theoretical Claims	Practical Claims
1) the [political economist] tells us that originally, and in theory, the whole produce of labour belongs to the worker.	However, at the same time he tells us that what the worker actually receives is the smallest part of the product, the absolute minimum necessary . . . (MEC 3, p. 239; EW, p. 287).
2) The political economist tells us that everything is bought with labour and that capital is nothing but accumulated labour,	but then goes on to say that the worker, far from being in a position to buy everything, must sell himself and his humanity (MEC 3, p. 239; EW, p. 287).
3) According to the political economist labour is the only means whereby man can enhance	However, according to this same political economy the landowner and the capitalist,

the value of natural products, and labour is the active property of man.	who as such are mere privileged and idle gods, are everywhere superior to the worker and dictate the law to him (MEC 3, p. 240; EW, p. 287).

The opposition of the worker's theoretical and practical claims indicates that 'the interest of the worker is never opposed to that of society. However, society is invariably and inevitably opposed to the interest of the worker.' (MEC 3, p. 240; EW, pp. 287f) Thus the worker is the heart and head of the future emancipation. At the end of the first stage in each column, Marx examines the relationship between the interests of each class and that of society. Given Marx's task in *A Contribution to the Critique of Hegel's Philosophy of Right: Introduction*, this examination means:

1. The capitalist and the landowner are losing the ability to dictate their conditions of subsistence as the laws to the society.

2. On the other hand, the worker is 'a sphere which has a universal character because of its universal suffering and which lays claim to no particular right because the wrong it suffers is not a particular wrong but wrong in general.' (MEC 3, p. 186; EW, p. 256) It is 'a sphere which cannot emancipate itself without emancipating itself from ... all the other spheres of society'. (MEC 3, p. 186; EW, p. 256)

As the proletariat is found to be the heart of 'radical revolution or universal emancipation' (MEC 3, p. 184; EW, p. 253), what is to be examined next is the mediation between the heart and the head of the emancipation, i.e., philosophy which enables individual man to organise 'his own forces as social forces so that social force is no longer separated from him in the form of political force'. (MEC 3, p. 168; EW, p. 234) At the end of the first stage of this column, Marx writes:

> Let us now rise above the level of political economy and examine the ideas developed above, taken almost word for word from the political economists, for the answers to these two questions:
> 1. What is the meaning, in the development of mankind, of this reduction of the greater part of mankind to abstract labour?
> 2. What mistakes are made by the piecemeal reformers, who either want to raise wages and thereby improve the situation of the working class, or – like Proudhon – see equality of wages are the goal of social revolution? In political economy labour appears only in the form of wage-earning activity. (MEC 3, p. 241; EW, p. 289)

Some commentators assert that these two questions were not answered by Marx in EPM. Let us start by examining the character of the questions.

First, 'examine the ideas developed above' indicates that the ideas are given and the questions have already been implicitly answered.

Second, the 'abstract labour' in the quotation means not only the labour separated from capital and soil but also the monotonous and machine-like labour which results from the separation. Judging from the nature of this 'abstract labour', its standpoint 'the meaning, in the development of mankind' and the content in the second stage of this column, the first question asks for the positive aspects of wage-labour in history.

Third, Marx asks for the negative aspects of wage-labour, i.e., why and in what way wage-labour is to be abolished. As far as 'wage-earning activity' is concerned, this is explained in *Notes on James Mill*. Exchange begins between communities, and the more exchange develops, the more labour becomes 'wage-labour'. It becomes completely wage-earning activity under capitalist conditions, that is, when 'The man who purchases the product does not himself produce but only exchanges the produce of others.' (MEC 3, pp. 219f; EW, p. 268)

It is careless to jump from Marx's terminology here to the conclusion that Marx could not distinguish simple commodity production from capitalist commodity production, because he is not confusing the two. In fact, Marx grasps the similarity and dissimilarity between the two. Wage-labour in capitalist relations is the zenith of wage-earning activity in general. Marx sees wage-earning activity can be transcended by abolishing its peak form: wage-labour. I would like to remind readers that the second question asks about the mistakes of reformers who 'abolish economic estrangement within economic estrangement'. (MEC 4, p. 43)

From all the observations above, it is safe to say that the questions have already been answered in the critical analysis of the three conditions of society, in particular of 'the second condition'. Hitherto Marx has presented his ideas on the laws of capitalist society mainly through examples and questions from political economists. In the next stage he attempts theoretically to expound the laws.

MARX'S ANALYSIS OF THE MOVEMENT OF CAPITALIST SOCIETY

The Second Stage of the Column 'Profit of Capital'

In section 4 'The Accumulation of Capitals and the Competition among the Capitalists' of the column 'Profit of Capital', Marx expounds the idea that the accumulation of capitals results in monopoly. His competition theory is worth noting with regard to his theory of monopoly and the laws of movement of capital.

First, Smith does not recognise any inner relationship between competition and monopoly. In his theory both were abstractly separated and opposed, as Marx writes: 'the sole defence against the capitalist is competition, which in the view of political economy has the beneficial effect both of raising wages and cheapening commodities to the advantage of the consuming public'. (MEC 3, pp. 250f; EW, p. 300)

Here again Marx sees the lack of comprehension (*Begriffslosigkeit*) of political economists. Competition is possible only if capitals multiply and are held by many different people. However, under capitalist conditions, accumulation means concentration of capitals in few hands. Smith opposes competition to monopoly, because he cannot distinguish between accumulation of capitals and the concentration of capitals in a few hands. If we understand competition among capitalists as the over-accumulation of capitals for their use,[20] we also understand that competition is nothing but 'mobile and restless monopoly' (MEC 3, p. 267; EW, p. 319) and that 'multilateral accumulation inevitably turns into unilateral accumulation' (MEC 3, p. 251; EW, p. 300), i.e., monopoly.

Second, obviously Marx grasps that competition is the driving force of the laws of capital,[21] as he states:

> Accumulation, which under the rule of private property means concentration of capital in few hands, inevitably ensues if capitals are allowed to follow their own natural course. It is only through competition that this natural proclivity of capital begins to take shape. (MEC 3, p. 251; EW, p. 300)

This is best expressed in his phrase in the column 'Rent of land':

> Finally, it is inevitable under these conditions of competition that landed property, in the form of capital, should manifest its domination both over the working class and over the property owners themselves, inasmuch as the laws of the movement of capital are either ruining or raising them. (MEC 3, p. 267; EW, p. 319)

Based on this understanding of competition, it is easy to comprehend that 'Even if we ignore deliberate competition for the moment, a large capital accumulates more rapidly, in proportion to its size, than does a small capital.' (MEC 3, p. 251; EW, p. 300) The speed of accumulation is investigated with regard to the difference between large and small capitals because the matter is transformed into capital itself, or the matter of advantage between large and small capitals in accumulation. Thus Marx develops the accumulation process of capitals through the following two advantages of large capital:

1. The profit of capital is in proportion to the volume of capital. (See MEC 3, p. 248; EW, p. 296)
2. The relationship between fixed capital and circulating capital. (MEC 3, p. 253; EW, p. 302)

On 2) Marx asserts that 'The accumulation of large capitals is generally accompanied by a concentration and simplification of fixed capital, as compared with the smaller capitals' (MEC 3, pp. 253f; EW, p. 303), which means the saving of fixed capital, the increase of circulating capital and an increase in profits.[22] The following part of this column is taken up by quotations which fall into two categories and which answer the 'two questions' in the first stage.

Answers to 'What mistakes are made by the piecemeal reformers ... ?'

1. 'To hire out one's labour is to begin one's enslavement; to hire out the materials of labour is to achieve one's freedom ...' (MEC 3, p. 254; EW, pp. 304f)
2. 'The element of matter, which can do nothing to create wealth without the element of labour, acquires the magical property of being fruitful for them.' (MEC 3, p. 255; EW, p. 305)

3. 'The property owners have received from human law the right to use and abuse the materials of all labour, i.e., to do as they wish with them.' (MEC 3, p. 255; EW, p. 305)
4. 'Competition is simply an expression of free exchange, which is itself the immediate and logical consequence of the right of any individual to use and abuse all instruments of production … . The inevitable consequences are continual and spreading bankruptcies, … trade crises, unemployment, periodic surfeits and shortages …'. (MEC 3, p. 255; EW, pp. 305f)
5. 'Nations are merely workshops for production, and man is a machine for consuming and producing … . Economic laws rule the world blindly.' (MEC 3, p. 256; EW, p. 306)
6. 'The master who buys a worker's labour at a price so low that it is barely enough to meet his most pressing needs is responsible neither for the low wages nor the longer hours of work: he himself is subject to the law which he imposes …'. (MEC 3, p. 257; EW, pp. 306f)

To sum up, the capitalist employs workers and forces them to work for him. Marx asserts, unlike reformers, that this is the consequence of the 'use' of human rights but not the 'abuse' of it. And not only the worker but also the capitalist is controlled by blind economic laws.

Answers to 'What is the meaning … of this reduction of the greater part of mankind to abstract labour?'

1. 'The inhabitants of many different parts of Great Britain have not capital sufficient to improve and cultivate all their land.' (MEC 3, p. 257; EW, p. 307)
2. 'The annual produce of the land and labour of any nation can be increased in its value by no means but by increasing either the number of its productive labourers, or the productive powers of those labourers who had before been employed … . In either case, an additional capital is almost always required.' (MEC 3, p. 257; EW, p. 307)
3. 'As the accumulation of stock must, in nature of things, be previous to the division of labour, so labour can be more and more subdivided in proportion only as stock is previously more and more accumulated.' (MEC 3, p. 257; EW, p. 307)
4. 'As the accumulation of stock is previously necessary for carrying on this great improvement in the productive powers of labour, so that accumulation naturally leads to this improvement. The person who employs his stock in maintaining labour … endeavours, therefore, both to make among his workmen the most proper distribution of employment, and to furnish them with the best machines …'. (MEC 3, pp. 257f; EW, pp. 307f)
5. 'Hence overproduction'. (MEC 3, p. 258; EW, p. 308)
6. 'More extensive combinations of productive forces … in trade and industry through the unification of more numerous and more varied human and natural forces for undertakings on a larger scale. Also there are already a number of cases of closer links among the main branches of production themselves … . Finally, in the larger joint-stock companies which have become so numerous, we find extensive combinations of the financial resources of many shareholders with the scientific and technical knowledge and skills of others to whom the execution of the work is entrusted … . However, the greater ease with which capital can be

> employed fruitfully in the most varied fields inevitably increases the conflict between the propertied and the propertyless classes.' (MEC 3, p. 258; EW, pp. 308f)

To sum up, the accumulation of capital causes, on the one hand, the development of productive forces, and, on the other, overproduction and the conflict between the capitalist and the worker. It is noteworthy that Marx emphasises the positive aspects of accumulation. Without the universal development in productive forces, the universal emancipation of mankind (Marx's communism) is impossible.

The Second Stage of the Column 'Wages of Labour'

In accordance with the column 'Profit of Capital', the second stage of 'Wages of Labour' consists almost solely of quotations on the conditions of the worker in the accumulation of capital. In the first stage of this column Marx shows the positive and negative aspects of capital, but in the second stage, those of wage-labour.

Answers to the Meaning of Abstract Labour

1. '[W]hile the commensurate wage for mechanically uniform activity, in which anyone can be quickly and easily trained, has fallen, and inevitably so, as a result of growing competition. And it is precisely this kind of labour which, under the present system of labour organization, is by far the most common ... . Finally, ... for the English cotton workers the working day has been increased, ... since labour-saving machines were introduced.' (MEC 3, pp. 241f; EW, p. 289)
2. 'But even if it were as true as it is false that the average income of all clases of society has grown, the differences and relative intervals between incomes can still have grown bigger, so that the contrast between wealth and poverty becomes sharper ... . relative poverty can therefore grow while absolute poverty diminishes.' (MEC 3, p. 242; EW, p. 290)
3. 'But political economy knows the worker only as a beast of burden, as an animal reduced to the minimum bodily needs.' (MEC 3, p. 242; EW, p. 290)
4. 'If a people is to increase its spiritual freedom, it can no longer remain in thrall to its bodily needs, it can no longer be the servant of the flesh. Above all it needs time for intellectual exercise and recreation. This time is won through new developments in the organization of labour.' (MEC 3, p. 242; EW, p. 290)
5. 'The transition from complicated handicrafts preesupposes a breaking down of such work into the simple operations of which it consists. To begin with, however, only a part of the uniformly recurring operations falls into the machines, while another part falls to men.' (MEC 3, p. 243; EW, p. 291)
6. 'In the future life of the nations, however, the mindless forces of nature operating in machines will be our slaves and servants.' (MEC 3, p. 243; EW, p. 291)
7. 'So as a result of changes in the organization of labour, a wider area of employment opportunities has been opened up to members of the female sex ... more economic independence for women ... both sexes brought closer together in their social relations.' (MEC 3, p. 243; EW, p. 291)
8. 'True, the advances in mechanization, which remove more and more of the monotonous tasks from human hands, are gradually eliminating these ills. However, standing in the way of these more rapid advances is the fact that the

capitalists are in a position to make use of the energies of the lower class, right down to children, very easily and very cheaply, and to use them instead of machinery.' (MEC 3, p. 243; EW, pp. 291f)

To sum up, with these quotations from economists and socialists Marx illustrates that labour produces, by becoming abstract labour, the possibility and the necessity: of shortening a working day, of the disposable time (free time) for intellectual development; of the socialisation of labour, means of production and human beings; of women's liberation. Although the possibility appears only in an alienated form to the worker under present conditions, the accumulation process of capital is producing this possibility before our eyes. It is also noteworthy that this criticism is made as a critique of Wilhelm Schulz's *Die Bewegung der Produktion* (Zürich, 1843), and as a critique of Proudhon's standpoint on simple commodity production. This means that the 'two questions' and the answers should be understood in connection with the criticism of Proudhon. The 'two questions' are connected.

Answers to the Mistakes of Reformers

1. 'The evil that millions are only able to eke out a living through exhausting, physically destructive and morally and intellectually crippling labour; that they are even forced to regard the misfortune of finding such work as fortunate.' (MEC 3, p. 243; EW, p. 292)
2. 'Servants – pay; workers – wages; clerks – salaries or emoluments.' (MEC 3, p. 243; EW, p. 292)
3. 'hire out one's labour', 'lend out one's labour at interest', 'work in another's space'. (MEC 3, p. 243; EW, p. 292)
4. 'This economic constitution condemns men to such abject employment, ... that by comparison savagery appears like a royal condition'. 'Prostitution of the non-owning class in all its forms'. (MEC 3, p. 244; EW, p. 292)
5. 'Political economy regards labour abstractly as a thing; labour is a commodity' .... 'Labour is life, and if life is not exchanged every day for food it suffers and soon perishes. If human life is to be regarded as a commodity, we are forced to admit slavery.' ... 'So if labour is a commodity, it is a commodity with the most unfortunate characteristics.' (MEC 3, pp. 244f; EW, p. 293)
6. Up to now industry has been in the situation of a war of conquest: 'The industrial war, if it is to be waged successfully, needs large armies which it can concentrate at one point and decimate at will. And neither devotion nor duty moves the soldiers of this army to bear the burdens laced upon them; what moves them is the need to escape the harshness of starvation' .... 'We are convinced ... that the large industrial towns would quickly lose their population of workers if they did not all the time receive a continual stream of healthy people and fresh blood from the surrounding country areas.' (MEC 3, pp. 245f; EW, pp. 294f)

Through these quotations the negative side of wage-labour is pointed out, i.e., the alienation of life activity. The problem is not the level of wages but the abolition of the alienation. From the observation above, I cannot agree with the widely-accepted assertion that Marx in 1844 was not able to answer the 'two questions' or that he could answer them only in the 'Estranged Labour' (i.e., 'FM: LP') or in the 'Third Manuscript' of EPM. Quotations in the second stage of columns 'Wages' and 'Profit' are not only on the negative but also on the positive aspects of capitalist society. The 'FM: FP' differs from the 'FM: LP' (the 'Estranged Labour') in its logical dimension. The 'two questions' are answered in both parts. However, the dimensions are different.

The Second Stage of the Column 'Rent of Land'

As we have already seen, the conflict of interests between the landowner and society was investigated at the end of the first stage of the column 'Rent of Land'. It ends with the conflict of interests among landowners. Here the competition between landlords, i.e., accumulation, is investigated. From the examination of the accumulation of capital in the column 'Profit of Capital', Marx writes that 'Generally speaking, large landed property and small landed property are in the same relation to one another as large and small capital.' (MEC 3, p. 264; EW, p. 315). However, there are special circumstances which lead without fail to the accumulation of large landed property and the swallowing up of small properties. Marx investigates the four of them and arrives at the abolition of the distinction between capitalist and landowner. (MEC 3, p. 266; EW, p. 317)

> This competition has the further consequence that a large part of landed property falls into the hands of the capitalists; thus the capitalists become landowners, just as the smaller landowners are in general nothing more than capitalists. In this way a part of large landed property becomes industrial. (MEC 3, p. 265; EW, p. 317)

The following should be noted with regard to this 'abolition of the distinction between capitalist and landowner'.

First, this abolition means that 'landed property, like every other kind of property, falls into the category of capital which reproduces itself with profit'. (MEC 3, pp. 315f; EW, p. 367) This is very important to be able understand theories of value and surplus value, because it shows rent and profit as developed forms of surplus labour.

Second, looking at the process more subjectively, the abolition means that 'With the transformation of the slave into a free worker, i.e., a hireling, the landowner himself is transformed into a master of industry, a capitalist.' (MEC 3, p. 286; EW, p. 338)

Third, this abolition is not developed for the first time here, but has already been clarified in the first stage. Here it is dealt with from the standpoint of how feudal landed property relations are transformed into modern capital relations based on the principles of private property.

Fourth, this abolition should be understood as a critique of Hegel's *Philosophy of Right*. In this work Hegel asserts that 'property' is the outside position (*fremdes Dasein*) of 'free will' and the developing process of freedom from 'abstract law' (family asset) to 'Moral' (private property) and to

'Humanity' (landed property). In Hegel's system, landed property is the 'sphere of realised freedom' (§4) and the abolition of private property, or capitalist society. Marx, however, demonstrates through his analysis of capitalist society that 'landed property' and Hegel's assembly of estates of the realm (*Stände*) cannot supersede capital and capitalist society. Landed property, as distinct from capital, is merely 'capital which is not yet fully developed'. (MEC 3, pp. 288f; EW, pp. 340f) Hegel's supersession of capitalist society is nothing less than utopian or reactionary.

Consequently, the whole of Marx's analysis of capitalist society in the three columns should be understood as a critique of Hegel. In particular, the transformation theory of feudal property into capitalist property and of capital into 'association, applied to the land' in the future makes a strong criticism.

Last, according to Marx, the abolition also means the development of the alienation from mere 'estrangement' to 'contradiction'. As he writes in the 'Third Manuscript':

> Estrangement appears not only in the fact that the means of my life belong to another and that my desire is the inaccessible possession of another, but also in the fact that all things are other than themselves, that my activity is other than itself, and finally – and this goes for the capitalist too – an inhumane power rules over everything. (MEC 3, p. 314; EW, p. 366)

Estrangement in this broad sense can be found in every society throughout history. However, the alienation of labour in capitalist society is more than this simple 'estrangement' and is to be understood as self-contradiction of labour. It is a symptom of the 'growing estrangement which is hastening towards its own abolition'. (MEC 3, p. 316; EW, p. 368).[23]

From this point of view, Marx refuses 'to join in the sentimental tears which romanticism sheds on' the causes of this 'abolition', i.e., the transformation of land into a commodity. He criticises the romanticism because it overlooks 'the dominion of the earth as of alien power over men' in feudal landownership and that the transformation of landed property into capital is 'entirely reasonable and, within the system of private property, inevitable and desirable'. (MEC 3, p. 266; EW, p. 318) The rule of private property begins with property as land, which is its basis and reaches its peak with capital, the manifestation of the domination of private property 'both over the working class and over the property owner themselves'. (MEC 3, p. 267; EW, p. 319)

With regard to the 'controversy over whether or not to divide up landed property' (MEC 3, p. 267; EW, p. 319), Marx observes that the division of landed property 'corresponds to the movement of competition in the industrial sphere' (MEC 3, p. 267; EW, p. 319) and inevitably leads to further accumulation, i.e., 'monopoly will inevitably reappear in an even more repulsive form – unless, that is, the division of landed property itself is negated or abolished.' (MEC 3, p. 268; EW, p. 329)

According to Marx, 'the first abolition of monopoly [the division of landed property] is always to generalise and extend its existence.' (MEC 3, p. 268; EW, p. 329) The second abolition or the negation of the abolition, i.e., 'association ... applied to the land', however, is the complete destruction of monopoly. Association, that is, Marx's concept 'social property', is defined as follows:

> Association, when applied to the land, retains the benefits of large landed property from an economic point of view and realises for the first time the tendency in the division of land, namely equality. At the same time association restores man's intimate links to the land in a rational way, ... because the earth ceases to be an object of barter, and through free labour and free enjoyment once again becomes an authentic, personal property for man. (MEC 3, p. 268; EW, p. 320)

In the succeeding paragraphs Marx proves the historical movement of private property in England and concludes the column, or his analysis of capitalist society, with the prospect of revolution.

VALUE THEORY IN THE 'FIRST MANUSCRIPT'

Marx's View on the Law of Value

Much ink was used on Marx's value theory in the early 1840s but only a few commentators have clarified the formation of Marx's own value theory. A widely accepted assertion goes, on the following two grounds, that Marx 'negated' or 'rejected' the classical labour theory of value:

1. Marx was under the influence of Engels' *Outlines of a Critique of Political Economy* which attaches too much importance to competition and negated the law of value as an 'abstraction'.[24]
2. Marx agreed with Proudhon's value theory which defines 'value' as 'cost of production' but 'price' as 'cost of production' plus 'tribute'.[25]

Even a quick look at Engels' and Proudhon's works reveals that these grounds contradict each other. Engels did not support Proudhonian value theory. Neither of them understood that profit emerged from unequal exchange in the process of circulation. Obviously, these grounds and their assertions are very questionable. However, there is space here only for Marx's value theory in the 'FM: FP'. Although no clear definition of 'value' can be found in this text, we can examine the two grounds from two aspects: Marx's views of competition and 'natural price'.

Marx's View on Competition

As far as 'competition' is concerned, I have already shown that Marx clearly grasped it as the driving force of the laws of capital in the 'FM: FP'. Consequently, the laws of capital are more scientifically comprehended by Marx and the first ground, (1) above, does not hold true in the 'FM: FP'. This requires only two quotations:

Accumulation, which under the rule of private property means concentration of capital in few hands, inevitably ensues if capitals are allowed to follow their own natural course. It is only through competition that this natural proclivity of capital begins to take shape. (MEC 3, p. 251; EW, p. 300)

Even if we ignore deliberate competition for the moment, a large capital accumulates more rapidly, in proportion to its size, than does a small capital. (MEC 3, p. 251; EW, p. 300)

Marx's View on Natural Price

Smith and Ricardo determined 'value' in terms of 'natural price'. In the 'FM: FP', without doubt, Marx accepts the 'natural price', when he states: 'So the worker is sure to lose and to lose most from the gravitation of the market price towards the natural price.' (MEC 3, p. 236; EW, p. 283) Judging from the authorial purpose evident here, Marx does not and cannot negate the law of value in Smith's and Ricardo's sense. As Marx says at the beginning of the so-called part 'Estranged Labour', the 'FM: FP' aims to conceptualise economic laws in political economists' own words: 'We have started out from the premises of political economy. We have accepted its language and its laws. We presupposed private property; ... competition; the concept of exchange value, etc. From political economy itself, we have shown that ...'. (MEC 3, p. 270; EW, p. 322)

Thus we can say with certainty that Marx had already reached the level of Smith and Ricardo in the determination of value. What is to be noted is that it is only from the 'Estranged Labour' (i.e., 'FM: LP') onwards that Marx rises above the level of political economists and expounds his criticism of political economy, i.e., in the working out of the conceptions and ideas into concepts.

The 'Cost of Production' in the 'FM: FP'

In the 'FM: FP' Marx uses the term 'production costs' (*Productionskosten*) three times. Let us devote some space here to clarify this aspect of Marx's value theory in the 'FM: FP' by examining how he uses the term. The investigation of 'cost' requires great care because political economists used the term in three ways:

1. the cost of production to the capitalist (c+v),
2. 'the immanent cost of production' of the commodity (c+v+s), which is identical with the 'value' of commodity,
3. the price of production (c+v+average profit). Thus the point is, to which of these are Marx's 'production costs' equivalent.

Sample 1

Investigating the two means by which capitalists can keep the market price above the natural price, Marx writes:

Firstly, by secrets in trade, ... Secondly, by secrets in manufacture, which enable the capitalist to cut production costs and sell his goods at the same price, or even at a lower price than his competitors, while making a bigger profit. (MEC 3, p. 249; EW, p. 297)

In fact, this passage is Marx's summary of *The Wealth of Nations*. Thus the secrets 'which enable the capitalist to cut production cost' in Sample 1 correspond to Smith's 'dyer who has found the means of producing a particular colour with materials which cost only half the price of those commonly made use of'.[26] Here the capitalist's extraordinary gains are directly derived from the cut in production costs. The first point to note is that Marx's 'production costs' concerns the process of production. It does not consist of average profit nor average rent and differs from Smith's 'natural price' and Ricardo's 'cost, including profit' (3).

Sample 2

Investigating Smith's two factors in the determination of rent, Marx also writes: 'These propositions of Smith are important, because they reduce the rent of land, where production costs and size are equal, to the degree of fertility of the soil.' (MEC 3, p. 260; EW, p. 311)

Similarly, the phrase 'when production costs and size are equal' in Sample 2 corresponds to Smith's 'the capitals are equal and equally well applied'[27] which was quoted earlier (Sample 2). Here again, 'production costs' is literally the cost in the process of production. The second point to note is that the term may mean the cost for the capitalist to produce the commodity, or 'cost price' in *Capital*, Volume 3 (where 'cost' is used in the sense of (1)).

Sample 3

Examining the special circumstances which lead to the accumulation of large landed property and the swallowing up of small properties, Marx says:

Nowhere does the number of workers and the amount of equipment decline so greatly in proportion to the size of the stock as in landed property. Similarly, nowhere does the possibility of many-sided exploitation, the saving of production costs and the judicious division of labour increase more in proportion to that stock than in this sphere. (MEC 3, p. 264; EW, pp. 315f)

In Sample 3, an increase in rent is directly derived from the saving of the production costs, albeit indirectly in Sample 2.

From all the observations above, we can say with certainty: that Marx's 'production costs' means costs for individual capitalists to produce commodities, i.e., the 'cost price' in *Capital*, Volume 3; that Marx does not presuppose the natural price but is explaining how it emerges through the gravitation of market prices; and that Marx does not presuppose the average profit nor the natural price and is completely free from the proposition that

'production costs' + 'average profit' = 'natural price'

Rather, he thinks that

'market price' – individual 'cost of production' = individual 'profit'

and that the 'market price' gravitates towards the 'natural price' through the gains and losses of wages, profits and rents. This is supported by my observation in the second section. Here again we can confirm that Marx does not negate the 'natural price' at all.

The Origin of Profit

Here I examine the second reason for the widely accepted assertion above, i.e., whether or not Marx explains profit from unequal exchange. The answer is yes and no. Marx explains profit through the unequal exchange in the production process but not in the circulation. As I have already described in the second section, in the first stage of the column 'Profit of Capital', Marx re-reads and re-interprets Smith's concept 'command' from 'the power of purchasing' into 'the power to command labour' which the capitalist exercises in the production process (MEC 3, p. 247; EW, p. 295). Consequently, confining himself to the propositions of political economy itself, he remarks:

> He [the capitalist] profits in two ways: firstly from the division of labour [read as 'collective forces of workers'], and more generally, from the growing role played by human labour in fashioning the natural products. The larger the human share in a commodity, the larger the profit of dead capital. (MEC 3, p. 249; EW, p. 298)

CONCLUSIONS

Kyuzo Asobe asserted[28] that Marx developed his analysis of capitalist society (the 'FM: FP') in the following order: (1) political economists (thesis), then (2) socialists (antithesis) and then (3) his views (synthesis); but that, in fact, Marx could not indicate his views. To begin with, Asobe failed to distinguish the two stages in the 'FM: FP'. Next, he did not understand the authorial purpose of the 'FM: FP'. Political economists and socialists are quoted not to introduce nor to criticise their views but to conceptualise the economic laws of capitalist society. As Marx states several times in the 'FM: FP', he defines the economic laws of the structure and the development of capitalist society, confining himself within the propositions of political economists and socialists. It is not until almost the second stage of each column that Marx 'rises above the level of political economy' (MEC 3, p. 241; EW, p. 288) and socialism.

In fact, even in the 'FM: FP' Marx is already above the level of political economists, but is still only at the starting-point of his real task, that is, a critique of political economy, or the working-up of observation and conception into concepts. From the 'FM: LP' (the so-called part 'Estranged Labour') onwards, Marx starts to comprehend the economic laws as necessary laws of private property by extracting the 'essence of private property'.

Consequently, the position of the 'FM: FP' in EPM is just a conceptualisation of capitalist society which is comprehended in the 'FM: LP' (the 'Estranged Labour'). However, this comprehension becomes possible only on the basis of this conceptualisation.

In broad outline, the following are conceptualised as the laws of the structure of capitalist society:

1. Rent is a derivation from the profit of capital.
2. The landlord falls into the category of the capitalist.
3. Thus capitalist society consists of two main classes: the worker and the capitalist.
4. Wage is the price of the worker who has become a commodity, though Marx distinguishes the wage-labourer from slave. The worker is free in a two-fold sense: from feudal compulsions and from the means of production.
5. The capitalist profits from employing the worker, i.e., commanding the labour and the products of the worker in the process of production.
6. Only the interest of the worker coincides with that of society.

Marx closes this first stage by posing questions concerning the positive and negative aspects of wage-labour.

In the second stage, he defines the laws of development, such as:

1. The accumulation of many capitals results in monopoly.
2. The political emancipation of man completes his estrangement.
3. Marx answers the questions concerning the positive and negative aspects of wage-labour. (The merchandising of labour is a modern slave system. The exploitation of labour results from free exchange itself. However, it builds material bases for really humane emancipation of man.)
4. Estranged labour can be abolished only by abolishing the 'capital–wage-labour relation', especially the large-scale monopoly of landed property and capital, with 'association' applied to the land:

> Association, when applied to the land, retains the benefits of large landed property from an economic point of view and realizes for the first time the tendency inherent in the division of land, namely equality. (MEC 3, p. 268; EW, p. 320)

With regard to these analyses, the following three points are noteworthy.

First, capital is the zenith of private property, which develops from landed property. Capital is the power to command the labour and the products of other men and its subjective essence is 'estranged labour', that is, the labour under the command of another man. Thus the abolition of capital is the abolition of all sorts of private property and enslavement. The analysis of the 'capital–labour' relation provides insights into past and future societies.

Second, Marx's critique of political economy, of German philosophy and of French socialism are not three different things but three aspects of the same thing. Marx's critical analysis of capitalist society itself is his critique of Hegel's and Proudhon's critique of capitalist society. Marx's theory of revolution, the abolition of private property at the peak of its development is a critique of the Hegelian state theory and of the Proudhonian romanticism which advocates simple commodity production. The second stage of the column 'Rent of Land' should be read in this context.

Third, Smith has two types of value theory: the 'dissolving' and the 'composing'. Marx's conceptualisation in the 'FM: FP' is based on the 'dissolving' type. The following serve as evidence:

1. Marx's quotations from *The Wealth of Nations*. They are strictly limited to the passages based on the 'dissolving' type.
2. Marx's summary of the 'FM: FP' at the beginning of 'FM: LP' (the 'Estranged Labour').
3. Marx's rent and profit theories in the 'FM: FP'.
4. There is no evidence to suggest that Marx negated the labour theory of value.
5. Marx's theory of alienation. Unless it is based on the 'dissolving' type, the definition of 'estranged' labour is impossible, as Shigeji Wada asserts:

> If the 'composing' type of value theory were correct, the labourer would produce only the equivalent to his wage, and the definition of 'estranged labour' would become completely impossible. Thus whether value and price are to be explained as the dissolving type or not was the central and the pressing issue for Marx, which concerns the basis of his formulation of the problem.[29]

As a matter of fact, Engels does not negate the proposition that 'price is determined by the reciprocal action of production costs and competition', (MEC 3, p. 427) on the contrary, he admits that 'It is ... quite correct, and a fundamental law of private property.' (MEC 3, p. 427) The point Engels makes is that 'everything in economics stands on its head'. He writes: 'Value, the primary factor, the source of price, is made dependent on price, its own product.' (MEC 3, p. 427)

Ricardo's value, like Smith's, is the 'natural price' and consists of the average wage and the average profit. This concept cannot explain price, because it is a price , i.e., the 'central price' in the fluctuations of market price. This is the so-called 'confusion of value and price' in political economy. According to Engels, value is the concept from which price is to be explained. In Marx's terminology in *Capital*, 'value' defined by political economists is 'production cost' in Volume 3 and is quite different from 'value' in *Capital*, Volume 1.

Consequently, Engels' critique of value determination by Smith and Ricardo is right, albeit it has a weak point too.[30] I wonder whether we can transcend the Old Marx when very few can appreciate the 26-year-old Marx's new horizon.

7 A TWO-FOLD ANALYSIS OF THE CAPITALIST PRODUCTION PROCESS

As Lenin said, Marx's system is a critique of English political economy, German classical philosophy and French socialism.

Surprisingly, however, the logical structure of this three-part enterprise has never been made clear. Once this simple structure has been clarified, the critique as a whole becomes easier to understand. In my view the EPM is the first and simplest attempt at this critique, and it is the logical place to begin. To defend this view I shall begin by critically summarising the research on the EPM to date.

Commentators on EPM agree on the following three points: first, EPM is Marx's first critique of political economy; second, the central concept in EPM is 'alienated labour' through which English political economy, German philosophy and French socialism are criticised; third, 'alienated labour' also has a function in economic analysis. However, most Marxist economists do not regard 'alienated labour' as an important concept in Marx's mature thought, as seen in *Capital*. Consequently, they have not regarded EPM, his first critique, as very important. I shall argue that the concept 'alienated labour' is essential to Marx's whole system at every stage. An investigation into the first two manuscripts of EPM will show that 'alienated labour' is not at all extraneous to Marx's critique. Commentators have generally analysed the EPM in three parts:

1. 'First Manuscript: Former Part' ('FM: FP').
2. 'First Manuscript: Latter Part' ('FM: LP').
3. 'First Manuscript: Former Part' taken together with 'Second Manuscript'.

A formal examination of the two manuscripts will make clear how the EPM should be understood as the first draft of Marx's critique.

THE POSITION OF THE FIRST AND SECOND MANUSCRIPTS

The Relation of the 'First Manuscript: Latter Part' and the 'Second Manuscript'

There are two suppositions concerning the content of the missing parts of the 'Second Manuscript'. The first supposes that the description of the three stages of exchange in history would be developed in order to explain the historical forms of private property in the 'Second Manuscript'. Evidence for this includes the fact that most of the *Notes on James Mill* presumes that Marx had done this himself. This fact is then linked to the distinction between movable and immovable property, the sketch concerning the movement of capital and labour in the 'Second Manuscript', and the discussion of 'two problems' at the end of the 'FM: LP'. Mitzutani asserts: 'It might not be wrong to conclude that the task of the 'Second Manuscript' is to make clear the meaning of alienated labour and private property in human history by giving an account of their historical development.'[1]

According to this view the content of the 'Second Manuscript' has nothing to do with that of the 'First Manuscript', and the conclusion is inevitable that economic theories are not developed anywhere in EPM. This has given rise to three critical questions. First, what is the basis for supposing that the *Notes on James Mill* would have been quoted in the 'Second Manuscript'? The only evidence comes from outside the EPM. Second, could Marx really have been concerned with history qua history after the 'FM: LP'? After that point he seems only concerned with the comprehension (*Begreifung*) of the laws of private property. Third, does not the content of the 'Third Manuscript' prove that the analysis of the 'Second Manuscript' had to be at the logical level? For example, Marx writes:

> We have already seen how the political economist establishes the unity of labour and capital in a variety of ways: (1) Capital is accumulated labour. (2) The determinations[2] of capital within production partly, reproduction of capital with profit, partly .... (MEC 3, p. 312; EW, p. 364)

On the other hand, a second view supposes that the 'FM: LP' and the 'Second Manuscript' form two components of the analysis of the immediate process of capital. The basis of this view is the content (particularly MEC 3, pp. 287f; EW, pp. 339f) of the 'Second Manuscript'. The only weak point in this view is that its adherents do not make plain the logical structure of the first two manuscripts. Typically they say: 'We should not forget that the real historical process is reflected in "political economy" and will be made clear through the critique of "political economy" by Marx.'[3] This is correct, but it is not enough to persuade commentators adhering to the first view. I will develop this view after the following formal considerations concerning the relationship between the first two manuscripts. Marx repeated his comments on the relation of 'private property' eight times in the 'FM: LP' and twice in the 'Second Manuscript'. I quote some of these comments in order to draw conclusions:

Comments in the 'First Manuscript: Latter Part'

Extract 1 Through estranged, alienated labour, the worker produces the relationship to this labour of a man alien to labour and standing outside it. The relationship of the worker to labour creates the relation to it of the capitalist or whatever one chooses to call the master of labour. (MEC 3, p. 279; EW, pp. 331f)

Extract 2 Alienated labour has resolved itself for us into two components which depend on one another, or which are but different expressions of one and the same relationship. Appropriation appears as estrangement, as alienation; and alienation appears as appropriation, estrangement as true naturalisation. (MEC 3, p. 281; EW, pp. 333f)[4]

Extract 3 Having seen that in relation to the worker who *appropriates* nature by means of his labour, this appropriation appears as estrangement, his own spontaneous activity as activity for another and as activity of another, vitality as a sacrifice of life, production of the object as loss of the object to an alien power, to an *alien* person, – we shall now consider the relation to the worker, to labour and its object of this person who is alien to labour and the worker. (MEC 3, pp. 281f; EW, p. 334)

Comments in the 'Second Manuscript'

Extract 4 The relations of private property contain latent within them the relation of private property as labour, the relation of private property as *capital*, and the *mutual relation* of these two to one another. (MEC 3, p. 285; EW, p. 336)

Extract 5 The character of private property is expressed by labour, capital, and the relation between these two. (MEC 3, p. 289; EW, p. 341)

Conclusions Drawn from These Extracts

First, 'private property' or 'alienated labour' consists of two aspects: the 'relation of the worker to labour and to the production of his labour' (or 'the relation of private property as labour') and the 'relation of the non-worker to the worker and to the product of his labour' (or 'the relation of private property as capital'). That means these two aspects are 'two components which depend on one another, or which are but different expressions of one and the same relationship'.

Second, that these two aspects are defined as 'appropriation'. This appears as estrangement, as 'alienation'; alienation appears as appropriation, estrangement as true naturalisation.

Third, 'appropriation appears as alienation, estrangement' defines the 'relation of private property as labour'. 'Alienation appears as appropriation, estrangement as true naturalisation' must define the 'relation of private property as labour'. The analysis in the 'FM: LP' is limited to 'the relation of private property as labour', which logically produces the other relation. Thus the 'FM: LP' ends by posing the analysis of the other relation as a topic for the following manuscript.

Last, the reconfirmation of 'both relations' in the 'Second Manuscript' shows that the 'relation of private property as capital' must have been analysed there.

We can now conclude the following:

(a) the 'relation of private property' consists both of the alienation of the worker from his work and from his product and of the appropriation of work and product by the non-worker;
(b) the object of analysis in the 'Second Manuscript' is the same as that in the 'FM: LP', i.e., the immediate production process of capital. These are the only immanent interpretations of the 'FM: LP' and the 'Second Manuscript', and confirm the second view on the content of the 'Second Manuscript'.

Following through on these conclusions, we can now confirm that the logical position of the 'Second Manuscript' in the EPM is the same as that of the 'FM: LP', i.e., the derivation of economic laws from the principle of private property, that is, the genetic development of economic categories from 'the general essence of private property'. In the 'FM: LP' Marx has already developed a conception (*Vorstellung*) of the structural and dynamic laws of the capitalist economy through the works of political economists and socialists. At the beginning of the 'FM: LP' he demonstrates that the basic flaw in classical economics is that the economists did not comprehend the inner, necessary relationships of their categories. They had no conception that the economic categories should be explained step-by-step from the abstract up to the more complex and concrete. Thus Marx set himself the task of comprehending these laws in the manuscript which followed:

> Political economy starts with the fact of private property; it does not explain it to us. It expresses in general, abstract formulas the material process through which private property actually passes, and these formulas it then takes for laws. It does not comprehend these laws, i.e., it does not demonstrate how they arise from the very nature of private property. (MEC 3, pp. 270f; EW, p. 322)

Thus Marx's task is to deduce the 'general nature of private property' and then to develop each economic category from this as a more precise definition. This is the real meaning of the phrase in which Marx recommends grasping economic categories as scientific reflections of historical, transcendent economic relations of production. He writes:

> Just as we have derived the concept of private property from the concept of estranged alienated labour by analysis, so we can develop every category of political economy with the help of these two factors; and we shall find again in each category, e.g., trade, competition, capital, money, only a particular and developed expression of these first elements. (MEC 3, p. 281; EW, p. 333)

The Position of the First and Second Manuscripts

As Marx himself put it, his work in the 'FM: LP' and the following manuscripts was supposed to expose the 'essence of private property' and to demonstrate how economic laws arise from its very nature. However to understand this work it is important to grasp two points:

(a) the 'separation of labour, capital and landed property', which had been presupposed earlier in the 'FM: LP', must now be explained;

(b) this exercise has nothing to do with the historical 'original accumulation of capital'. This separation is rather produced regularly every year and must be explained as the 'separation of wages, profit of capital and rent'.

From the 'FM: LP' onwards Marx's task was the genetic development of economic categories. Hence he criticised the explanation of the origin of profit as given by classical political economists. Marx writes:

> Political economy throws no light on the cause of the division between labour and capital, and between capital and land. When, for example, it defines the relationship of wages to profit, it takes the interest of the capitalist to be the ultimate cause, i.e., it takes for granted what it is supposed to explain. (MEC 3, p. 271; EW, pp. 322f)

In classical political economy the origins of wages, profit and rent were not discussed. David Ricardo, as well as Adam Smith, took it for granted that capitalists must receive profit, or else 'capitalists had no interest to invest their money in business'. This is not a scientific explanation for the origin of profit. Rather the economists 'assume as a fact, in historical form, what has to be explained'.

Marx, however, starts his explanation with the analysis of an 'actual economic fact', which he confirmed as a concept (*Vorstellung*) in the 'FM: FP':

> The worker becomes all the poorer the more wealth he produces, the more his production increases in power and size. The worker becomes an ever cheaper commodity the more commodities he creates. The devaluation of the world of men is in direct proportion to the increasing value of the world of things. Labour produces not only commodities: it produces itself and the worker as a commodity – and this at the same rate at which it produces commodities in general. (MEC 3, pp. 271f; EW, pp. 323f)

LOGIC IN THE 'FIRST MANUSCRIPT: LATTER PART'

Distinguishing Alienation and Estrangement from Objectification

Let us move on to consider the content of the critique of political economy in EPM. Marx analyses this 'fact' by taking the metabolism between men and nature, that is, the relation of the worker to work and to the product of his labour', as his basic viewpoint. Ontologically 'the product of labour is labour which has been embodied in an object'. Production is the realisation of labour, which is also its objectification, and in addition the appropriation of nature by the worker. This 'fact', however, means that 'objectification appears as loss of the object and bondage to it; appropriation as estrangement, as alienation' in capitalist society (MEC 3, p. 272; EW, p. 324). Marx calls this situation the 'estrangement or alienation of the worker from his product'. In other words, 'realization' is ontologically equal to 'objectification' and to the 'appropriation (*Aneignung*) of nature', but 'under these (capitalist) economic conditions' it appears as a 'loss of the object and bondage to it' of 'estrangement, alienation'.

An Analysis of the Worker's Relation to Nature

When the product of the worker's labour does not belong to him, Marx calls this alienation from the product. This is the first aspect of alienation. Moreover, when the product of labour does not belong to the worker, this is only possible because his labour itself does not belong to him; his labour is not done for himself but for someone else. The alienation of the worker from his product comprises the alienation of the worker from his labour. The estrangement of the object of labour merely summarises the estrangement of the activity of labour. Note that objectification and alienation are compared in three dimensions:

(a) realisation appears as loss of realisation;
(b) objectification appears as loss of object and bondage to it;
(c) appropriation appears as estrangement, as alienation.
(MEC 3, p. 272; EW, p. 324)

The third aspect of the alienation of labour is a reflection of the second. This aspect is very important, because it is the turning point in evaluating the whole of the EPM. First we should understand the difference in the logical dimension between the first two aspects and the third. That aspect was 'deduce(d) from the two already considered'.

The third aspect shares the same object as the first two, but the viewpoint is different. Up to then production had been considered only as a realisation of private life. However, according to the new viewpoint production is also the realisation of human nature. Human beings also need nature as the object of their material and spiritual means of living. In that sense human beings are natural beings like other animals. Nature is the inorganic body of human beings, who cannot live without it, yet it does not exist already prepared for consumption by humans. Human beings, however, are not quite the same as other animals who must relate to nature within a limited range of activities. Only humans relate to nature over a full range, which means that each human being is a species-being (*Gattungswesen*). Humans can address the species as an object, and can produce quite apart from the demands of hunger, even, according to the standards of beauty, and so they can produce universally.

The third aspect of alienation indicates that human beings sell their productive activities to get their means of life, something which is possible only for them. As human beings they are free beings; they can sell their productive activities under certain conditions and can fall under the control of other human beings. Thus the third aspect of alienation indicates the alienation of the worker from human nature.

Economically this aspect is the basis of exchange and the formation of 'commercial society'. As only human beings can exchange products and form a commercial society, these phenomena must be explained from human nature itself. Moreover, Marx also used this aspect of alienation to explain a commodity-producing society as alienated social relations, yet only through that means, in his view, could human beings increase their social power and individual abilities.

An Analysis of the Relation between Men

The fourth aspect of alienated labour is the alienation of man from some other man. This aspect of alienated labour represents the answer to an important question: if labour and the product of the worker do not belong to the worker himself, to whom do they belong? In society, or rather, in social relations, the alienation of the worker from his product and from his labour can appear only through his relation with some other man. The worker's product and labour must belong to someone else. In other words, the alienation of the worker is the logical representation of the appropriation of his labour and product by someone else. 'The property relation of non-worker to the worker and labour' is reproduced daily by 'the alienated relation of the worker to labour and to his product.' (MEC 3, p. 281; EW, p. 334) Without the labour of others, the capitalist cannot be a capitalist; the capitalist cannot reproduce his money with profit. Thus this fourth aspect marks the transcendence of 'private property as labour' to 'private property as capital'. This is illustrated in the following passages:

> If the product of labour does not belong to the worker, if it confronts him as an alien power, this can only be because it belongs to some *other man than the worker*. (MEC 3, p. 278; EW, p. 330)
>
> If the worker's activity is a torment to him, to another it must give *satisfaction* and pleasure. (MEC 3, p. 278; EW, pp. 330f)
>
> Thus, if the product of his labour, his labour objectified, is for him an alien, hostile, powerful object independent of him, then his position towards it is such that someone else is master of this object, someone who is *alien*, hostile, powerful, and independent of him. (MEC 3, p. 278; EW, p. 331)
>
> If he treats his own activity as an unfree activity, then he treats it as an activity performed in the service, under the dominion, the coercion, and the yoke of another man. (MEC 3, pp. 278–9; EW, p. 331)
>
> Just as he creates his own production as the loss of his reality, as his punishment ... so he creates the dominion of the person who does not produce over production, and over the product. (MEC 3, p. 279; EW, p. 331)
>
> Just as he estranges his own activity so he confers upon the stranger from himself, an activity which is not his own. (MEC 3, p. 279; EW, p. 331)

Through 'estranged labour' the worker not only creates his relationship to the object and to the act of production as a relationship to powers that are alien and hostile to him, he also creates the relation in which another man stands to his production and to his product, and the relationship in which he stands to the other man. It is very important to confirm that 'the concept of private property', which is derived by analysis from the 'concept of alienated labour', is the 'relation of the non-worker to the worker and to the product of his labour'. The concept of 'private property' used here is the 'property relation of the non-worker to the worker and to labour'. (MEC 3, p. 281; EW, p. 334).[5] Marx analysed the immediate process of production of capital into two component parts: 'the relation of private property as labour' and 'the relation of private property as capital'. He showed that the latter is merely a logical and necessary result of the former. Although the latter relation itself has not yet been analysed, the most important points to note are the following: Marx grasped capital as a social relation, a production relation and a commanding power over other men's labour and their products. The first two aspects of alienated labour are not merely found in *Capital* but are crucial to comprehending capital as 'self-realising value'.[6]

LOGIC IN THE 'SECOND MANUSCRIPT'

An Analysis of Private Property as Capital

The extant pages of the 'Second Manuscript' consist of the following four parts:

(a) 'The worker produces capital, and capital produces him; hence he produces himself, man as worker, as a commodity ... '. (MEC 3, p. 283; EW, p. 335)
(b) Capitalist 'production produces him in keeping with this role as a mentally and physically dehumanised being'. (MEC 3, p. 284; EW, p. 336)
(c) 'The real course of development ... results in the necessary victory of the capitalist over the landed owner.' (This describes the antagonism between movable property and landed property.)
(d) Description of 'the movement through which these constituents (labour and capital) have to pass'.

The 'Second Manuscript' as extant begins with a paragraph stating that capital and labour are a negation of each other: 'The worker is the subjective manifestation of the fact that capital is man wholly lost to himself, just as capital is the objective manifestation of the fact that labour is man lost to himself.' (MEC 3, p. 283; EW, pp. 334f) This relation of capital and labour is not a simple negation. It is a contradiction in the strict sense: that they need each other, produce each other and yet still exclude each other. A worker can be a worker when he gets a job and thus he becomes capital in the production process. The worker is a most miserable commodity and has to starve to death if his commodity cannot be sold to the capitalist. He can exist as a worker only when he becomes a part of capital and reproduces capital with profit. Wages, as is the same with the price of any other commodity, are determined by their 'cost'. Human activity is considered within political economy merely as a material commodity and as nothing more.

> The wages of labour have thus exactly the same significance as the maintenance and servicing of any other productive instrument, or as the consumption of capital in general, required for its reproduction with interest, like the oil which is applied to wheels to keep them turning. Wages, therefore, belong to capital's and the capitalist's necessary costs, and must not exceed the bounds of this necessity. (MEC 3, p. 284; EW, p. 335)

In short, in capitalist relations of production, the worker reproduces not only capital with profit but also himself as a commodity. This antithesis of capital and labour is not a simple antithesis. It is the highest form of antithesis, that is, contradiction, because in the form of capital, private property has reached its peak of development. In capital, private property has become 'totally indifferent to its real content'. (MEC 3, p. 285; EW, p. 336) Capital is the peak form which contains all forms of private property within its essence.

> There is the production of human activity as labour ... On the other hand, there is the production of the object of human activity as capital ... This contradiction, driven to the limit, is of necessity the limit, the culmination, and the downfall of the whole private property relationship. (MEC 3, p. 285; EW, pp. 336f)

Let us reconfirm the content of the 'Second Manuscript' with the following paragraph in the 'Third Manuscript', which refers to the 'Second Manuscript':

> *We have already seen how the political economist establishes the unity of labour and capital in a variety of ways*: (1) Capital is *accumulated labour*. (2) The determinations of capital within production – partly, reproduction of capital with profit, partly, capital as raw material (material of labour), and partly, as an automatically *working instrument* (the machine is capital directly equated with labour) – is *productive labour*. (3) The worker is a capital. (4) Wages belong to the costs of capital. (5) In relation to the worker, labour is the reproduction of his life-capital. (6) In relation to the capitalist, labour is an aspect of his capital's activity. Finally, (7) the political economist postulates the original unity of capital and labour as the unity of the capitalist and the worker; this is the original state of paradise. The way in which these two aspects as two persons, confront each other, is for the political economist an *accidental* event, and hence only to be explained by reference to external factors. (MEC 3, p. 312; EW, p. 364)

First, the italicised phrase in the extract above shows that Marx has already considered the determinations of capital within production in the 'Second Manuscript'. The definitions in the 'Second Manuscript' confirm this statement: they coincide with the content of the 'Second Manuscript'.

Second, (2) above shows that it is only labour that reproduces capital with profit. Two things are now obvious: Marx distinguishes three phases of capital within production: labour, raw materials and machines. In relation to labour, Marx states that it reproduces capital with profit, because raw materials and machines, which have no life, cannot reproduce themselves.

Last, (7) above shows that Marx grasped the production process of capital as a transcendent unity of capital and labour followed by their separation. Criticising the economic trinity (capital producing profit, wages of labour and rent of land), Marx identifies rent as a part of profit. Landed property as such has vanished and it has become capital. Here we see the outlines of his analysis of the economic categories, which had been already demonstrated in the 'FM: FP' in purely conceptual form (*Vorstellung*).

With the above consideration in mind, we can conclude that in the 'Second Manuscript' Marx considered another component of the production process of capital from the standpoint of capital itself: 'the relation of private property as capital'. History as such has nothing to do with the analysis from that point in the 'FM: LP' onwards.

The third type of discussion in the 'Second Manuscript', the discussion of 'the necessary victory of the capitalist over the landowner', which follows the paragraphs above, is a logical insight based on the essence of capital (MEC 3, p. 288; EW, p. 340). This essence of capital logically contains the essence of all former types of private property and thus comprehends the necessary development of private property. Just as in the 'First Reference' in the 'Third Manuscript', antagonism between immovable and movable property and so on is grasped by their essences. In the form of capital, private property has become totally indifferent to its content. It contains all kinds of private property in its essence. Capital is the highest abstraction of this content. From this point of view the historical development from landed property to capital must be grasped as 'necessary'. This is of course consistent with the task which Marx set himself in the 'FM: LP'.

Marx's Genetic Description of Capital

Marx uses 'capital' positively for the first time in the 'Second Manuscript'. In the 'FM: LP' 'capitalist' is used only once negatively. Although 'capital' is often used in the 'FM: FP', this is only because of its position in the EPM, that is, an idea pertaining to the economic laws of capitalism. However, 'capital' is not used at all in the 'FP: LP', in which the production process is analysed from the standpoint of 'labour'. Here 'capital' is a category to be developed from the 'general essence of private property'. In the 'Second Manuscript', for the first time, 'capital' is used positively within an analysis of the production process. Starting his analysis with an 'actual fact' – that the worker produces the 'commodity' – Marx came to the conclusion that the worker produces the 'private property' through 'alienated labour': the 'property relation' of the non-worker to labour and to its product. 'Private property' as used in the 'FM: LP' means 'property relation' or 'commodity' (or 'product') in the hands of the non-worker: 'private property as the material and embracing expression of estranged labour ...'. (MEC 3, p. 281; EW, p. 334)

In the 'Second Manuscript', through a two-fold analysis of the production process of capital, Marx defines the worker as reproducing 'capital with profit'. There are two meanings that Marx assigns here to 'commodity' and 'capital'. First, they mean 'accumulated labour' reproduced with 'profit'. It takes only one example of this usage to make the point: 'Land as land, and rent as rent, have lost their distinction of rank and have become insignificant capital and interest – or rather, capital and interest that signify only money.' (MEC 3, p. 285; EW, p. 337)

Second, in connection with the first, Marx calls 'private property' 'capital' when it has become indifferent to its content. Capital is private property in which any social meaning, which landed property once had, has been lost.

Its only reference is to money, which is the extreme form of abstraction of its material content. For example:

immovable private property	movable private property
. . . landed property (aristocratic feudal life) and [industry] itself continues to bear the feudal character of its opposite in the form of monopoly, craft, guild, corporation, etc., within which labour still has a *seemingly* social significance, . . . (MEC 3, p. 286; EW, p. 337)	But liberated industry, industry constituted for itself as such, and *liberated capital*, are the necessary *development* of labour. (MEC 3, p. 286; EW, p. 337)
The landowner lays stress on the noble lineage of his property, on feudal souvenirs or reminiscences, the poetry of recollection, on his romantic disposition, on his political importance, etc.; and when he talks economics, it is *only* agriculture that he holds to be productive. (MEC 3, pp. 286f; EW, p. 338)	a sly, hawking, carping, deceitful, greedy, mercenary, rebellious, heartless and spiritless person who is estranged from the community and freely trades it away, who breeds, nourishes and cherishes competition, and with it pauperism, crime, and the dissolution of all social bonds, . . .(MEC 3, p. 287; EW, p. 338).
undeveloped, immature private property (MEC 3, p. 288; EW, p. 340)	developed private property (MEC 3, p. 288; EW, p. 340)

In short 'capital' is used when every relation is turned into a 'value relation'. Capital is used as private property indifferent to its content, i.e., 'abstract', and without any social significance.

From the investigation so far we can now conclude the following.

First, 'commodity' is in 'fact' the starting point of analysis in the 'FM: LP', which has been developed step-by-step with the progress of the analysis into 'private property' and 'capital'. As was predicted near the end of the 'FM: LP' 'capital' is developed through the help of two factors: 'alienated labour', and 'private property'.

Second, in the 'Second Manuscript' a new standpoint of 'value' has been introduced and Marx has discovered the way in which 'accumulated labour' realises itself in 'capital'.

Third, it is also shown that the production process of 'capital' is not only the reproduction process but also the reproduction process of wage labour, i.e., the capitalist 'relation of production' itself, which forms the basis of the 'separation of capital, labour and landed property'.

Last, the content of 'a critique of political eeconomy' in EPM is the genetic description of 'wages' and 'profit' (in the broad sense of 'surplus-value') through a two-fold analysis of the immediate production process of capital.

Capital as the Limit of the Development of Private Property

We have examined the first two sections of the 'Second Manuscript', and now we move on to the examination of the last two. These two are connected with the 'two problems' set up at the end of the 'FM: LP'. The first supposition concerning the content of the 'Second Manuscript' was based on it. In the following passages these three will be examined one by one.

Meaning, Character and Method of the 'Two Problems'

For a careful reader it is obvious that these 'two problems' are new forms of the 'two questions' which were set up and answered in the 'FM: FP'.[7] Why did Marx set these two up on a more profound logical level? Marx argues that we have to stop looking at 'private property' as a material object existing outside us and must grasp it instead as a definite mode of existence or a definite mode of labour. Private property is not a material object in itself, it is a social relation within the production process. Only when we grasp this essence does it become possible for us to abolish it.

In other words, the theory of value and theory of surplus-value explain the meaning of private property in human history. In the history of economic theory, this was facilitated partly by the agricultural system. It was François Quesnay[8] who took the first important step towards this. Adam Smith followed and David Ricardo completed this view within classical political economy. Quesnay, criticising the mercantile system, for which only precious metal was wealth, put the subjective essence of wealth partly into human labour, i.e., 'agricultural labour'. Smith grasped the 'essence of' labour in general, but he could not develop his theory consistently. Smith has a two-fold value theory: 'dissolving value theory' and composing value theory'. Ricardo criticised the latter and developed his theories solely in terms of the former.

However, Ricardo did not understand the profound confusion in Smith' s value theory. This was the distinction between 'simple commodity production' and 'capitalist commodity production'. Ricardo neglected this historical distinction and regarded 'capitalist commodity production' as 'simple commodity production'. In this sense, Ricardo's version of value theory was also a step backwards in understanding history.

Ricardo' s retreat from Smith can be seen in his understanding of 'capital'. Smith defined capital as accumulated labour reproduced with profit, but Ricardo deprived any historical *differentia specifica* from capital and understood it as accumulated labour in general. Why and how 'accumulated labour' is turned into 'capital' was not explained by Ricardo. In other words, Ricardo did not grasp the substance and form of labour which determines 'value'.

Smith and Ricardo understood the subjective essence of private property as labour in general, but did not grasp this essence as 'alienated labour'. They defined labour which determines value as labour in accordance with human nature. In other words, they confused 'alienation' with 'objectification' in general.

On the other hand, Marx understood the subjective essence of private property as alienated labour, i.e., human labour opposed to human nature. This means that Marx understood the substance of value as the alienated form of social labour and understood capital as the appropriation of the labour of others.

The next question is what this 'alienation' and its abolition mean for the development of human beings. These are the reasons why Marx set up 'two questions' and 'two problems' in the 'FM: FP'.

The above analysis reveals the logical, theoretical character of the 'two tasks'. It has nothing to do with history as history. These 'two problems' do not form a basis for anyone to derive some historical content from the 'Second Manuscript'. What we have to take into account when we think about the answers to these 'two problems' is the way in which the 'FM: LP' ends. Following these tasks, Marx wrote 'As to (1)' noting that his analysis had been limited to one of the two component parts of 'the relation of private property': 'Now we are going to consider the relation of man, who is alien to work and of the worker, to the worker,' (MEC 3, p. 282; EW, p. 334)

This suggests that Marx tried to answer these problems through the analysis of this relation in the 'Second Manuscript'. The extant pages of the manuscript contain no direct answer. Thus the next question for us is how the answer is likened to the analysis of the 'relation of private property as capital'. It seems to me that they are connected through the comprehension of the 'essence of capital'. This connection can be shown by considering the fourth section of the 'Second Manuscript'.

The Description about the Antithesis of Movable and Immovable Property

> There is the production of human activity as *labour* – that is, as an activity quite alien to itself, to man and to nature, and therefore to consciousness and the expression of life – the *abstract* existence of man as a mere *workman* who may therefore daily fall from his filled void into the absolute void – into his social and therefore actual, non-existence. On the other hand, there is the production of the object of human activity as *capital* – in which all the natural and social characteristic of the object is *extinguished*; in which private property has lost its natural and social quality (and therefore every political and social illusion, and is not associated with any *apparently* human relations); in which the *selfsame* capital remains the *same* in the most diverse natural and social manifestations, totally indifferent to its *real* content. This contradiction, driven to the limit, is of necessity the limit, the culmination, and the downfall of the whole private property relationship. (MEC 3, p. 285; EW, pp. 336f)

This paragraph tells us two things: private property has reached its limit subjectively (labour in general) and objectively (value) in the form of capital; this limit is the contradiction of capital and labour, and therefore the downfall of private property in general.

Let us begin with the explanation of the former statement. The loss of any natural and social quality in capital means not only that human activity is separated (or abstracted) from other means of production and is regarded as a mere labour force or 'hands' but also that it does not matter in which branch of production or to what use it is bestowed. It is only quantity that counts. The historical development of private property (from landed property to capital) is now grasped as a development in abstraction from its content. 'Development' here means that the latter form has become more abstract and universal in its essence and that it contains in itself the preceding form. Labour in general, as the subjective essence of capital, includes agricultural labour as well as the essence of landed property. The following passage in the 'Third Manuscript' indicates this:

> It is clear that if the subjective essence of industry is now grasped ... , this essence includes within itself its opposite. For just as industry incorporates annulled landed property, the subjective essence of industry at the same time incorporates the subjective essence of landed property. (MEC 3, p. 293; EW, p. 344)

The so-called description of the antithesis, which occupies nearly half of the extant pages of the 'Second Manuscript', is not history qua history. What Marx is trying to show is why the 'civilised victory' of capital over landed property is logically necessary. It is the victory of completed, universal private property over immature, local private property. Read carefully the following comparison, moving in turn from the left to the right column:

movable property	immovable property
The real course of development . . . results in the necessary victory of the *capitalist* over the *landowner* – that is to say, of developed	over undeveloped, immature private property – just as in general,
movement must triumph	over immobility;
open, self-conscious baseness	over hidden, unconscious baseness;
cupidity	over self-indulgence;
the avowedly restless, adroit self-interest or enlightenment	over the parochial, world-wise, respectable, idle and fantastic self-interest of superstition;
and money	over the other forms of private property (MEC 3, p. 288; EW, p. 340).

The real historical development of private property is understood by Marx even in the 'FM: FP', the purpose of which is to get a first glimpse of the economic laws of capitalism. None the less, historical matters are not relevant here, since his purpose is to comprehend economic laws from the 'essence of private property'. No matter what their historical form, private property is based on appropriating (or commanding) another's labour and product: 'alienated labour'. Seen from the 'general essence of private property':

> ...the distinction between capital and land, between profit and rent, and between both and wages, and industry, and agriculture, and immovable and movable private property – this distinction is not rooted in the nature of things, but is a historical distinction, a fixed historical moment in the formation and development of the contradiction between capital and labour. (MEC 3, p. 285; EW, p. 337)

What is important is that if we grasp the 'essence of private property', the 'civilised victory' of the capitalist over the landowner will become comprehensible as a necessary one.

The Movement through which the two Constituents must Pass

Let us start by quoting the whole description of the fourth type in the 'Second Manuscript' in order to investigate the content more closely. Marx writes at the end of the 'Second Manuscript':

> The character of private property is expressed by labour, capital, and the relation between these two. The movement through which these constituents have to pass is:
>
> *First. Immediate or mediated unity of the two.* Capital and labour are at first still united. Then, though separated and estranged, they reciprocally develop and promote each other as *positive* conditions.
>
> [Second.] *The two in opposition*, mutually excluding each other. The worker knows the capitalist as his own non-existence, and vice versa: each tries to rob the other of his existence.
>
> [Third.] *Opposition* of each other to itself. Capital = stored-up labour = labour. As such it splits into *capital itself* and its *interest*, and this latter again into *interest and profit. The capitalist is completely sacrificed. He falls into the working class, whilst the worker (but only exceptionally) becomes a capitalist.* Labour as a moment of capital – its *cost*. Thus the wages of labour – a sacrifice of capital.
>
> Splitting of labour into *labour itself* and the *wages of labour*. The worker himself a capital, a commodity.
>
> *Clash of mutual contradiction.* (MEC 3, p. 289; EW, p. 341)

At first glance this may look like a historical analysis. However, if we look closely at the latter half, particularly at the emphasised section, we can see clearly that this is a sketch for the development of the economic categories. The same sketch can be found in the conspectus of Engels' *Outlines of a Critique of Political Economy* by Marx, and in his *Notes on James Mill.*

Second, the content is consistent with that of the 'Second Manuscript', that is, 'the worker is the subjective manifestation of the fact that capital is man wholly lost to himself, just as capital is the objective manifestation of the fact that labour is man lost to himself'. (MEC 3, p. 283; EW, pp. 334f)

Furthermore, in his reference to the preceding page (now missing), Marx notes that 'the antithesis between labour and capital, ... grasped in its active connection, in its internal relation, ... grasped as a contradiction. (MEC 3, pp. 293f; EW, pp. 343f) Thus, 'The two in opposition' in [Second] means that the production process of capital is the opposed process of capital and labour, and thus it is a self-contradicting process. The immediate production process of capital is the opposed process of accumulated labour and living labour through which the 'antithesis' between lack of property and possession of property becomes a 'contradiction'. When the description in [Second] corresponds to the content in the 'Second Manuscript', what part of EPM does the preceding phrase, i.e., [First], correspond to? It must be either the 'FM: LP' or the first stage of exchange between capital and labour, which precedes the production process by capital. I think that it must be the 'FM: LP'. There are reasons for my view.

First, 'unity of capital and labour' is the way that political economists see the production process. They saw only this aspect, in which Marx saw both unity and opposition. Second, Engels also wrote about this unity in his *Outlines of a Critique of Political Economy*, which Marx valued very highly as a sketch of the economic categories. Third, so long as [Second] corresponds to the 'Second Manuscript', it is natural to interpret [First] with respect to the 'FM: LP'.

In fact, this unity is shown in the 'FM: LP' when Marx describes 'nature' (as material and as means of production) as the inorganic body of a human 'with which he must remain in continuous interchange if he is not to die'. (MEC 3, p. 276; EW, p. 328) I believe that the 'immediate or mediated unity of the two' indicates that the capitalist process of production is not merely the unity of the two but also their separation (MEC 3, p. 289; EW, p. 341). The fact that a relation of production, i.e., the capital-labour relation, is also reproduced through this production process, was grasped by Marx for the first time, yet was overlooked by other political economists.

Last, with respect to the underlined sentences in [Third], the idea there has already been formulated in the 'FM: FP' as the accumulation of capital that increases in intensity among competing capitals; this leads to a decrease in the rate of profit and rent, which leads to a decline of small capitalists and moneyed classes. Thus this section indicates a decrease in the rate of profit and rent in the development of the economic categories themselves. Marx understood this law as proof of the following two corollaries: capital is the 'limit' of private property so long as this law is a result of capital accumulation, and the 'downfall' of private property so long as this law means the decrease of impetus within capital, i.e., profit. Thus the emphasised section must have the same meaning as the following passage, which refers to the 'Second Manuscript':

> The decrease in the interest rate is therefore a symptom of the annulment of capital only in as much as it is a symptom of the growing domination of capital – of the estrangement which is growing and therefore hastening to its annulment. This is indeed the only way in which that which exists affirms its opposite. (MEC 3, p. 316; EW, pp. 367f)

Now we may conclude that Marx reveals the limit of private property, i.e., capital, and that this is also its downfall through the development of the economic categories. What is important is to grasp 'the general essence of private property', which is deduced from the two-fold analysis of the production process of capital, i.e., the limit of private property. This essence makes it possible for Marx to develop the economic categories genetically. Through this development, economic laws are comprehended as laws of the self-alienation of labour. Thus capitalist society is comprehended as a society in which the individual and the species are separated and in which there are dynamic relations driving towards a resolution (see MEC 3, pp. 293f; EW, pp. 344f).

'It is clear, therefore, that only when labour is grasped as the essence of private property, can the economic process as such be analysed in its real concreteness.' (MEC 3, p. 317; EW, p. 369) Here we witness the birth of Marx' s dialectical method. It is the 'essence of private property', particularly the first two determinations of 'alienated labour', which makes it possible for us to comprehend the structural and dynamic laws of modern civil society through critical, genetic analysis of the economic categories.

CONCLUSIONS

What we have clarified through this investigation into the 'FM: LP' and the 'Second Manuscript' can be summarised in the following three points.

First, the 'FM: FP' was undertaken to form an 'idea' (*Vorstellung*), that is, to grasp the structural and dynamic laws of capitalist society through the works of socialists and political economists. The 'Third Manuscript' is a reference to the 'Second Manuscript'. The 'FM: LP' and the 'Second Manuscript' are works of conceptualisation in which the 'idea' which was formed in the 'FM: FP' is developed. It is these sections which should be known as Marx' s first critique of political economy.

Second, Marx analysed two components of the immediate production process of capital in the 'FM: LP' and the 'Second Manuscript'. These components are (1) 'the relation of the worker to his work and product' and (2) 'the relation of the non-worker to the worker and to the product of labour', or (1) 'the relation of estranged worker to himself' and (2) 'the property relation of the non-worker to the worker and labour' which is the necessary result of the former.

Through these two-fold analyses Marx showed the reproduction of capital with profit to be the reproduction of 'relations of production' as well.

Thus in this first critique of political economy not only the theory of surplus-value but also the theory of accumulation appear for the first time. This reminds careful readers that there is a chapter, 'Transformation of Money into Capital', in the Contents of *Manuscripts of 1861–1863*. The Contents of EPM is not the same as that of *Capital*, but is like that of *Manuscripts of 1861–1863*. This apparent likeness reveals the maturity of Marx in 1844. This is no wonder, since Marx worked on the principles of his system in EPM. The difference between EPM and *Manuscripts of 1861–1863* is merely a further maturity in the development of the economic categories. There is no difference in principle.

Last, the essence of capital allows the comprehension of both the structural laws and dynamic laws of private property, i.e., the comprehension of the birth, development and termination of capital. The critique of political economy in EPM shows the birth of Marx's dialectical method.

8 COMPREHENDING CAPITALIST LAWS AND CONFLICTS

Here I am concerned with the position of the 'Third Manuscript' in the EPM: its intrinsic connection with the 'First Manuscript' and the 'Second Manuscript'.[1] The 'Third Manuscript' consists of the following sections: 'Private Property and Labour', 'Private Property and Communism', 'Need, Production and Division of Labour', 'Critique of Hegel's Dialectic and Philosophy in General', 'Money' and the 'Preface', which are so-termed by the editor of the 1927–32 MEGA1. In the following I shall examine each section except the 'Preface'.[2]

The first paragraphs of the 'Private Property and Labour' and 'Private Property and Communism', and the second paragraph of the 'Private Property and Communism' refer to pages to which they are to be added, i.e., 'ad. XXXVI', 'ad. XXXIX' and 'ad ibidem' respectively. Unfortunately, these pages are no longer extant. The 'Critique of Hegel's Dialectic and Philosophy in General' is a collection of Marx's three comments which are written separately in 'Needs, Production and Division of Labour'.[3] 'Money', is an independent comment which follows the 'Preface'.

In form, the position of the 'Third Manuscript' is evident, that is, addenda to the missing pages of the 'Second Manuscript'. As I shall demonstrate below, this is supported by its substance. The 'Third Manuscript' is concerned with the 'subjective essence of private property', i.e., 'estranged labour', which was derived through a two-fold analysis of the process of capitalist production in the 'FM: LP' and the 'Second Manuscript'.

THE COMPREHENSION OF NECESSITIES

'Private Property and Labour'

The theme of this part is to comprehend the necessity for the development of private property and the economic system from the subjective essence of industry: 'labour in general'.

To begin with, Marx explains that it is only Smith who recognised labour as its principle and 'therefore no longer regarded private property as nothing more than a condition external to man' (MEC 3, p. 290; EW, p. 341); and that to the enlightened Smith, 'the supporters of the monetary and mercantile system, who look upon private property as a purely objective being for man, appear as fetishworshipers, as Catholics'. (MEC 3, p. 291; EW, p. 342) Thus Marx calls Smith 'the Luther of political economy'. (MEC 3, p. 291; EW, p. 342) Just as Luther transcended external religiosity by recognising 'religion and faith as the essence of the external world' and making religiosity the inner essence of man, Smith transcends external private property by recognising labour as the essence of private property and by making labour the inner essence of man.

This also explains that the principle of political economy or of modern civil society does not and cannot emancipate but exploits human beings to its logical conclusion. Just as Luther 'in consequence confronted Catholic paganism', Smith brings man himself into the province of private property. He recognises labour only in its present form, i.e., wage-labour, and man only as a wage-labourer. Wage-labour is thought to be the natural and thus eternal form of life-activity as such. Consequently, political economists, whose principle is labour, appear to recognise man but deny man more than mercantilists. This is what Marx names the 'cynicism of political economy'.[4]

According to Marx, Smith is 'the Luther of political economy', and the 'physiocratic doctrine of Dr Quesnay forms the transition from the mercantile system to Adam Smith'. (MEC 3, p. 292; EW, p. 343) Agricultural products and agriculture are regarded by Quesnay as wealth and the source of wealth. In his system the 'object of wealth' has 'attained the greatest degree of universality possible within the limits of nature' (MEC 3, p. 292; EW, p. 343) and 'the subjective essence of wealth is already transferred to labour' (MEC 3, p. 292; EW, p. 343). However, unlike Smith, both essences have not yet been grasped in their universal and abstract forms.

Marx grasps the development of these economic systems as being necessary, because objectively and subjectively, the essence of capital includes that of landed property and any other sort of private property in a more developed form. 'Labour in general' includes agriculural and industrial labour. It follows the 'civilised victory of movable capital' (MEC 3, p. 288; EW, p. 340) and 'a world-historical power' (MEC 3, p. 293; EW, p. 345) of capital. It is very surprising that those commentators who were attracted by Marx's phrase in *Grundrisse* (Manuscripts of 1857–58), such as 'The simple concept of capital has to contain its civilising tendencies etc. in *themselves*',[5] pay little attention to a similar phrase in the manuscript of 1844. The point is that 'capital = civilisation' can be fully understood only from the 'essence of capital', which was derived from the 'FM: L P' and the 'Second Manuscript'.

'Private Property and Communism'

The first paragraph of this section deals with the necessity for the resolution of private property by grasping the antithesis between labour and capital as the 'developed relation of contradiction'. The antithesis between propertylessness and property can be found even in the Roman age; but it was not a 'contradiction', i.e., each presupposes and excludes the other. However, as Marx analysed in the 'Second Manuscript', 'The worker produces capital and capital produces him, which means he produces himself; man as a worker, as a commodity, is the product of this entire cycle.' (MEC 3, p. 283; EW, p. 335) As capital is accumulated labour, the contradiction between capital and labour is that of estranged labour itself. The capital-labour relation is the zenith of private property and 'a vigorous relation, therefore, driving towards resolution'. (MEC 3, p. 294; EW, p. 345)

In the second paragraph and thereafter, Marx examines forms of the abolition of estrangement, which can be divided into the following:

(a) The three forms of communism.
(b) The meaning of estranged labour in history.
(c) The two historical necessities for private property.

The Three Forms of Communism and the Movement of History

Just as in *The German Ideology*, by 'communism' here Marx means 'the real movement which abolishes the present state of things' but not 'a state of affairs which is to be established, an ideal to which reality [will] have to adjust itself'.[6] In *The German Ideology* Marx does not explain the reason but here he does, distinguishing 'communism' from 'socialism as such'. (MEC 3, p. 306; EW, p. 357) According to Marx, capitalist private property, founded on the exploitation of the labour of other men, is the negation of individual private property founded on its proprietor's own labour. As the negation of capitalist private property, communism is the 'the negation of the negation' (MEC 3, p. 306; EW, p. 358) and, as such, needs such mediation. Thus 'Communism is the necessary form and the dynamic principle of the immediate future, but communism is not, as such, the goal of human development – the form of human society'. (MEC 3, p. 306; EW, p. 358) The future society which stands on its own feet and 'no longer needs such mediation [negation]' (ibid.) is named 'socialism as such'. (MEC 3, p. 306; EW, p. 358)

The point for the full understanding of this terminology is the term 'social = human' which is frequently used here. 'Social = human' indicates a state of the existence of individual suitable to its essence. Man becomes 'social' when 'in his most individual existence he is at the same time a communal being'. (MEC 3, p. 296; EW, p. 347) Human being becomes 'social = human' in proportion to 'the extent to which his human essence has become a natural essence for him', to which 'his human nature has become the nature of him' and 'man's needs have become human needs, hence ... the other, as a human being, has become a need for him'. (MEC 3, p. 296; EW, p. 347)

'Social' is wider ranging than 'communal' which means the direct, 'real association with other men'. (MEC 3, p. 298; EW, p. 350) 'Communal' is a form, but not the only form, of 'social= human'. Marx illustrates this with the activity 'in the field of science' which can seldom be performed in direct association with other men. In this case, the activity is individual and is performed as a human being for human beings. Marx states:

Man, however much he may therefore be a *particular* individual – and it is just this particularity which makes him an individual and a real *individual* communal being – is just as much the *totality*, the ideal totality, the subjective existence of thought and experienced society for itself; he also exists in reality as the contemplation and true enjoyment of social existence and as a totality of vital human expression. (MEC 3, p. 299; EW, p. 351)

On the other hand, we should note that 'social' in daily sense is not 'social = human'. To overlook this is to misunderstand Marx's socialism. Marx remarks, for example in the 'Needs, Production and Division of Labour':

Society, as it appears to the political economists, is *civil society*, in which each individual is a totality of needs and only exists for the other as the other exists for him – in so far as each becomes a means for the other ... .

The *division of labour* is the economic expression of the *social nature of labour* within estrangement. (MEC 3, p. 317; EW, p. 369)

This does not mean that Marx in EPM is an idealist who presupposes an idea of 'human nature', but that he analyses existences and distinguishes their ahistorical essences and their historical forms, just as in the case of 'species-being'. 'Species-being' and 'communal-being' are ontological concepts which are derived from his analysis of capitalist relations of production.[7]

Now let us return to Marx's communism. As the negation of capitalist private property, the forms of communism are determined by their understanding of the 'essence of private property'. In Marx's phrase in EPM: 'The supersession of self-estrangement follows the same course as self-estrangement.' (MEC 3, p. 294; EW, p. 345). From this viewpoint communism is classified as follows (1) to (3) being positive points and I to III negative:

1. The abolition of capital 'only in its objective aspect' (MEC 3, p. 294; EW, p. 345): Proudhon attempted to abolish 'capital' only, without superseding 'commodities' or 'money' which are not only the conditions but also the results of capital.
2. The abolition of estranged labour by 'the particular form of labour' (MEC 3, p. 294; EW, p. 345): Fourier regarded agriculture as the best form of labour, while Saint-Simon considered 'industrial labour as such' (MEC 3, p. 294; EW, p. 345) is the essence.
3. The abolition of private property by 'universal private property'.

I. A 'generalization and completion' (MEC 3, p. 294; EW, p. 346) of private property, e.g., 'the community of women'. This crude communism 'threatens everything which is not capable of being possessed by everyone as private property' (MEC 3, p. 294; EW, p. 346), e.g., 'talent'.

II. Communism which has 'understood the concept but not yet the essence of private property' nor 'the human nature of need'. (MEC 3, p. 296; EW, p. 348) Communism still of a political nature.

III. Communism as 'the positive supersession of private property as human self-estrangement, and hence the true appropriation of the human essence through and for man; it is the complete restoration of man himself as a social (human) being, a restoration which has become conscious and which takes place within the entire wealth of previous periods of development'. (MEC 3, p. 296; EW, p. 348)

> This is Marx's communism which understands both the concept and the essence of private property.[8]

The Meaning of Estranged Labour in History

From Marx's viewpoint of 'estranged labour as the essence of capital', the development of private property (landed property to capital) is man's transformation from standing 'in an external relation of tension to the external substance of private property' into becoming 'the tense essence of private property' (MEC 3, p. 291; EW, p. 342), and thus, inversely, the creation of communism: 'The entire movement of history is therefore both the *actual* act of creation of communism – the birth of its empirical existence – and, for its thinking consciousness, the *comprehended* and *known* movement of its *becoming*; ...'. (MEC 3, p. 297; EW, p. 348)

First, we should note that Marx is not overlooking the estrangement in the sphere of consciousness. Although Marx deals with only the 'material, immediately sensuous private property, i.e., the material, sensuous expression of estranged human life' (MEC 3, p. 297; EW, pp. 348f), because it embraces the subjective estrangement. 'Religion, the family, the state, law, morality, science, art, etc., are only particular modes of production and therefore come under its general law.' (MEC 3, p. 297; EW, p. 349) The objective estrangement 'embraces both aspects'. (MEC 3, p. 297; EW, p. 349)

Second, we should note that the supersession of the objective estrangement also 'embraces both aspects'. The transcendence of estranged labour, or the sensuous appropriation of the human essence, should not be understood 'only in the sense of direct, one-sided consumption, of possession, of having. Man appropriates his integral essence in an integral way, as a total man.' (MEC 3, p. 299; EW, p. 351)

The Two Historical Necessities of Private Property

Initially, all human senses and attributes require the existence of objects. Human senses are developed in proportion to the volume and the range of production and consumption. However, 'Private property has made us so stupid and one-sided that an object is ours only when we have it ... . when we use it.' (MEC 3, p. 300; EW, p. 351) Under present conditions, 'all the physical and intellectual senses have been replaced by the simple estrangement of all senses – the sense of having.' (MEC 3, p. 300; EW, p. 352) The senses and enjoyment of objects must be emancipated and changed into the appropriation of nature and the confirmation of human reality. This is possible only when objects are produced and exchanged not for money but for other men's confirmation of human reality.[9] The movement of production and consumption must be changed into the way in which 'the object, which is the direct activity of his individuality, is at the same time his existence for other men, their existence and their existence for him'. (MEC 3, p. 300; EW, p. 349) In this sense, communism is also needed for the emancipation of all the organs of his individuality. 'The supersession of private property is therefore the complete *emancipation* of all human senses and attributions ...'. (MEC 3, p. 300; EW, p. 352)

'The *cultivation* of the five senses is the work of all previous history.' (MEC 3, p. 302; EW, p. 353)

Fully developed and human senses are produced only through the appropriation of objects which are produced for the confirmation of man's human reality, i.e., only through the fully developed and human movement of production and consumption. This is not the starting-point but the arrival-point in history. Here Marx sees the historical necessity for the formation and abolition of private property, i.e., the theoretical answers to the 'two questions' set up in the 'FM: FP'.

> We have seen how, assuming the positive supersession of private property, man produces man, himself and other men; how the object, which is the direct activity of his individuality, is at the same time his existence for other men, their existence and their existence for him. Similarly, however, both the material of labour and man as subject are the starting-point as well as the outcome of the movement [of production and consumption] (and the historical *necessity* of private property lies precisely in the fact that they must be this starting-point). (MEC 3, p. 298; EW, p. 349)

Unlike Smith, Marx does not think that the labour under the command of other men is a natural, eternal form of productive activity – praxis – but only historical and transitory. Praxis is an essential activity for man to become a social = human being. Production and consumption is not to be understood only in an economic sense (in the sense of creation and use of material wealth), but in the sense of the objectification and confirmation of human nature. Through the movement of production and consumption, human nature, human abilities and human senses are developed and cultivated. As production is always the co-operation of several individuals, social = human production is the creation of social organs. 'Apart from these direct organs, *social* organs are therefore created in the *form* of society.' (MEC 3, p. 300; EW, p. 352)

Last, we should note the propositions above in their philosophical context. Marx writes in the 'Critique of Hegel's Dialectic and Philosophy in General' that 'Feuerbach is the only person who has a serious and critical attitude to the Hegelian dialectic and who has made real discoveries in this field'. (MEC 3, p. 328; EW, p. 381) Here Marx specifies his position in relation to Feuerbach. The quotation below summarises the relationship between Feuerbach and Marx, that is, Marx's 'critique' of Feuerbach.

> *Sense perception* (see Feuerbach) must be the basis of all science. Only when science starts out from sense perception in the dual form of *sensuous* consciousness and *sensuous* need – i.e., only when science starts out from nature – is it *real* science. (MEC 3, p. 303; EW, p. 355)

Feuerbach, for the first time in German philosophy, attaches great importance to sense perception, but not in the dual form of sensuous consciousness and sensuous need. His 'nature' is only 'the sensuous external world' (MEC 3, p. 273; EW, p. 325) and is not the material in which the worker's labour realised itself. Thus he does not investigate the movement of production and consumption. However, Marx considers the mutual relationship between nature and man. As Marx expounded in the 'FM: LP', man needs nature as a means of his living and subsistence, but, on the other hand, he manufactures nature to human needs which is expressed in the history of industry. 'It can be seen how the history of *industry* and the *objective* existence of industry as it has developed is the *open* book of the essential power of man, man's psychology present in tangible form ...'. (MEC 3, p. 302; EW, p. 354)

From this point of view, science becomes 'real science' only when it starts out from nature and 'there will be one science' (MEC 3, p. 304; EW, p. 355), i.e., the science of industry.[10] Social sciences, separated from natural sciences, and natural sciences, separated from the science of industry, are both abstract. The two are elements of a totality but neither of them, as such, can be a totality.

To sum up, here again we confirm that the essence of private property, estranged labour, is the basis of this section. In form and substance, 'Private Property and Communism'[11] is an addendum to the 'Second Manuscript'. The history of industry is the process of the creation of 'a total man' and the capitalist 'social formation brings ... the prehistory of human society to a close' by yielding huge productive forces, that is, the means of production and the fully developed co-operation of workers.

'Needs, Production and Division of Labour'

This section opens with a paragraph, a summary of the 'Private Property and Communism', which carries number '(7)'. This number provides evidence of the continuity of the 'Private Property and Communism', the 'Critique of Hegel's Dialectic and Philosophy in General' and the 'Needs, Production and Division of Labour' in form and in substance. (1) to (5) comprise the 'Private Property and Communism' and (6) is the first part of the 'Critique of Hegel's Dialectic and Philosophy in General' (usually printed subsequently). In opposition to the 'Private Property and Communism', here Marx examines, under the circumstances of private property, 'what significance the wealth of human needs has' (MEC 3, p. 306; EW, p. 358), or 'what significance a new mode of production and a new object of production have' (MEC 3, p. 306; EW, p. 358) in the following order:

(a) Their significance under the system of private property.
(b) Evidence: the contradictory character of political economy.
(c) Theoretical conflicts and contradictions among political economists can only be solved by praxis. The meaning and the limitations of communism as the solution.

The Significance of Needs under Capitalist Relations

Under the system of private property their significance is reversed. Under the system of socialism, the wealth of human needs, a new mode of production and a new object of production signify 'A fresh confirmation of human power and a fresh enrichment of human nature'. (MEC 3, p. 306; EW, p. 358) However, their significance under the system of private property is reversed. Marx writes:

> [1] Each person speculates on creating a *new* need in the other, with the aim of forcing him to make a new sacrifice, placing him in a new dependence and seducing him into a new kind of *enjoyment* and hence into economic ruin. [2] Each attempts to establish over the other an alien power, in the hope of thereby achieving satisfaction of his own selfish needs. [3] With the mass of objects grows the realm of alien powers to which man is subjected, and each new product is a new *potentiality* of mutual fraud and mutual pillage. (MEC 3, p. 306; EW, p. 358; numbers mine).

Consequently, under the present conditions, 'Man becomes ever poorer as a man, and needs ever more *money* if he is to achieve mastery over the hostile being.' (MEC 3, p. 306; EW, p. 358) The growth of new objects increases the power of money and decreases that of man as such. The need for money is the only need produced under the system of private property. Since money is an abstract being,[12] 'Lack of moderation (*Maßlosigkeit*) and *intemperance* (*Unmäßigkeit*) become its true standard (*Maß*).' (MEC 3, p. 306; EW, p. 358) This 'lack of moderation and intemperance' is manifested subjectively in the facts:

1) the expansion of production and needs become 'the *inventive* and ever *calculating* slave of inhumanity, refined, unnatural and *imaginary* appetites – for private property does not know how to transform crude need into *human* need'. (MEC 3, p. 307; EW, p. 359)
2) 'the refinement of needs and of the means of fulfilling them give rise to a bestial degeneration and a complete, crude and abstract simplicity of need; or rather, that it merely reproduces itself in its opposite sense'. (MEC 3, p. 307; EW, p. 359)

The Contradictory Character of Political Economy

Marx sees the evidence of the significance of needs under the conditions of private property in the contradictory character of political economy. Marx examines how political economists prove that:

> ...the multiplication of needs and the means of fulfilling them give rise to a lack of needs and of means ... (1) By reducing the worker's needs to the paltriest minimum necessary to maintain his physical existence and by reducing his activity to the most abstract mechanical movement ... [and] (2) By taking as his standard – his universal standard – in the sense that it applies to the mass of men – the worst possible state of privation which life (existence) can know. (MEC 3, p. 308; EW, p. 360)

As Smith and Ricardo clarified, the lowest and the only necessary rate for wages is 'that required for the subsistance of the worker during work and enough extra to support a family and prevent the race of workers from dying out'. (MEC 3, p. 235; EW, p. 283) Thus 'Political economy, this science of wealth [for the capitalist], is therefore at the same time the science of denial, of starvation, of saving [for the worker]' (MEC 3, p. 309; EW, p. 360) and

'This science of the marvels of industry [for the capitalist] is at the same time the science of *asceticism* [for the worker]'. (MEC 3, p. 309; EW, pp. 360f)

As political economists do not show the intrinsic connection between the increase of needs and the means of fulfilling them on the capitalist's side and the decrease of them on the worker's, conflicts among political economists follow:

(a) A controversy in the field of political economy: 'One school (Lauderdale, Malthus, etc.) advocates luxury and execrates thrift. The other (Say, Ricardo, etc.) advocates thrift and execrates luxury.' (MEC 3, p. 309; EW, p. 361)
(b) The contradiction between moral and political economy. Michel Chevalier accuses Ricardo of abstracting from morality.
(c) Comparison between France and England, i.e., those nations which are still dazzled by the sensuous glitter of precious metal and those which are fully developed money nations.[13]

The point is that each side of each conflict sticks to one moment of the laws of estranged labour and that these conflicts can be solved only by the abolition of the laws of estranged labour as such.

The Two Historical Necessities for Private Property

Communism is the solution of theoretical contradictions.

> The extent to which the solution of theoretical problems is a function of practice and is mediated through practice, and the extent to which true practice is the condition of a real and positive theory is shown, e.g., in the case of fetish-worship. (MEC 3, p. 312; EW, p. 364)

The sense perception of a fetish-worshipper is different from that of a Greek because his sensuous existence is different. Thus Marx adds that 'The abstract hostility between sense and intellect is inevitable so long as the human sense for nature, the human significance of nature and hence the natural sense of man, has not yet been produced by man's own labour.' (MEC 3, p. 312; EW, p. 364)

Furthermore, Marx writes that 'It goes without saying that the supersession of estrangement always emanates from the form of estrangement which is the dominant power.' (MEC 3, p. 312; EW, p. 364). Thus in Germany, self-consciousness; in France, equality, because of politics: in England, real, material, practical need, which only measures itself. Self-consciousness and equality are two different expressions for the same thing, i.e., in his remarks in *The Holy Family*:

> Equality is the French expression for the unity of human essence, for man's consciousness of his species and his attitude towards his species, for the practical identity of man with man, i.e., for the social and human relation of man to man. (MEC 4, p. 39)

This quotation shows that Marx's term 'social and human' is a re-casting of the 'equality' of French socialists and the 'self-consciousness' of the Young Hegelians. The German, the French and the English are attempting to transcend estranged labour but from limited angles, philosophically, politically and practically.

Marx, on the other hand, claims to transcend the real estrangement of real individuals and appropriate human essence by real action. Here the significance and the limits of communism become clear.

> If we characterise *communism* itself – which because of its character as negation of the negation, as appropriation of the human essence which is mediated with itself through the negation of private property, is not yet the *true*, self-generating position, but one generated by private property … . (MEC 3, p. 313; EW, p. 365)

The appropriation of human essence through the movement of production and consumption is possible only in socialism as such.

Later Marx determines estrangement in a broad sense, outlines the history of estrangement and concludes that 'Clearly, then, it is only when labour is grasped as the essence of private property that the development of the economy as such can be analysed in its real determination.' (MEC 3, p. 317; EW, p. 369)

Last, with regard to this, Marx's view on the division of labour is noteworthy. It is natural for political economists to see the division of labour as one of the main driving forces in the production of wealth, because they see labour as the essence of private property. However, they are 'very unclear and self-contradictory about the essence of the division of labour'. To be accurate, they do not care about its essence; but Marx understands its essence with regard to estrangement.

> The *division of labour* is the economic expression of the *social nature of labour* within estrangement. However, since *labour* is only an expression of human activity within alienation, … the *division of labour* is nothing more than the *estranged, alienated* position of human activity as a *real species-activity* or as *activity of man as a species-being*. (MEC 3, p. 317; EW, p. 369)

Let us refer to *Notes on James Mill* and explain this remark. 'The process of exchange both of human activity in the course of production and of human products is equal to species-activity and the species-enjoyment.' (MEC 3, pp. 216f; EW, p. 265)[14] It is a complementing act. Capitalist commodity production enlarges the process but in a way in which human beings alienate their own mediating power with other men (social power) to commodities and money. 'The bond which unites the two owners is the specific nature of the object which constitutes their private property' (MEC 3, p. 218; EW, p. 267) but not their individuality. Thus the present form of exchanging human activity and human products is a social activity and social enjoyment within estrangement. 'Just as the reciprocal exchange of the produce of *human activity* appears as *barter, horse-trading*, so the reciprocal complementing and exchange of human activity itself appears in the form of: the *division of labour*.' (MEC 3, p. 220; EW, p. 269) 'The very unity of human labour is regarded only in terms of division because man's social nature is realised only as its antithesis, as estrangement.' (MEC 3, pp. 220f; EW, p. 269) The division of labour and exchange are 'perceptible alienated expressions of human activity and essential powers as species-activity and species-power'. (MEC 3, p. 321; EW, p. 374) As we have already seen, Marx calls the completing activities 'social=human' activity and enjoyment when they are carried out consciously and authentically.

> The process of *exchange* both of human activity in the course of production and of *human products* is equal to species-activity and the species-enjoyment whose real, conscious and authentic existence consists in *social* activity and *social* enjoyment. (MEC 3, pp. 216f; EW, p. 265)

The most important point to be made here is that Marx sees in the development of the division of labour a two-fold necessity of capital: the necessity for its formation and its supersession.

> To say that the *division of labour* and *exchange* are based on *private property* is simply to say that *labour* is the essence of private property – an assertion that the political economist is incapable of proving and which we intend to prove for him. It is precisely in the fact that the *division of labour* and *exchange* are configurations of private property that we find the proof, both that *human* life needed *private property* for its realization and that it now needs the abolition of private property. (MEC 3, p. 321; EW, p. 374)

Let us investigate the meaning of this remark. Judging from Marx's critical 'Comments on Skarbek' (MEC 3, pp. 319f; EW, pp. 371ff), 'private property' in the opening sentence of this quotation means the 'right of exclusive private property'. (MEC 3, p. 319; EW, p. 372) Thus 'based upon' (*beruhn auf*) means that the right of exclusive private property transforms the life-activity and the complementing activity of man into 'labour' and 'the division of labour'. This is partly true. The capitalist employs workers and the wage-worker enters into the process of production by employment (exchange). Naturally, Marx admits the fact. Thus, by stating that 'the division of labour and exchange are based on private property', 'Skarbek is here giving expression in objective form to that which Smith, Say, Ricardo, etc., say when they designate '*egoism* and *private self-interest* as the basis of exchange and *haggling* as the *essential* and *adequate* form of exchange.' (MEC 3, p. 321; EW, p. 373) However, the point is to explain the right of private property as such, that is, the origin of profit. From this viewpoint, the assertion that 'the division of labour and exchange are based on private property' is equivalent to Marx's statement that '(estranged) labour is the essence of private property'.

Next, why is it that political economists, who reveal that labour is the essence of wealth, cannot prove this assertion? It is because they take 'labour' as natural and eternal. None of the political economists has clarified the historical character of the labour which produces exchange value. Even the idea of proof does not enter their minds. The assertion that the 'division of labour and exchange are configurations of private property' means that the right of exclusive private property is the basis of the division of labour and exchange in capitalist society. Both human labour and human products are mutually complemented in a way to confirm the right of private property. Neither of them is a gift nor a tribute, requiring an equivalent, i.e., exchange value. 'The division of labour' and 'exchange' are perceptible expressions of 'the right of private property'.[15]

How then can Marx find the two kinds of proof? The answer is related to 'the historical necessity of private property' (MEC 3, p. 297; EW, p. 349) in 'Private Property and Communism'. Man becomes human as the needs and the means of fulfillment increase, which is the result of the development in the social character of human labour. As capital – 'private property in the products of another's labour' (MEC 3, p. 246; EW, p. 295, the opening words of the column 'Profit of Capital') – being 'Universal exploitation[16] of communal human nature' (MEC 3, p. 307; EW, p. 359), it develops the social character of human labour to its logical conclusion within alienation, i.e., in the form in which workers are controlled by their products such as commodities, money and capital. Thus capital produces objective conditions for the real emancipation of man. On the other hand, for the real creation of 'a total man', capital is to be positively transcended. This means that the division of labour and exchange must be transformed into 'social = human' complementing activity and enjoyment as the species-activity and the species-enjoyment: labour under the command of the capitalist must be abolished.

To sum up, the significance and the limitation of capital in history lies in the social character of labour. Capital is needed for the development of human social labour and now needs to be superseded for its further development. Now I hope we can appreciate more deeply Marx's proposition that 'This social formation [capitalist society] brings, therefore, the prehistory of human society to a close.'[17] In form and in substance, this part is a series of 'Private Property and Communism' and is also an addendum to the 'Second Manuscript'. As I have already mentioned, the first and the second paragraphs of 'Private Property and Communism' carry the page numbers to which they are to be added. On the other hand, there is a strong intrinsic connection between 'Private Property and Communism' and 'Needs, Production and Division of Labour'. I wonder why the editors of EPM placed the first and second paragraphs of 'Private Property and Communism' together under the same title and why they separated 'Private Property and Communism' and 'Needs, Production and Division of Labour'. There seems to be no adequate reason for this separation except that Marx's critical comments on the Hegelian philosophy are scattered throughout 'Needs, Production and Division of Labour'. It might be better if these two were collated in one section entitled 'The Abolition of Estranged Labour'.

'Money'

The aim of this section is not to investigate the essence nor the functions of money but the ontological relationship between human feelings, passions and their objects in contrast with those under the system of private property.[18]

Ontologically, feelings and passions are affirmations of man's essence (nature) and they affirm themselves in so far as their objects exist sensuously for them. Their mode of affirmation constitutes the particular character of their existence and of their lives. The ontological essence of human passion comes into being, both in its totality and in its humanity, 'only through developed industry', 'The meaning of private property, freed from its estrangement, is the existence of essential objects for man, both as objects of enjoyment and of activity.' (MEC 3, p. 322; EW, p. 375)

However, under the system of private property, which has already been mentioned in 'Needs, Production and Division of Labour', money becomes the real object of man. 'Money, inasmuch as it possesses the *property* of being able to buy everything and appropriate all objects, is the *object* most worth possessing.' (MEC 3, p. 323; EW, p. 375) The more commodity production and money systems develop, the more mighty money becomes and the less powerful individuals become.

> The universality of this *property* is the basis of money's omnipotence; hence it is regarded as an omnipotent being ... . Money is the *pimp* between need and object, between life and man's means of life. But *that* which mediates *my* life also *mediates* the existence of other men for me. It is for me the *other* person. (MEC 3, p. 323; EW, p. 375)

It follows that money is 'the visible divinity, the transformation of all human and natural qualities into their oppositions, the universal confusion and inversion of things'. (MEC 3, p. 324; EW, p. 377) As an individual, I am lame and ugly but money can buy me a luxury car and a beautiful woman, thus I am neither lame nor ugly. The stronger the power of my money, the stronger I am. Money rules the world; but the end of money is the end of love. She married my money, not me. Money becomes the bond which ties man to human life and society, i.e., the abilities to relate to nature and other men. Money is 'the alienated capacity of mankind'. Although Marx does not write this explicitly, in the expansion of the power of money he sees the development in the social capacities of individuals.

On the other hand, the supersession of private property, commodities, money and capital means that each of our relations to man and to nature must be a particular expression, corresponding to the objects of our will, of our real individual life. Marx concludes this part with the proposition that 'If we assume man to be man, and his relation to the world to be a human one, then love can be exchanged only for love, trust for trust, and so on.' (MEC 3, p. 326; EW, p. 379)

To sum up, the power of 'money, as the existing and active concept of value' (MEC 3, p. 326; EW, p. 379) is an alienated social power of individuals. In the increase of the power of money under the capitalist mode of production, Marx sees the development in the social power of individuals to communicate and complement each other. Consequently, this section also takes 'estranged labour' in the 'FM: LP' for granted and constitutes an addendum to the 'Second Manuscript'.

Critique of Hegel's Dialectic and Philosophy in General

This section is a collection of three critical comments scattered before and in 'Needs, Production and Division of Labour', as is shown by the number with which it opens: '(6) This is perhaps the place to make a few, remarks ... about the Hegelian dialectic.' (MEC 3, p. 326; EW, p. 379) 'This is ... the place' in the quotation means just after 'Private Property and Communism' – albeit 'The Abolition of Estranged Labour' is more suitable – in which Marx expounds on the significance and the limitation of communism as the negation of estranged labour: 'communism is the act of positing as the negation of the negation, and therefore a real phase, necessary for the next period of historical development, in the emancipation and recovery of mankind'. (MEC 3, p. 306; EW, p. 358) That which Marx refers to here is the creation of 'a total man' in 'socialism as such'. (MEC 3, p. 306; EW, p. 357) Consequently, the aim of this section is to clarify his relationship with the Hegelian dialectic and Feuerbach's critique of Hegelian philosophy.

As we have already seen in the preceding part, i.e., 'Private Property and Communism', Marx rates Feuerbach's work very highly and schematises his great achievement as follows:

1. 'To have shown that philosophy is ... equally [as religion] to be condemned as another form and mode of existence of the estrangement of man's nature.' (MEC 3, p. 328; EW, p. 381)
2. 'To have found true materialism and real science by making the social relation of "man to man" the basic principle of his theory.' (MEC 3, p. 328; EW, p. 381)
3. 'To have opposed to the negation of the negation, which claims to be the absolute positive, the positive which is based upon itself and positive grounded in itself.' (MEC 3, p. 328; EW, p. 381)

As is shown in the relationship between his communism and socialism, here Marx follows Feuerbach and understands 'communism as the negation of the negation' as not being the absolute positive. It requires the mediation of estranged labour. The absolute positive is 'socialism as such' which no longer needs such a mediation. Accordingly, Hegel's 'negation of the negation' is appreciated because:

> Hegel has merely discovered the abstract, logical, speculative expression of the movement of history. This movement of history is not yet the real history of man as a given subject, it is simply the process of his creation, the history of his emergence. (MEC 3, p. 329; EW, p. 382)

Although Marx investigates Hegel's *Phenomenology* – 'the true birthplace and secret of the Hegelian philosophy' (MEC 3, p. 329; EW, p. 383) – and analyses Hegel's theoretical inadequacy, he identifies in Hegel 'a double error' in two phrases:

1) First, Hegel's understanding of alienation. In Hegelian philosophy, 'Estrangement...is the opposition of *in itself* and *for itself*, of *consciousness* and *self consciousness*, of *object* and *subject*, i.e., the opposition within thought itself of abstract thought and sensuous reality or real sensuousness.' (MEC 3, p. 331; EW, p. 384) In the Hegelian sense 'estrangement' is by no means 'the fact that the human essence *objectifies* itself in an *inhuman* way, in opposition to itself, but that it *objectifies* itself in *distinction* from and in *opposition* to abstract thought'. (MEC 3, p. 331; EW, p. 384)
2) Second, Hegel's understanding of the abolition of alienation: the 'appropriation'. In Hegelian philosophy, it is the estrangement, i.e., the 'appropriation of man's objectified and estranged essential power', (MEC 3, p. 331; EW, p. 384) that is to be superseded, and takes place 'only in consciousness, in pure thought, i.e., in *abstraction*'. (MEC 3, p. 331; EW, p. 384) It is not understood as 'the vindication of the objective world for man'. (MEC 3, p. 332; EW, p. 385) Hegel does not understand that 'religion, wealth, etc., are only the estranged reality of human objectification, of human essential powers born into work, and therefore only the way to true human reality'. (MEC 3, p. 332; EW, p. 385)

On the other hand, Hegel is stronger than Feuerbach in his dialectic of negativity. In spite of its idealistic and mysterious form, Hegel 'conceived the self-creation of man as a process, objectification (*Vergegenständlichung*) as loss of object (*Entgegenständlichung*), as alienation and as supersession of this alienation. He therefore grasps the nature of labour and conceives objective man ... as the result of his own labour.' (MEC 3, pp. 332f; EW, p. 386) With regard to this, the following is to be noted in terms of the intrinsic connection between Marx's critique of political economy and of the German philosophy:

(1) For the present, let us observe that Hegel adopts the standpoint of modern political economy. (2) He sees *labour* as the *essence*, the self-confirming essence, of man; (3) He sees only the positive and not the negative side of labour. (4) Labour is *man's coming to be for himself* within *alienation* or as an *alienated man*. (5) The only labour Hegel knows and recognises is *abstract mental* labour. (MEC 3, p. 333; EW, p. 386; numbers are mine)

The 'standpoint' in (1) refers to the view on labour or the essence of labour, as is indicated in the following part. The 'modern political economy' in (1) implies British political economists. As we have already seen in 'Private Property and Labour', Marx understands that Smith, Ricardo and James Mill share the same view on labour. Thus we can safely say that the 'standpoint of modern political economy' indicates Smith's, Ricardo's and Mill's views on labour.

In 'Private Property and Labour', Marx writes that political economists have 'revealed – within the system of private property – the subjective essence of wealth' (MEC 3, p. 290; EW, p. 342) and make 'man as a non-being (*Unwesen*) the essence (*Wesen*)'. (MEC 3, p. 292; EW, p. 343) This means that Smith makes labour the essence of wealth by making man the essence of private property. As is indicated in (4), labour hitherto has been 'estranged' labour and is 'man's coming to be for himself within alienation or as an alienated man'; but Smith does not understand this and appears to think that this form of labour is natural and eternal. He does not see that the man as the essence of private property is a 'man as a non-being', that is, estranged man. In this sense Smith 'sees only the positive and not the negative side of labour'. This holds true in Hegelian philosophy. As (5) says, the only labour Hegel knows and recognises is abstract mental labour. As his concept 'estrangement' shows, Hegel sees only 'objectification' in labour. He does not and cannot distinguish objectification from estrangement, i.e., from loss of object. He considers the capitalist form of labour as natural and eternal. Both modern political economists and Hegel see in labour only objectification but not alienation. Hegel adopts the standpoint of modern political economy.

In short, here again we see that the 'Critique of Hegel's Dialectic and Philosophy in General' is, both in form and in substance, an addendum to the 'FM: LP' and the 'Second Manuscript': 'estranged labour', which is a two-fold analysis of the process of production.

CONCLUSIONS

As I have demonstrated in form and in substance, the 'Third Manuscript' is an addendum to the 'Second Manuscript', and thus to the 'FM: LP'. In each section of the 'Third Manuscript', the concept of 'estranged labour' – labour under the control of other man – is presupposed and the ramifications of the concept are developed. Surprisingly, Marx is faithful to his principle and all his arguments have intrinsic connections. No wonder that Marx says excitedly 'the wealth and diversity of the subjects to be dealt with would have fitted into a single work only if I had written in aphorisms, and an aphoristic presentation' (MEC 3, p. 231; EW, p. 281) in the Preface of EPM. EPM is really worth calling the representation of his system in the 1840s. On some points, EPM is more instructive than *Grundrisse* and *Capital*, as his system is less complete in them.

The core of his system is the concept of 'alienated labour', i.e., the 'essence of private property in general' derived from a two-fold analysis of capital – the zenith of the development of private property. The concept of 'alienated labour' is the principle of his critique of political economy, French socialism and German philosophy.

This principle and the structure of Marx's trinity have been hidden and access to it was obstructed by Soviet Marxists and their Western followers. Marx is still unknown, not because the number of studies is limited, but because the number of such studies is too large.

9 RICARDO, ENGELS AND MARX IN 1844

Friedrich Engels, with whom, since the appearance of his brilliant sketch on the criticism of the economic categories (in the *Deutsch-Französische Jahrbücher*), I maintained a constant exchange of ideas by correspondence, had by another road (compare his *The Condition of the Working Class in England* in 1844) arrived at the same result as I ... .[1]

The Preface to *A Contribution to the Critique of Political Economy* (1859) quoted above indicates:

1. that in 1844 Marx appreciated Engels' *Outlines of a Critique of Political Economy* (1844) – hereafter OCPE – as 'a brilliant sketch',
2. that Marx maintained this appreciation in 1859; and
3. that Marx appreciated OCPE only as a brilliant 'sketch' on 'the criticism of the economic categories'.

This Preface of 1859 shows how highly Marx thought of OCPE and is very instructive for rethinking how Marx formed 'the decisive points of our [Marx's] view'[2] from their formation process – movement. However, large numbers of studies, which have been made over the last few decades, have completely failed to explain the meaning of OCPE in Marx's formation process. This is due to the methodological inadequacies of those studies, which is best declared in their interpretation of OCPE. Thus I am concerned here with a methodological critique of them.

Up to now, the studies on the development of Marx's thought and theories have been under the strong influence of Soviet Marxism. They interpreted all Marx's and Engels' works preceding GI as 'self-clarified' through the formation of the so-called 'materialist interpretation of history' in GI. The only aim of their effort was to negate one concept in Marx's EPM, i.e., 'estranged labour', which contains a profound criticism of Soviet society. They have tried to justify their ideology by arguing against Marx's value theory in the early 1840s. They have asserted that Marx, in the works preceding GI, 'negated' or 'rejected' the Ricardian labour theory of value, which was subsequently withdrawn by the later Marx.[3] The reasons they have given are:

1. In 1844 Marx was under the strong influence of Engels, who overestimated 'the effect of competition' and negated the concept 'value' by criticising 'value' as an 'abstract' notion.

2. In 1844 Marx agreed with Proudhon's value theory which negates equal exchange.

The first point to note is that both reasons originated solely in Marx's criticism of the Ricardian value theory in *Notes on Ricardo* (1844), which is concerned with the concept of 'abstraction'. Other works in the early 1840s do not support any of these interpretations.

The second point is that these arguments contradict each other. A close look at OCPE would reveal that Engels disagrees with the Proudhonian value theory and accepts the law of value in the classical sense, as he states: 'It is, however, quite correct, and a fundamental law of private property, that price is determined by the reciprocal action of production costs and competition.' (MEC 3, p. 427)

The third point to note is the methodological inadequacy of their studies. They understand Marx's concept 'value' in *Capital*, Volume 1, as almost the same as Ricardo's. They evaluate the works preceding *Capital* by this Ricardian standard. This is the explanation why they formulate the development of Marx's value theory; from the negation (or rejection) to the affirmation (or acceptance) of the Ricardian value theory. In short, they assert that in 1844 Marx was not a Ricardian but later became a Ricardian. That which is to be clarified is how Marx became Marx, i.e., the formation of the *differentia specifica* of Marx's value theory. However, even if their assertion was correct, the process they have clarified would have been the prehistory of Marx's formation, because they assert that Marx became a Ricardian, i.e., Marx was not 'Marx' yet. This results from their methodological inadequacies.

1. In Marx's 'genetic presentation' of economic categories, the order of inquiry and that of presentation are opposite.[4] Thus the definition of value as the *Anfang* is formed later than that of surplus-value. The chapter on 'The Commodities' is first formed only after *Grundrisse*: the manuscripts of 1857–58. This, however, does not mean that Marx accepted the classical value theory in 1858, but that Marx completed his criticism of the classical value theory, which is retroactive to 1844. Consequently, the concept 'value' in the chapter 'The Commodities' cannot become the criterion for Marx's formation of value theory.

2. The definition of 'value' in Chapter 1 of *Capital*, Volume 1, is the *Anfang* of Marx's 'genetic presentation' of economic categories and is merely the first and an abstract definition of 'value'. As Marx writes in his letter to Kugelmann,[5] value is the capitalist form of 'social labour' or of 'the social character of labour'. This means that 'value' is defined further in the following chapters until the end of *Capital*, Volume 3. On the other hand, Ricardo's 'value' is a species of 'price', i.e., the 'natural price' which consists of the average wage and average profit. Thus, Marx's value is far from Ricardo's, and it is this *differentia specifica* which is to be clarified.

3. Although in *Capital* Marx stresses that his value theory is in the Ricardian line, this does not mean at all that his value theory is the same as the Ricardian. In the Ricardian value theory, 'value' is the equivalent expression of 'exchangeable value' and is defined as 'cost, including profit'. His concept 'labour bestowed in production' is one of the two sources of 'exchangeable value'. He does not say that 'value' (in Marx's sense) is determined by 'the amount of labour bestowed in production' but that commodities are exchanged 'almost in proportion to' the amount of labour expended in production, meaning the sum total of wages by 'the amount of labour'.

4. Ricardo, like Smith, confused 'value' with 'price'. This means that their definition of value as 'natural price' is nothing but a tautology, because it consists of that which has yet to be explained, i.e., average profit and average rent. The classical value theory is to be criticised as a 'value' determination. This does not mean that the concept is useless as the definition of 'price'. In short, they have not grasped the distinction between 'value' and 'price' well enough, which is criticised by Marx as the 'confusion of value with price'. Soviet Marxists fail to understand the problem of 'natural price ' as the definition of 'value'. They have overlooked the reason why the criticism by Marx and Engels is focused on Chapter 1, § 4, Chapter 2 and Chapter 4 of Ricardo's *Principles of Political Economy and Taxation* (1817) but not on the first three sections of Chapter 1.

MARX AND ENGELS ON 'A CRITIQUE OF POLITICAL ECONOMY'

Engels' Critique of Political Economy

Engels' Task

According to Engels, both the mercantile system and modern liberal economics are 'political economy', that is, 'an entire science of enrichment' (MEC 3, p. 418) which came into being as 'a natural result of the expansion of trade' (MEC 3, p. 418); 'born of the merchant's mutual envy and greed, bears on its brow the mark of the most detestable selfishness'. (MEC 3, p. 418) Naturally, Engels recognises an advance in the development of political economy from bullionism via the mercantile system to the classical economy. If the principle of bullionism, which everywhere prohibited the export of 'precious' metals, 'had been rigorously carried through trade would have been killed'. Thus people began to go beyond this first stage. They came to appreciate a more sociable system: the mercantile system. The eighteenth century, the century of revolution, also revolutionised economics and produced Smith's liberal system. 'But just as all the revolutions of this century were one-sided and bogged down in antitheses ... likewise the economic revolution did not yet go beyond antitheses', (MEC 3, p. 419) because 'It did not occur to economics to question the validity of private property.' (MEC 3, p. 419)

'The new economics does not disavow its own premises, i.e., commerce, and is obliged to have recourse to sophistry and hypocrisy so as to cover up the contradiction in which it became entangled.' (MEC 3, p. 419) 'The mercantile system still had a certain artless Catholic candour and did not in the least conceal the immoral nature of trade.' (MEC 3, p. 422) Nevertheless

> Protestant hypocrisy took the place of Catholic candour. Smith proved that humanity, too, was rooted in the nature of commerce; that commerce must become 'among nations, as among individuals, a bond of union and friendship' instead of being 'the most fertile source of discord and animosity'. (MEC 3, pp. 422f)

It is in this sense that Engels names Smith 'the economic Luther'. (MEC 3, p. 422) The nearer the economists come to the present time, the more sophistry necessarily increases. This is why Ricardo is more guilty than Smith, and McCulloch[6] and James Mill are more guilty than Ricardo. The most guilty, according to Engels, is Malthus.[7] Hence, Engels' task in OCPE becomes to disclose the hypocrisy of economists: the invalidity of private property and the immorality of commerce which drove them to hypocrisy and sophistry.

Engels' Method

It follows from his task that the method of his critique of political economy is taking up the economic categories one by one and disclosing the sophistry of the economists in their definitions. 'In the critique of political economy, therefore, we shall examine the basic categories, uncover the contradiction introduced by the free-trade system, and bring out the consequences of both sides of the contradiction.' (MEC 3, p. 421)

Engels writes that he proceeds from a 'purely human, universal basis', meaning that only this viewpoint can criticise 'the premises common to both [contradicting economists] and can assign to both their proper position'. (MEC 3, pp. 420f)

Engels' View on Economic Categories

The first point to note is that it looks as if Engels does not understand economic categories as theoretical expressions of capitalist relations of production and commerce. His 'value' is a good example.

> ... and once this [private property] is superseded, there can no longer be any question of exchange as it exists at present. The practical application of the concept of value will then be increasingly confined to the decision about production, and that is its proper sphere. (MEC 3, p. 426)

However, to be fair, the second point to note is that he writes in a preceding part that trade is the 'immediate consequence of private property' (MEC 3, p. 422) and 'value' is the 'next category established by trade'. (MEC 3, p. 424). Thus it would be more than just an empty compliment and not his misunderstanding that leads Marx to write in *The Holy Family* (1845) as follows:

> Proudhon does not consider *the further creations of private property*, e.g., wage, trade, *value, price*, money, etc., as forms of private property in themselves, *as they are considered*, for example, *in* the *Deutsch-Französische Jahrbücher* (see *Outlines of a Critique of Political Economy by F.Engels*) … . (MEC 4, p. 32 Emphasis added)

The third point to note relates to his 'critique' of political economy. Understanding the economic categories as the theoretical expressions of capitalist relations of production and commerce, naturally does not mean accepting the definitions of the categories made by political economists. Actually, it means redefining economic categories after examining how far they successfully express capitalist relations. From this point of view, classical economic categories are not scientific enough, e.g., 'value' is confused with 'price'. Now let us return to the subject.

As we have already seen, Engels, on the one hand, understands economic categories as the theoretical expressions of capitalist relations, but, on the other, he writes as if the proper sphere of economic categories were in future society. The problem is how we should understand the statements. In my opinion, Engels make a distinction between an historical form and an ahistorical essence, and plans a new and more rational form of the essence in future society. It seems to me to be the best interpretation of his viewpoint 'which … proceeds from a purely human, universal basis'.

Therefore, his value theory can be understood as follows: the value of commodities consists of two factors: 'the real inherent utility' (MEC 3, p. 426) and 'production costs'. The first 'application of value is the decision as to … whether utility counterbalances production costs', (MEC 3, p. 426) but 'under the dominion of private property, by competition', 'utility of an object' is hard to determine. Thus the two factors of value are separated and opposed by political economists: 'cost of production' by Ricardo and 'utilities' by Say. In the following part, let us examine Engels' critique of economic categories.

First, Engels criticises the determination of 'real value' of political economists. To begin with, Engels clearly admits that 'price is determined by the reciprocal action of production costs and competition' (MEC 3, p. 427) and that the 'real value' of political economists is 'the price at the time when competition is in a state of equilibrium'. (MEC 3, p. 427) The point Engels makes here is that the price is not value but 'is merely a definite aspect of price'. (MEC 3, p. 427) He is recasting 'value': from the quotient of 'price' into its source. This is the core of his criticism, but has been misunderstood as the 'negation' of labour theory of value. 'Thus everything in economics stands on its head. Value, the primary factor, the source of price, is made dependent on price, its own product.' (MEC 3, p. 427)

Engels then goes on to criticise the determination of 'real value', distinguished from 'central price', by both Ricardo and Say as being one-sided. Note that he does not agree with either of them. This needs only one example: 'Let us try to introduce clarity into this confusion. The value of an object includes both factors, which the contending parties arbitrarily separate – and, as we have seen, unsuccessfully.' (MEC 3, p. 426)

Second, Engels criticises the determination of 'production costs' by economists. As capital is accumulated labour, Engels reduced the three component elements of 'production costs' – profit, rent and wage – to the two sides: the natural, objective side, land; and the human, subjective side, labour.

Engels starts by criticising economists: that they do not think about the third factor, i.e., 'the mental element of invention, of thought, alongside the physical element of sheer labour'. (MEC 3, p. 427) He then criticises economists in that they do not explain the causes of the separation of those three elements, i.e., profit, rent and wage. According to him, 'the functions of these three elements are completely different'. (MEC 3, p. 431)

> What share land, capital and labour each have in any particular product cannot be determined. The three magnitudes are incommensurable ... Therefore, when it comes to dividing the proceeds among the three elements under the existing circumstances, there is no inherent standard; as it is an alien and with regard to them fortuitous standard that decides – competition, the cunning right of the stronger. (MEC 3, p. 431)

In contrast to the political economists, Engels plans to present economic categories in the following way:

> 1. We have already seen that capital and labour are initially identical; we see further from the explanations of the economist himself that, in the process of production, capital, the result of labour, is immediately transformed again into the substratum, into the material of labour; and that therefore the momentarily postulated separation of capital from labour is immediately superseded by the unity of both.
> 2. Yet the economist separates capital from labour, and yet clings to the division without giving any other recognition to their unity than by this definition of capital as 'stored-up labour'. The split between capital and labour resulting from private property is nothing but the inner dichotomy of labour corresponding to this divided condition and arising out of it.
> 3. After this separation is accomplished, capital is divided once more into the original capital and profit – the increment of capital, which it receives in the process of production;
> 4. although in practice profit is immediately lumped together with capital and set into motion with it.
> 5. Indeed, even profit is in its turn split into interest and profit proper. (MEC 3, p. 430; numbers are mine)

In short, economic categories are to be presented in the order: the process of capitalist production as the unity of capital and labour; separation between wage and profit; profit and rent in the process of circulation. The feature of his presentation is clear when we compare it with Say's *Treatise of Political Economy*: principles of the nature of wealth and circulation (the right of private property, wealth, value and price, etc.), principles concerning production (three elements and method of production, etc.) and the sources of income and distribution (cost of production, profit, wage, rent, rent for tenancy, etc.).

Furthermore, Engels expounds through this presentation of categories that, on the one hand, trade crises necessarily arrive regularly as the great plagues did in the past, as long as the producers produce as 'dispersed atoms without consciousness, of [their] species'; (MEC 3, p. 434) and that, on the other, the development of private property will bring 'a total transformation of social conditions', (MEC 3, p. 441) or 'the reconciliation of mankind with nature and with itself'. (MEC 3, p. 424) Later we shall see that in EPM Marx also shares the same plan as Engels. Engels' presentation of economic categories is the reason why Marx rated OCPE as a 'brilliant sketch on the critique of economic categories' in the Preface of 1859.

Marx's Critique of Political Economy

Marx's Task

The first point to notice is the difference between 'FM: FP' and 'FM: LP' (the part so-called 'Estranged Labour'). In the opening paragraph of 'FM: LP', Marx summarised the laws of capital which he conceptualised in 'FM: FP'. In the second and third paragraphs of 'FM: LP', he specifies the fundamental inadequacy of political economists as follows:

> Political economy proceeds from the fact of private property. It does not explain it. It grasps the material process of private property, the process through which it actually passes, in general and abstract formula which it then takes as laws. It does not comprehend these laws, i.e., it does not show how they arise from the essence (*Wesen*) of private property. (MEC 3, pp. 270f, EW, p. 322)

The second point to notice is that hereafter Marx 'rise[s] above the level of political economy', (MEC 3, p. 241; EW, p. 288) in a strict sense. According to Marx, the propositions of political economists serve only as his starting-point. Political economists do not comprehend the economic laws which they formulated as necessary laws of private property, because they do not show the intrinsic connection between the laws and the 'essence of private property'. Thus in the fourth paragraph, Marx sets his task in 'FM: LP' and thereafter to comprehend the laws, as necessary laws, of private property, i.e., to work up the conceptions into concepts:

> We now have to grasp the essential connection between private property, greed, the separation of labour, capital and landed property,[8] exchange and competition, value and the devaluation of man,[9] monopoly and competition, etc. – the connection between this entire system of estrangement and the money system. (MEC 3, p. 271; EW, p. 323)

The importance of this difference in authorial purpose between 'Former Part' and 'Latter Part' of 'First Manuscript' arises, because it has been ignored by Soviet Marxists and their Western followers.

Marx's Method

The first point to notice is the relationship between 'private property' and 'capital'. Private property begins with landed property and reaches its peak with capital. As Marx aims to comprehend the historical development of landed property to capital as being the necessary law of private property and to abolish all sorts of private property, he starts his work by extracting the 'essence (*Wesen*) of private property in general', by analysing capital, i.e., the two-fold analysis of the process of capitalist production in 'FM: LP' and 'Second Manuscript'. Through this analysis, Marx specifies 'the essence of capital', i.e., the 'essence of private property in general', as the 'estranged labour' or the labour under the command of other man.[10] There are three points to be made with regard to this 'essence of capital'.

First, the essence enables Marx to comprehend economic laws as necessary laws of capital. Through the genetic presentation of economic categories, Marx shows the intrinsic connection between the 'essence' and the economic categories. Political economists understand that, on the one hand, labour is the sole source of exchange-value and the active source of use-value. On the other, the same economists conceive 'capital as the regulator of production, the source of wealth and the aim of production', whereas labour is regarded as wage-labour, whose representative and real instrument is inevitably a pauper.[11] Marx in 1844 (and also in 1863) understands that 'In this contradiction, political economists merely expressed the essence of capitalist production or, if you like, of wage-labour, of labour alienated from itself, which confronted by the wealth it has created as alien wealth ...'.[12] The separation between wage and profit, between profit and rent, can be comprehended as necessary laws of capital only from this essence of capital, that is, estranged labour. The essence of capital enables Marx to comprehend the economic laws of political economists as necessary laws of capital through the presentation of economic categories, as Marx states:

> Just as we have arrived at the concept of *private property*[13] through an *analysis* of the concept of *estranged, alienated labour*, so with the help of these two factors it is possible to evolve all economic *categories*, and in each of these categories ... we shall identify only a *particular* and *developed expression* of these basic constituents. (MEC 3, p. 281; EW, p. 333)

Second, the essence of capital enables Marx to comprehend the development of landed property to capital as the necessary law of private property. In this regard we should note the implication of his proposition: 'Human anatomy contains a key to the anatomy of the ape'.[14] In 'capital-labour' relation, objectively and subjectively, wealth has arrived at its peak form: in capital as well as in 'labour in general', 'all the natural and social individuality of the object [and subject are] extinguished'. (MEC 3, p. 285; EW, p. 336) It is only from the 'essence of capital', as the 'essence of private property in general', which enables us to understand the development of private property as a necessary law of private property. Without this essence, Marx's concept, the 'civilised victory of movable capital'[15] cannot be fully understood.

Third, the 'essence of capital' enables Marx to understand the necessity for the developments in economic theories from mercantilists via Quesnay to Smith. If the essence of capital is grasped as being 'labour in general', it is obvious that it contains the essence of landed property and any sort of private property.

> Clearly, once the *subjective essence* is grasped of industry's constituting itself in opposition to landed property, i.e., as industry, this essence includes within it that opposition ... so this process is repeated in the scientific comprehension of the *subjective* essence of private property, of *labour*; labour appears at first only as *agricultural labour*, but later assumes the form of *labour in general*. (MEC 3, p. 293; EW, p. 344)

With regard to this 'essence of capital', I would like to point out a difference between Marx and Engels. As we have already seen, Engels named Smith 'the economic Luther', similarly, in EPM Marx terms Smith 'the Luther of political economy'. However, we should not overlook the fact that this similarity also contains the dissimilarity between them. Marx re-read and re-interpreted Engels, giving a deeper meaning. Engels called Smith 'the economic Luther' because Smith brought Protestant hypocrisy into economics. On the other hand, Marx's reason is

> Therefore the supporters of the monetary and mercantile system, who look upon private property as a *purely objective* being for man, appear as *fetish-worshippers*, as *Catholics*, to this enlightened political economy, which has revealed – within the system of private property – the *subjective* essence of wealth. Engels was therefore right to call Adam Smith the Luther of political economy. (MEC 3, p. 290; EW, p. 342)

Smith opens his *Wealth of Nations* with the statement that labour is the only source of wealth. On the other hand, his propositions demonstrate that the labourer suffers most and the non-worker profits most. He does not recognise any contradiction between his principle and his propositions, because he understands the present form of labour (estranged labour) as natural, thus, as eternal. This is what Marx calls the 'cynicism' of political economy. Marx's task also includes the comprehension of this cynicism. This is very important not only because it has been overlooked by Soviet Marxists but also because it shows their methodological deficiency. Theoretically,[16] all sections of EPM have strong connections with each other by this essence of private property, estranged labour. 'Estranged labour' is the core of Marx's critique of political economy.[17]

There is another noteworthy point. Marx's critique of political economy is characterised by his early concern with his critique of the Hegelian philosophy of law. It is well-known that Marx explains a certain form of state from the certain form of civil society which underlies it. Marx's understanding of money and of capitalist relations of production as 'alienated' communities,[18] and his concept 'the abolition of [estranged] labour', can be fully grasped only in this connection. In other words, his presentation of economic categories demonstrates the alienation of social labour or the social character of labour.

Marx's View on Economic Categories

Marx in the early 1840s clearly understands economic categories as theoretical expressions of the capitalist relation of production and commerce. There is actually no evidence which disproves this. As this is very important, let us quote a couple of examples here.

> The most decisive expression of the insight of the English into pauperism – and by the English we mean the English bourgeoisie and the government – is to be found in *English Political Economy, i.e., the scientific reflection of the state of the economy in England.* ('Critical Notes on the Article: The King of Prussia and Social Reform', appeared on the 7 August 1844 in the *Vorwärts*, No. 63. See MEC 3, p. 193; EW, p. 406)

> Just as we have arrived at the concept of *private property* through an *analysis* of the concept of *estranged, alienated labour*, so with the help of these two factors it is possible to evolve all economic *categories*, and in each of these categories ... we shall identify only a *particular and developed expression* of these basic constituents. (MEC 3, p. 281; EW, p. 333)

> Proudhon does not consider the further creations of private property, e.g., wage, trade, value, price, money, etc., as forms of private property in themselves, as they are considered, for example, in the *Deutsch-Französische Jahrbücher* ... . (MEC 4, p. 32)

The second point concerns Marx's genetic presentation of economic categories. As we have already seen, Engels planned to present the economic categories by analysing the process of capitalist production and then the process of circulation. Marx shares similar plans, for example:[19]

> The relation of *private property* is labour, capital and the connections between these two. The movement through which these parts (*Glieder*) have to pass is:
>
> First – Immediate or mediated unity of the two.
>
> Capital and labour at first still united; later separated and estranged, but reciprocally developing and furthering each other as *positive* conditions.
>
> Second – *Opposition of the two*. They mutually exclude each other; the worker sees in the capitalist his own non-existence, and vice-versa; each attempts to wrench from the other his existence.
>
> Third – *Opposition* of each to itself. Capital = stored-up labour = labour. As such it divided into *itself* (capital) and its *interest*; this latter divides into *interest and profit*. Complete sacrifice of the capitalist. He sinks into the working class, just as the worker – but only by way of exception – becomes a capitalist. Labour as an element of capital, its *costs*. i.e., wages a sacrifice of capital.
>
> Labour divides into *labour itself* and *wages of labour*. The worker himself a capital, a commodity. *Hostile reciprocal opposition*. (MEC p. 3, 289; EW, p. 341)

The last point to notice is how far Marx achieved this presentation of economic categories. Despite his words 'it is possible to evolve all economic categories', Marx actually developed only 'estranged labour', 'private property' (read: 'commodities'), 'capital' ('profit' in a broad sense) in EPM. However, this does not mean that his words are a mere boast, but that he has obtained the principle of his presentation of economic categories. The incompleteness of Marx's presentation is a result of lack of time but not of a methodological inadequacy. This refers to his rating Engels' OCPE highly and his contract for publication.[20]

MARX AND ENGELS ON VALUE

Engels' Concept of 'Real Value'

As we have seen, the task of OCPE is to 'examine the basic categories, to uncover the contradictions introduced by the free-trade system, and to bring out the consequences of both sides of the contradiction'. (MEC 3, p. 421) Before investigating his critique of the classical concept 'real value', as an example of it, let us confirm a couple of points.

To begin with, as I have already shown, Engels understands economic categories as theoretical expressions of capitalist relations of production and commerce. Next, Engels distinguishes value from price. Value is recast into 'the primary factor, the source of price'. In other words, price should be evolved from value. Value is grasped as 'the relation of production costs to utility' (MEC 3, p. 426), whereas price is determined 'by the reciprocal action of production costs and competition'. (MEC 3, p. 427) Thus Engels never negated the law of value as such and is still free from the classical confusion of value with price. In the following, let us examine his concept of 'value' by examining its two factors.

First, by 'production costs' Engels means the expenditure 'which cost him [the capitalist] to produce it' (MEC 3, p. 425) or the 'tremendous exertion' (MEC 3, p. 425) to produce it. There are two points to be made. One is that his 'production costs' concerns 'supply', for 'no one will sell for less than what he has himself invested in production'. (MEC 3, p. 426) The other point is that this concept differs from the Ricardian 'cost' which consists of average wage and average profit.

Second, by 'competition' Engels means 'utility' so long as it appears in the sphere of exchange, as he states: 'The only possible way to arrive at a more or less objective, apparently general decision on the greater or lesser utility of an object is, under the dominion of private property, by competition; ...'. (MEC 3, pp. 425f) With regard to this, by 'utility' Engels means the object for 'desire' which is 'something purely subjective, something which cannot be decided absolutely'. (MEC 3, p. 425) Thus, by a 'general decision on the greater or lesser utility of an object' and 'the real inherent utility of the thing', Engels means 'demand' of the whole society.

Third, we should note that Engels criticises both parties in the dispute over value determination, i.e., both Ricardo's and Say's determination of value is one-sided. 'Let us try to introduce clarity into this confusion. The value of an object includes both factors ('production costs' of Ricardo and 'utility' of Say), which the contending parties arbitrarily separate – and as we have seen, unsuccessfully.' (MEC 3, p. 426) According to Engels, Ricardo determined value only by production costs and Say only by utility, and neither of them succeeded. In short, he determines value by both factors, namely production costs and utility. Engels clarifies this by examining the 'abstraction[s]'[21] or 'confusion[s]' of both parties.

Fourth, we should note that 'the proper sphere' (MEC 3, p. 426) of the concept of value is understood to be 'the decision about production' (MEC 3, p. 426) or 'the decision as to whether utility counterbalances production costs'. (MEC 3, p. 426) This remark sounds as if he had failed to understand 'value' as a capitalist relation. However, it is strongly connected with his method, his views of the law of value and communism. According to Engels, under the dominion of private property, suppliers do not know the volume of demand, and 'demand and supply strive to complement each other, and therefore never do so'. (MEC 3, p. 433) 'Supply always follows close on demand without ever quite covering it.' (MEC 3, p. 433) The law of competition, or supply and demand, is 'purely a law of nature and not of the mind' (MEC 3, p. 433) and 'a law which can only assert itself through periodic upheaval'. (MEC 3, pp. 433f) Thus, the concept of value cannot be practically applied under the present conditions, but in 'community' (MEC 3, p. 435) or 'a world worthy of mankind'.[22] (MEC 3, p. 435) By the misleading phrase, Engels did not mean that value is not a capitalist relation. He meant that it is the capitalist form of the social distribution of labour, by 'uncover[ing] the contradiction introduced by the free-trade system'. (MEC 3, p. 421) He sees 'The truth of the relation of competition is the relation of consumption to productivity' (MEC 3, p. 421) in the law of value. This is the only possible consistent interpretation of 'value' in OCPE.

From all the observations above, we can conclude with fair certainty that 'value' in OCPE concerns the social distribution of labour, or the distribution of social labour among the branches of production.

Marx's Concept of 'Real Value'

At first sight Marx in 1844 seems to be following Engels word for word, but this proves to be wrong upon a second look. There are big differences between them, as was the case of 'the Luther of political economy'. Marx uses Engels' words by re-casting and giving them deeper meanings. 'Value' is no exception. This hardly needs any examples. A comparison of Marx's brief summary of Engels' OCPE[23] with Engels' original text reveals that value is grasped as a capitalist relation more clearly by Marx than by Engels. This is not an accident but is rather a result of Marx's methodological advantage over Engels. As we have already seen, Marx understands economic categories as a theoretical expression of capitalist relations of production and commerce more clearly than Engels. This makes the first point.

The second point is that Marx, like Engels, distinguishes value from price and evolves price from value. This requires an example: 'The problem of defining this *value*[24] more precisely, as well as showing how it becomes *price*, must be dealt with elsewhere.' (MEC 3, p. 219; EW, p. 268)

The third point is that Marx, like Engels, determines value by cost of production and utility and criticises both Ricardo and Say. This requires only the notorious passage in *Notes on Ricardo*:

'In the determination of value Ricardo adheres to production costs only, whereas Say to utility (usefulness) only.' (MEGA2, IV-2, p. 392)

As this note forms the grounds for the assertion that Marx in 1844 negated the Ricardian value theory, let us devote some space to this problem.

To begin with, Marx keeps to this proposition through his life. The point is that for Marx the determination of value by production costs is equivalent to that by supply and demand.[25] The same criticism is repeated in *Wage-labour and Capital* (1849) and *Notes on Ricardo* (1851–52).

> Similarly, the labour which the worker sells as a *use value* to capital is, for the worker, his *exchange value*, which he wants to realize, but which is already *determined* prior to this act of exchange and presupposed to it as a condition, and is determined like the value of every other commodity *by supply and demand*; or, in general, which is our concern here, *by the cost of production, the amount of objectified labour* ... . (G, p. 306)

However, it would be useful to quote the opening paragraph of *Notes on James Mill* and show how Marx has been misinterpreted by commentators.

> 1) Both on the question of the relations of money to the value of metal and in his determination that the cost of production is the sole factor in the determination of value Mill succumbs to the error, made by the entire Ricardo school, of defining an *abstract law* without mentioning the fluctuations or the continual suspension through which it comes into being. 2) If e.g., it is an *invariable* law that in the last analysis – or rather in the abstract coincidence of supply and demand – the cost of production determines value, 3) then it is no less an *invariable law* that these relations do not obtain, i.e., that value and the cost of production do not stand in any necessary relation. 4) Indeed, supply and demand only ever coincide momentarily thanks to a previous fluctuation in supply and demand, to the disparity between the cost of production and the exchange value. And in like fashion, the momentary coincidence is succeeded by the same fluctuations and the same disparity. This is the *real* movement, then, and the above-mentioned law is no more than an abstract, contingent and one-sided moment in it. (MEC 3, p. 211; EW, pp. 259f; numbers are mine)

In 2) and 3) Marx criticises both Ricardo's and Say's determinations of value, making an antithesis. 1) and 4) show Marx's own view and form the ground of his criticism. The point is that both Ricardo and Say are one-sided, which is indicated by the antithesis: 'abstract' and 'real' movements. In Hegelian philosophy, 'reality' is the sum total of many elements, and 'abstraction' is separating an element from the other elements. Critics, however, cannot understand this and so misinterpreted 'abstraction' as a total negation of 'reality'.

Now let us move on to the fourth point concerning the only difference in the determination of value between Marx and Engels: the determination of 'production costs'. Although Engels did not specify it, Marx reduced it to 'labour-time' in *The Holy Family* (1845).[26]

> As far as immediate material production is concerned, the decision whether an object is to be produced or not, i.e., the decision on the value of the object, will depend essentially on the labour time required for its production. For it depends on the time whether society has time to develop in a human way. (MEC 4, p. 49)

In a preceding paragraph, Marx, on the one hand, criticises Proudhon's confusion between the 'measures of wage' and of the 'value of a product', and, on the other, agrees with his not counting profit or rent in the measure. This suggests that in 'the labour time required for its production' Marx counts not only 'the immediate existence of human activity as activity' but also the amount of labour embodied in the means of production. With regard to this, the following quotation illustrates how Marx re-cast the Ricardian 'cost of production'. In 1844 Marx read the French edition of *The Principles of Political Economy* which contains Say's notes. Marx left an interesting note on the Ricardian proposition in Chapter 2 'On Rent', using Say's note to it.

> 1) Here Say notes: so far as rent is not a part of the sum total cost for the production of a commodity, rent is not a component part of the natural price but of the market price of the commodity.
>
> 2) Generally, it is very interesting: 3) According to Smith, natural price consists of wage, rent and profit. 4) Land is necessary for production but rent does not enter into the necessary part of production costs. 5) Profit does not either. 6) The necessity of land and capital for production is counted into costs only so far as they require some labour in their maintenance, i.e., only its re-production costs. (Numbers are mine)[27]

Using Say's logic, Marx excludes profit and rent from 'production costs' in a strict sense, or the sense in which form and substance coincide. As a result, 'production costs' are determined by 'wages' and the 'reproduction costs of land and capital', which is equivalent to labour time expended on production.

Last, Marx's value leads us to his theory of 'disposable time', the dialectic of free time. In the latter part of the quotation above and the following paragraph, he expounds the embryo of his view. In this respect, his value can be said to be the capitalist form of the decision of social production

CONCLUSIONS

Marx in 1844 looks as if he were following Engels word for word. However, a closer look clarifies Engels as re-read and criticised by Marx. Engels' value theory in OCPE is summarised by Marx but without the expression 'if private property is superseded'. Value is clearly grasped as a capitalist relation, determined in the process of capitalist production and the source of price. The difference originates in their task, method and views on categories.

However, OCPE served for Marx as 'a brilliant sketch' on the criticism of economic categories. Engels was closer than anyone else to Marx's critique of political economy. This is why they formed a life-long friendship.

The widely accepted interpretation of the early Marx, however, does not explain this basis of their friendship nor Marx's intellectual development. 'Development' is not a mere 'change' but a type of change in which the later stage includes the former stage as its embryo. For the formation of Marx's value theory, similarities and dissimilarities between the early and the late Marx must be understood beforehand. The late Marx must be re-examined also, first in relation to the early Marx; but no positive meanings in the works of the early Marx have been recognised, e.g., EPM, *Notes on Ricardo*.

In the formation of Marx's value theory, i.e., in examining the difference in his critique of 'costs of production' between the early and the late Marx, we see only a 'development' but not a 'rupture'. Here we also see the reasons why Marx rated OCPE as 'brilliant', but only a 'sketch', on the criticism of economic categories.

Part Three

The Totality of Marx's System

10 MARX'S CONCEPT OF 'SOCIAL PROPERTY'

This chapter is devoted to clarifying Marx's concept of 'individual property' and 'social property' in *Capital* (1867), Volume 1.[1] Marx's communism[2] is one of the most basic subjects in Marxology and has been discussed by a large number of commentators. However, I believe Marx's view is still little known or, at least, not known well enough for the following three reasons.

First, Engels is partly to be blamed. There are significant differences between Marx and Engels on some basic points of their communism. As we shall see later, Engels misinterpreted Marx's 'negation of negation', 'realm of freedom', 'individual property' and 'social property' in *Capital*. However, this has not been understood until now because Engels has been regarded as the most authoritative commentator on Marx's theories. That which we know as Marx's theories is Engels' interpretation of them and may be quite different.

Second, Stalinism is to be blamed. Soviet Marxists were reluctant to publish some of Marx's works, including the EPM and the letter to Vera Zassoulitch (1881),[3] which indicates that they have published only those parts favourable to them. Engels' interpretation of Marx's works was more to their liking than the originals. They could justify their oppressive political system with some parts of Engels' works.

Third, commentators themselves are to be blamed. They have been influenced by commentaries from Engels and from the Institute of Marxism-Leninism, both in Moscow and in Berlin. Consciously or unconsciously, they have not supported the peoples of Eastern Europe but rather the ruling classes, the Communist Parties in those countries. Whatever the reason, the time has come to understand Marx in his own words.

First, we are now completely free from the influence of Soviet Marxism. Second, and more importantly, the present is similar to the time in which Marx developed his thought and theories. The 1840s saw many different socialisms in France, which Marx criticised as a 'bungled job', and also in Germany. Also there was Owen's pilot community ('New Harmony') and its failure. However, it was the time when Marx formulated his communism in EPM which has been neglected, or rather prohibited completely by Soviet Marxism. This suggests that we had better make a fresh start from EPM to understand Marx's communism in his own words.

It may sound reasonable to categorise Marx's words under 'state property' and 'planned economy', but this is to be trapped by Soviet Marxism. I would like to start instead by comparing Engels' *Anti-Dühring* (hereafter AD, (MEC 25, pp. 5–309)) and Marx's *Capital* to extract some apparent differences between their communism, and to follow this by inquiring into their genesis.

Although *The German Ideology* (1845–46) and *The Communist Manifesto* (1847–48) are widely known to have been written by both Marx and Engels, I treat them here as Marx's views and as though they were written by him alone, because both differ from Engels' *Principles of Communism* (1847) and AD. Also I treat all Marx's works as consistent with each other. The so-called inconsistency between the 'Young Marx' and the 'Old Marx' is but a fiction set up by Soviet Marxism and its followers. This chapter will illustrate the controversy.

MARX V. ENGELS ON COMMUNISM

Communism in *Anti-Dühring*

What marks AD is its method: Engels explains that the 'contradiction between socialised production and capitalistic appropriation' manifested itself as the 'antagonism of proletariat and bourgeoisie', as the 'antagonism between the organisation of production in the individual workshop and the anarchy of production in society in general' and as 'crises'. By the 'contradiction' he means that the 'means of production of the individual' has been transformed into the 'social means of production only workable by a collectivity of men', and that 'production itself changed from a series of individual into a series of social acts, and the products from individual to social product', but 'the old forms of appropriation remained in full swing' and 'the owner of the instruments of labour always appropriated to himself the products ... of the labour of others'.

This revolt of the productive forces makes the capitalist class treat the forces more and more as 'social productive forces, so far as this is possible under capitalist conditions': they merge into 'the different kinds of joint-stock companies' and into 'state property'.[4] However, they are not the abolition of 'the capitalistic nature of the productive forces' at all. On the contrary, 'state ownership' is nothing but 'the zenith' of the capitalist relation. State ownership is not and cannot be the 'solution of the conflict, but concealed within it are the technical conditions that form the elements of that solution'.

> This solution can only consist in the practical recognition of the social nature of the modern forces of production, and therefore in the harmonising of the modes of production, appropriation and exchange with the social character of the means of production. And this can only come about by society openly and directly taking possession of the productive forces .... (MEC 25, p. 266)

The real solution of the conflict is summarised as: 'the proletariat seizes political power and turns the means of production in the first instance into state property'. As 'the taking possession of the means of production in the name of society' is the first and the last act as a state, 'state property' becomes 'the direct social appropriation'. (MEC 25, p. 267)

Similarities between *Anti-Dühring* and *Capital*

It is clear that the outline of AD is the same as that of *Capital*. The two share similar terms and statements. On closer examination, however, there are differences between the two works even on some significant points. I would like to illustrate some of these in the next section.

Dissimilarities between *Anti-Dühring* and *Capital*

'Realm of Necessity' and 'Realm of Freedom'

The most significant and the most apparent dissimilarity between AD and *Capital* is in the concepts 'realm of freedom' and 'realm of necessity'. Engels writes:

> Man's own social organisation, hitherto confronting him as a necessity imposed by nature and history, now becomes the result of his own free action .... Only from that time will man himself, with full consciousness, make his own history, only from that time will the social causes set in motion by him have, in the main and in a constantly growing measure, the results intended by him. It is humanity's leap from the realm of necessity to the realm of freedom. (MEC 25, p.270)

On the other hand, *Capital*, Volume 3, says:

> With his development this realm of physical necessity expands as a result of his wants; but, at the same time, the forces of production which satisfy these wants also increase. Freedom in this field can only consist in socialised man (*der vergesellschaftete Mensch*), the associated producers (*die assoziierten Produzenten*), rationally regulating their interchange with nature, bringing it under their common control, instead of being ruled by it as by the blind forces of Nature; and achieving this with the least expenditure of energy and under conditions most favourable to, and worthy of, their human nature. But it nonetheless still remains a realm of necessity. Beyond it begins the development of human energy which is an end in itself, the true realm of freedom, which, however, can blossom forth only with this realm of necessity as its basis. The shortening of the working-day is its basic prerequisite. (CAP 3, p. 959)

The 'realm of freedom' of Engels is the realm of conscious and planned control of the social metabolism by the associated producers.[5] However, this still belongs to the 'realm of necessity' in *Capital*. 'The realm of freedom', writes Marx, 'actually begins only where labour which is determined by necessity and mundane considerations ceases; thus in the very nature of things it lies beyond the realm of actual material production' (ibid.). Marx's 'realm of freedom' is the sphere of 'free time' or 'disposable time' beyond the working-day. It is not the leisure time as compensation for estrangement in the working-day. It is 'time for free development of the workers for society, i.e., civilisation'; (G, p. 634) the appropriation of surplus-time by the capitalist is the appropriation of civilisation by the capitalist.

Now we come to the following conclusions: 'Realm of freedom' in AD differs from that in *Capital*. AD lacks the 'realm of freedom' in *Capital*.

'Social Property'

'Negation of Negation' in Anti-Dühring

The second remarkable difference between AD and *Capital* is their concepts of 'social property' and 'individual property'. Dühring understands Marx's 'negation of negation' as the 'property which is at once both individual and social' and criticises him by saying that Marx 'leaves it to his adepts to solve for themselves this profound dialectical enigma'. (MEC 25, p. 120) Engels' explanation of it is his critique of Dühring's interpretation. He says that 'this means that social ownership extends to the land and the other means of production, and individual ownership to the products, that is, the articles of consumption'. (MEC 25, p. 121) He repeats his view on page 267. Let us formulate their interpretations before we quote Marx's original and examine which is correct.

Dühring: individual property = social property ≠ common property
Engels : individual property ≠ social property = common property

'Negation of Negation' in Capital

The second German edition[6] of *Capital*, Volume 1, says:

> The capitalist mode of production and of appropriation, accordingly capitalist private property, is the first negation of individual private property, as founded on the labour of its proprietor; but capitalist production begets ... Its own negation. This is the negation of negation. It re-establishes *individual property on the basis of* the achievements of the capitalist era: namely *cooperation of free workers and their possession in common of the land and the means of production produced by labour itself* ... . [The] transformation of capitalist private property which in fact rests on the carrying on of production by society, into *social property*. (CAP 1, pp. 929f; italics mine)

The French version begins with 'the capitalist mode of production and of appropriation that corresponds to it is ...' and omits the 'free workers'. The present German and the English versions were rewritten or modified by Engels. As far as we can distinguish a mode of appropriation from its basis and understand it in its context, we cannot agree with Dühring more.

'individual private property (as founded on the labour of its proprietor)' is negated by 'capitalist private property (which rests on the exploitation of alien, but formally free labour)' and then by
'individual property (on the basis of ... cooperation and the free workers' possession in common of the land and the means of production produced by labour itself)'
= 'social property'

Let us formulate this and compare it with that of Engels:

Marx : individual property = social property ≠ common property
Engels: individual property ≠ social property = common property

Thus we arrive in this roundabout way at the starting point, the controversy between Dühring and Engels: what kind of property it is which is 'at once both individual and social'; but one thing has become clear, Engels is not correct. So let us make a fresh start with the examination of his faults.

First, Engels misunderstands Marx's 'social property'. 'Social property' is set against 'capitalist private property' and cannot be equivalent to 'common property', which is a mere basis of 'individual property'. 'Social property' should be understood as equivalent to 'individual property'. That is the problem which misled Engels. He understands by appropriation 'appropriation of the means of production and of the products' (MEC 25, p. 269) or 'the taking possession' (*Besitzergreifung*) of them. However, he meant originally 'appropriation of productive forces', did he not?

Second, Engels failed to understand Marx's 'individual property' fully. No wonder that part of the product is consumed by individuals as means of subsistence. However, Engels failed to explain why the second negation is described as the 'reestablish [ment]' of individual property. There must be something more in it than 'the ownership to .... the articles of consumption'. He failed to tell us that 'individual private property' is 'the foundation of small-scale industry, and small-scale industry is a necessary condition for the development of social production and of the free individuality of the worker himself'. (CAP I, p. 927) The 're-establish[ment]' or the second negation must succeed individual property 'on the basis of the achievements of the capitalist era'. We have examined Engels' remarks within Chapter 32 of CAP 1. If we take Marx's other works into account, it will become clearer that Engels' interpretation of 'individual property' is defective. From 1844 onward, Marx describes the future social relations as 'association'. The EPM, *The German Ideology*, *The Poverty of Philosophy*, *The Communist Manifesto* and J. Most's *Capital and Labour by Marx* (corrected by Marx himself) says '*eine Assoziation*' (an association) or '*eine Vereinigung*' (a union) of free workers is established by the 'negation of negation'. *Capital and Labour by Marx*, for example, says:

> Thus individual property is re-established, but on the basis of the achievements of the modern mode of production. So we have an association of free workers who possess in common the land and the means of production produced by labour itself. (MEGA2, II-8, p. 783)

This shows us that Marx's 'individual property' is equivalent to 'an association of free workers' which links 'individual property' to 'social property' by bringing us back to the end of Chapter 1 of CAP volume 1. There Marx writes:

> Let us finally imagine, for a change, an association of free men, working with the means of production held in common, and expending their many different forms of labour-power in full self-awareness as one single social labour force. (CAP 1, p. 171; italics mine)

That which Engels quoted as the grounds for his argument turns into the grounds for an argument against him, if we understand by 'appropriation' the 'relations of production and forms of intercourse (*Verkehrverhältnisse*) that corresponds to it' (CAP 1, p. 90). Anyway, we can now formulate Marx's four concepts as follows:

individual property = an association of free workers = social property ≠ common property

We now come to a conclusion that AD differs from *Capital* even on some basic points. AD has been thought to be the best introduction to Marx's *Capital*, his thoughts and theories, but we should stop reading it as such. In the next section I make Marx's socialism clearer by showing where these dissimilarities come from and what causes them.

INDIVIDUAL, SOCIAL AND COMMON PROPERTY

The Labour Process and 'Individual Property'

The General Character of the Labour Process and of Appropriation

Physically and mentally human beings need nature and can live only through a metabolism between themselves and nature. Nature, in this sense, is the inorganic body of human beings, but it does not satisfy human needs as it is. Labour is a process between human beings and nature, a process by which man mediates, regulates and controls the metabolism between himself and nature. Man changes external nature using his physical and mental powers in order to appropriate (*aneignen*) the materials of nature in a form adapted to his own needs.[7] This action is not only a change of form for the materials of nature but a realisation (*Verwirklichung*) of his own purposes.[8] Man changes his own nature through this purposeful action. In this process he uses an instrument to direct his activity on to objects. The instrument becomes 'one of his organs of his activity, which he annexes to his own bodily organs'.[9]

The simple elements of the labour process are 1) purposeful activity, 2) the object on which that work is performed, and 3) the instruments of that work. Without any one of these elements, no production is possible.

With regard to the result, the product, both the instruments and the object of labour are means of production and the labour itself is productive labour. Production is the relation of productive labour to means of production. It is man's realisation of his physical and mental powers, that is, himself and his life, and the development of his powers through it. The labour process is an appropriation of what exists in nature for the requirements of men. The labour process in its simple elements is the universal condition for the metabolic interaction (*Stoffwechsel*) between man and nature. It is worth repeating that *Eigentum* (appropriation) in this sense is abstract but is also its first and original meaning.[10] We should understand by 'appropriation' the relationship of the worker to his means of production but not the relationship with the person to whom the products belong. 'Appropriation' should be understood as a process of production, or the whole of the relations of production, and the realisation and the confirmation of the worker's species-life.[11]

Incidentally, the labour process is not usually carried on by a single worker but by many workers. Workers usually co-operate in the process, which means that workers also develop 'the capabilities of his species (*Gattungsvermögen*)'[12] through their co-operation and the labour process.

Historical Features of the Capitalist Labour Process

The three elements of the labour process have become separated from each other. Under capitalist relations of production, immediate producers are separated from their means of production, and this separation is reproduced every day. The producers have to sell their labour-power (creative power and source of all wealth) to survive. They lose all other means of life. They cannot carry out the labour process alone any more. The labour process, production, is now carried out by capitalists only and it becomes a process by which capitalists consume the labour-power they purchase, or 'a process between things the capitalist has purchased' exhibiting two characteristic features:

1) the worker works under the control (command) of the capitalist to whom his labour belongs;
2) the product is the property of the capitalist and not of its immediate producer. 'Capital develop[s] within the production process until it acquired command over labour, i.e., over self-activating labour power, in other words the worker himself.'[13]

Working under the control of the capitalist is characteristic for human beings alone. It is possible only because man is a species-being. The animal is immediately one with its life activity and cannot make its life activity itself an object, but man can. Man can make his life-activity the object of his will and of his consciousness. In this case the strong point of man appears as his weak point, and man's life-activity loses any sense of the objectification of his species-life.

Working under the control of the capitalist means not only the alienation of labour-power but also social ability, an ability to have social intercourse with others. Co-operation in the production process is performed only under the command of the capitalist, not under the control of the workers themselves, and co-operation becomes part of the power of capital. It ceases to be a realisation of the workers' own social ability. Additionally, the products belong to the capitalist and are sold in the market. The social intercourse via products ceases to be a relation of producers to each other, becoming instead a relation of products to other products. The immediate producer loses his power to mediate relations with other men with his products. The capitalist mode of appropriation, based on the separation of productive labour from its means of production, should not be understood merely as the worker's loss of products, but also as the loss of his personal and social abilities.

Individual Property

Now let us go back to the 'negation of negation' in *Capital*, Volume 1. When we read the chapter carefully, the focus is on the proprietor of the means of production, on the immediate producer, and on production or appropriation as the combination of three elements of the labour process. That is so, whether 'the means of production and the external conditions of labour belong to private individuals' or not, 'whether these private individuals are producers or non-workers', and the general character of '(private) property': the mode of production or of appropriation. We can formulate the three modes of appropriation in this chapter as follows:

Character of Property	Individual as Proprietor	Individual as Producer
Individual Private Property	Yes	Yes
Capitalist Private Property	No	No
Individual Property	Yes (Common Property)	Yes (Co-operation)

'Individual property' is the new mode of appropriation into which capitalistic private property is transformed through a long process but not so long as that of the first negation. 'Individual property' means 'all production has been concentrated in the hands of associated individuals' (MEC 6, p. 505) who work with common property in the means of production. All individuals are proprietors of their means of production and are immediate workers. The original unity of labour with its external conditions is recovered on a new basis, which is the achievements of the capitalist era: namely 'cooperation of free workers and their possession in common of the land and the means of production produced by labour itself'.

I do not think I need to remind readers that 'individual property' also means the universal development of the workers' individuality. There is, however, one thing left which requires comment: 'social production'. Marx writes in relation to small-scale production that it is the basis of 'social production'. Before this mode of production there was only communal production, where all members of the community worked together at the same time and the members were not independent of the community itself but were immersed in it. Small-scale production, however, set the members free and made them independent individuals through commodity production. In that mode of production individuals worked separately and their labour was immediately private, not social or communal. Those private labours become social through an exchange of their products, by making up the whole quantity of labour that society needs. Exchange value of the commodity expresses a new historical way of conceptualising social labour or the social nature of labour.

Thus, the first negation, the supplanting of 'individual private property' by 'capitalistic private property', creates a universal development of human social intercourse by producing an 'immense collection of commodities'. Commodity production is fully developed on its own foundations, and universal (in this sense 'free') social relations of men are created, for the first time in opposition to the immediate producers themselves. This, however, forms the real basis for the full development of humanity.

> Personal independence founded on objective dependence is the second great form, in which a system of general social metabolism, of universal relations, of all-round needs and universal capacities is formed for the first time. Free individuality, based on the universal development of individuals and on the subordination of their communal, social productivity as their social wealth, is the third stage. The second stage creates the conditions of the third. (G, p. 158)

It is now clear that Marx's 'individual property' does not 'extend ... to the products, that is, the articles of consumption' at all but to the universal development of individuality of the individual workers. In the following section, we examine Marx's 'individual property' more closely by inquiring into the concepts 'appropriation of productive forces' and 'social property'.

'Appropriation of Productive Forces' and 'Social Property'

The German Ideology says that appropriation by free workers is determined by: 1) 'the object to be appropriated', 2) 'the persons appropriating' and 3) 'the manner in which it must be effected'. Thus in this section I would like to compare and examine Marx's and Engels' concepts of 'individual property' and 'social property' more precisely according to these criteria.

The Object to be Appropriated

The German Ideology says that 'the object to be appropriated' is 'the productive forces, which have been developed to a totality and which only exist within a universal intercourse' amongst individuals. 'Productive forces' does not only mean the 'means of production'. 'Productive forces' are said to 'exist within a universal intercourse'. On a preceding page, Marx also writes: that 'the social power, i.e., the multiplied productive force, which arises through the cooperation of different individuals as it is'.

Capital, Volume 1, is consistent with *The German Ideology* when it says in Chapter 32 that individual property is 're-established on the basis of the achievements of the capitalist era', i.e., 'cooperation of free workers and their possession in common of the land and the means of production'.

AD, however, is not consistent. Engels writes correctly that the proletariat succeeds the 'socialised productive power' in the capitalist mode of production. On the other hand, he describes the 'real solution', socialism, as 'taking possession of the means of production in the name of society', which leads him directly to 'social appropriation' extending to 'the land and the other means of production'. His concept of 'appropriation' does not include 'the cooperation' of the workers. His 'appropriation' is not 'production', but 'possession' of the products.

'The so-called community of property' (MEC 6, p. 348) of the early Engels shows that he had never counted 'cooperation' as a 'productive force'. This explains why Engels rewrites the opening sentence on 'negation of negation' (which I quoted on page 156) as follows in the present German and English editions: 'The capitalist mode of appropriation, which springs from the capitalist mode of production, produces capitalist private property.' This rewriting is based on the distinction between the mode of production and that of appropriation.

The Persons Appropriating and the Manner of Appropriation

The German Ideology says that 'the persons appropriating' are 'the proletarians'. It also says that 'the manner in which it must be effected' is 'a union, which ... can again only be a universal one, and through a revolution'. Seemingly *Capital* and AD are similar on this. However, if we examine both works closely and take 'the object' and 'the manner' of the appropriation into account, we will find that Marx considers the proletarians as 'individuals', and Engels considers them as a group, 'society'.

For Marx 'the persons appropriating' must be 'individuals', because workers in the capitalist mode of production 'have become abstract individuals, who are, however, by this very fact put into a position to enter into relations with one another as individuals'. (MEC 5, p. 87) Thus *The German Ideology* and *Capital* mention 'an association'[14] of 'free workers'. On the other hand, AD mentions the appropriation of all means of production 'by society'. (MEC 25, p. 268)

Here we must take into account the distinction between the different concepts of 'appropriation' held by the two. For Marx 'appropriation' is 'production', thus it is individuals who enter into co-operation in the production process. For Engels, however, 'appropriation' is 'possession' of the means of production, thus the subject who appropriates it has to be a group, i.e., 'society'. Keen-eyed readers may defend Engels by asserting that he uses 'the hands of the producers working together (*assoziierte Produzenten*)' (MEC 25, p. 267) once. This is, however, a supplement to the fourth edition of *Socialism: Utopian and Scientific* (1891) and extends only to the means of production.

Now it is safe to conclude that dissimilarities in the concepts of 'appropriation' and '(appropriation of) productive forces' led Marx and Engels to hold different concepts of 'individual property' and 'social property'.

Social Property

Let us summarise the concept of 'social property' in Marx and Engels. Marx's concept is equivalent to the 'appropriation of productive forces' developed universally in the capitalist era; it consists of co-operation amongst workers and of the means of production. Thus, it extends to their 'universal intercourse between men' (MEC 5, p. 49) which 'cannot be controlled by individuals, unless it is controlled by all'. (MEC 5, p. 88) This requires 'the association of individuals ... which puts the conditions of the free development and movement of individuals under their control'. (MEC 5, p. 80) Marx's 'individual Property', as the basis for the development of universal individuality, cannot exist except through this association in which individuals obtain freedom. Marx's individual property can exist only as 'social property'.

> Communism differs from all previous movements in that it overturns the basis of all earlier relations of production and intercourse, and for the first time consciously treats all naturally evolved premises as the creations of hitherto existing men, strips them of their natural character and subjugates them to the power of the united individuals. (MEC 5, p. 81)

Engels' concept of the 'appropriation of productive forces', however, is limited to 'taking possession' of the means of production. Thus he omits the co-operation amongst workers and, consequently, their association or their universal intercourse. Though he uses Marx's term 'associated workers', it does not link with other statements in his argument. It is necessary for Engels to explain Marx's 'social property' and 'individual property' as 'upon the one hand, direct social appropriation, as means to the maintenance and extension of production on the other, direct individual appropriation, as means of subsistence and of enjoyment'. (MEC 25, p. 267)

This dissimilarity also leads Marx and Engels to their different visions on communism. Engels is very optimistic and sounds as if taking possession of the means of production by 'society' would make everything all right. For example, he says: 'With the seizing of the means of production by society, production of commodities is done away with, and, simultaneously, the mastery of the product over the producer'. (MEC 25, p. 270) And:

> From the moment when society enters into possession of the means of production and uses them in direct association for production, the labour of each individual, however varied its specifically useful character may be, becomes at the start and directly social labour. (MEC 25, p. 294)

This optimism comes naturally from his concept of 'social'. Marx, on the other hand, is a bit more prudent. For example, he writes: 'Communism is for us not a state of affairs which is to be established, an ideal to which reality [will] have to adjust itself. We call communism the real movement which abolishes the present state of things.' (MEC 5, p. 49) And:

> Of course, in the beginning, this cannot be effected except by means of despotic inroads on the rights of property, and on the conditions of bourgeois production; by means of measures, therefore, which appear economically insufficient and untenable, but which, in the course of the movement, outstrip themselves, necessitate further inroads

upon the old social order, and are unavoidable as a means of entirely revolutionising the mode of production. (MEC 6, p. 504)

The author of *Capital* recognises very well through his analysis of the 'commodity' that even in 'an association of free men, ... expending their many different forms of labour-power in full self-awareness as one single social labour force',[15] their labour can be 'social' only when they fulfill the following two conditions:

(a) 'On the one hand, it must, as a definite useful kind of labour, satisfy a definite social need, and thus maintain its position as an element of the total labour'.
(b) 'On the other hand, it can satisfy the manifold needs of the individual producer himself only in so far as every particular kind of useful private [read this as: individual] can be exchanged with.'[16]

As far as the second point is concerned, 'labour-time would in that case play a double part' and may serve as the direct measure of distribution. The first point, however, is feasible only through 'a definite social plan' developed democratically by the individuals themselves. I would like to make Marx's concept of communism clearer by investigating his concept of the 'essence of private property' after a brief comment on his 'common property'.

Common Property

Common Property

Marx's concept of 'common property or communal property' (*Gemeineigentum*) extends, without any doubt, exclusively to the means of production. Thus, Engels does not differ from Marx on this concept. The only possible point of difference is whether the immediate workers have free access to the means of production or whether the means of production belong to some institution independent of the workers themselves.

In *Capital* Marx writes clearly: 'the free workers' possession of the land and the means of production produced by labour itself'. This leaves no room for any doubt. The producers are supposed to have free access to the means of production they need. According to Marx, what is important for the workers is to recover an original unity with the conditions of production and to develop their individuality universally, or else the revolution becomes meaningless.[17]

Although Engels sometimes seems to give 'society' priority over 'individuals', he also thinks that workers should have easy access to the means of production, because his concept 'community of property' is 'common use of all the instruments of production and the distribution of all products by common agreement'. (MEC 6, p. 348)

The Germanic Community

Both Marx and Engels write that workers must gain complete control over universally developed productive forces and over social powers, including those which arose from workers' labour but became opposed to them. Hence every individual is expected to be able to use 'common property'. Marx's description of the Germanic community, which preceded the capitalist mode of production, gives us a clear vision of 'common property'. In the Germanic relations of property, the independent unit at the bottom is the family, which 'settled in the forests, long distances apart', and the commune exists only in the periodic 'gathering-together (*Vereinigung*)' of the commune members (free landed proprietors) for shared purposes. 'The commune thus appears as a coming-together (*Vereinigung*), not as a being-together (*Verein*)' (G, p. 483) 'The commune exists only in the interrelations among these individual landed proprietors as such.' (G, p. 484) Communal property, as distinct from individual property, also occurs amongst Germanic tribes taking 'the form of hunting land ... etc., the part of the land which cannot be divided if it is to serve as means of production in this specific form'. It appears, however, 'merely as a complement to individual property' and 'is so used by each individual proprietor as such'. (G, p. 485)

The main point here is this: in the Germanic relations of property 'the existence of the commune and of communal property appears as mediated by, i.e., as a relation of, the independent subjects to one another'. (G, p. 484) Read instead the 'individual landed proprietor' as the 'free worker', the 'commune' as an 'association of free workers' and 'communal property' as the 'common property of free workers', then you obtain a clearer picture of Marx's 'individual property', 'social property' and 'common property'.

Summary

The capitalist mode of production and appropriation is based on the appropriation of alien labour, the social power of immediate workers. Marx's communism is the movement to replace this mode of production with 'an association of free men, working with the means of production held in common, and expending their many different forms of labour-power in full self-awareness as one single social labour force'. Thus the new mode of 'appropriation' as the mode of 'production' is both 'individual' and 'social' at once, so far as the 'association' is a 'society' mediated by its free individual members. The main points here are the following:

(a) 'Appropriation' should not be understood exclusively as 'possession of the means of production'.

(b) 'Individuals produce in society and for society as social-beings and subsume the community (cooperation and social intercourse among them) into themselves with the consciousness of a community-being.'[18]

(c) 'Individual = social property' is the mode of production which forms the basis of the free development of human abilities, organic and inorganic, and of the human senses, i.e., of the universal development of their individuality.

(d) Consequently, in due course, the meaning of 'social' will alter from mere relations among private men into the relations among individual human-beings who affirm each other as truly equal.[19]

THE NATURE OF CAPITAL AS THE PRINCIPLE OF MARX'S SYSTEM

The Nature of Capital and the Concept of Capital

'The Two-fold Proof' of Capital

In 1843 Marx left the *Rheinische Zeitung* to 'withdraw from the public stage into the study'. The reasons are clear: he faced a two-fold historical problem with private property; but his 'previous studies did not permit [him] even to venture any judgment on the content of the French tendencies'. On the one hand, private property was establishing itself in Germany, producing 'so-called material interests'. In England and in France, however, 'the content of the ... tendencies' was the abolition of private property. Thus Marx's withdrawal from the public stage means that he began to examine the two-fold proof of private property. On the one hand human life required it for the realisation of civilisation and on the other it now requires the supersession of it. To answer this question only Hegel's *Philosophy of Right*, an exceptional critique of modern civil society in Germany, would do.

> If we wanted to start with the German status quo itself, the result would still be an anachronism even if one did it in the only adequate way ... .
>
> Even the denial of our political present is already a dusty fact in the historical lumber-room of modern peoples. (MEC 3, p. 176)

To raise criticism to the level of 'the question of which the present age says: that is the question' is to criticise the socio-political circumstances of England and of France and address the controversy between political economists and French socialists. Marx aimed to analyse the nature of capital and to abolish it positively. The first work which he undertook for this solution was his EPM,[20] which will be examined closely in this chapter. I need not remind readers that Marx was never on the socialists' side, however strange it may sound. He has already declared himself against its 'amateurism' and had begun to study classical political economy critically.

The Nature of Capital and The Concept of Capital

The nature of something is clearer with its maturity than with its embryo. Capital is the high point of private property, which started historically with the form of landed property. Consequently, the nature of capital is the nature of private property of all forms. Classical political economy understood it as 'labour in general', as is well known. What about Marx? 'Estranged labour'! Let me show this by distinguishing the 'nature of private property' from the 'concept of private property' in EPM.

In the 'FM: LP' (so-called 'Estranged Labour') and in the 'Second Manuscript' of EPM, Marx analyses the immediate production process of capital in terms of 'two components which depend on one another, or which are but different expression of one and the same relationship' (MEC 3, p. 281):

1. 'the direct relationship between the worker and production' (MEC 3, p. 273)
   = 'relationship of labour to its products' and 'the relationship of the worker to the objects of his production' (MEC 3, p. 274)
   = the relation in which 'appropriation appears as estrangement, as alienation' (MEC 3, p. 281)
   = 'the relation of the worker to labour and to the product of his labour'
   = 'alienated labour in relation to the worker himself, i.e., the relation of alienated labour to itself' (MEC 3, p. 281)
   = 'the relation of private property as labour' (MEC 3, p. 285)
   = 'the production of human activity as labour that is, as an activity quite alien to itself, to man and to nature' (MEC 3, p. 285)
2. 'the relationship of the man of means to the objects of production and to production itself' (MEC 3, p. 274)
   = 'the relation to it [labour] of the capitalist' (MEC 3, p. 279)
   = the relationship in which 'alienation appears as appropriation, estrangement as truly becoming a citizen' (MEC 3, p. 281)
   = 'the relation of the non-worker to the worker and to the product of his labour'
   = 'the property relation of the non-worker to the worker and to labour' (MEC 3, p. 281)
   = 'the relation to the worker, to labour and its object of this person who is alien to labour and the worker' (MEC 3, pp. 281f)
   = 'the relation of private property as capital' (MEC 3, p. 285)
   = 'the production of the object of human activity as capital in which all natural and social characteristics of the object is extinguished' (MEC 3, p. 285)

It is already known that the second relation is the logical 'result, the necessary consequence' (MEC 3, p. 279) or 'the necessary outcome' (MEC 3, p. 281) of the first. It is not well known, however, that the second relation is the 'concept of private property'. Marx writes that 'just as we have derived the concept of private property from the concept of estranged, alienated labour by analysis', (MEC 3, p. 281) the second one is the concept of capital. This can be supported by his *Grundrisse* in which he criticised Smith by saying 'the appropriation of alien labour is not itself included in its [capital's] concept'. (G, p. 330) The appropriation of alien labour in the production process is the concept of capital.[21]

What is less known is that the first relation of alienated labour is the '(general) nature (*Wesen*) of private property'. (MEC 3, p. 281) In the English version of EPM, *Wesen* is translated as 'nature' in some cases and as 'essence' in others, preventing readers from following Marx's views. We find, if we read EPM very carefully, that Marx writes on the preceding page that 'private property thus results by analysis from the concept of alienated labour, i.e., of alienated man, of estranged labour, of estranged life, of estranged man'. (MEC 3, p. 279) The 'nature of private property' is the 'activity quite alien to itself, to man and to nature'. (MEC 3, p. 285)

This is supported by the concept of the 'subjective essence (*Wesen*) of private property' in the 'Third Manuscript' of EPM and is consistent with the description in the 'FM: FP' of EPM. The column 'Profit of Capital' begins by saying 'what is the basis of capital, that is, of private property in the products of other men's labour?', followed by a re-reading of Smith's concept of 'command'. Marx concludes 'capital is thus the governing power over labour and its products'.[22] (MEC 3, pp. 273f) Marx's *Manuscripts of 1861–1863* also support this, because Marx comments 'here at last, the nature of capital is understood correctly' as he notes Hodgskin's remark that 'fixed capital is bringing its owner a profit ... but because it is a measure of obtaining command over labour'.[23]

Let me repeat.The 'nature of capital' is 'command over labour', the 'alien activity of the worker' or the 'alienated labour', if you like. The 'concept of capital', that is, the property relation of the capitalist to the worker, is a mere result of this 'nature'.

Some commentators criticise Marx's use of 'private property' rather than 'capital' by saying that the early Marx cannot distinguish capital from private property in general. However, the 'nature of capital', derived from the immediate production process, is the 'nature of private property in general' or the 'general nature of private property', which allows Marx to analyse 'the economic process as such ... in its real concreteness'. (MEC 3, p. 317)

First, 'It is clear that if the subjective nature of industry (read as: capital) is now grasped (as 'labour in general'), this nature includes within itself its opposite', (MEC 3, p. 293) i.e., agricultural labour. Consequently, we can see 'how it is only at this point that private property can complete its dominion over man and become, in its most general form, a world-historical power', (MEC 3, p. 293) and how 'this process repeats itself in the scientific analysis of the subjective nature of private property' as the development from Quesnay to Smith.

Second, if the subjective nature of private property is grasped as estranged labour, we can easily see that the abolition of capital is the abolition of all forms of private property, in other words all class struggles. 'From the relationship of estranged labour to private property it follows further that the emancipation of society from private property, etc., from servitude, is expressed in the political form of the emancipation of the workers ...'. (MEC 3, p. 280)

Third, if the subjective nature of capital is grasped as 'estranged labour', as labour not in its natural or eternal form but in its historical form, we can resolve the controversy between the political economists and the French socialists by following Marx in EPM.

The Nature of Capital and Marx's Critique of French Socialism

Contradiction between Capital and Labour

Labour is the real source of wealth. This is the principle of classical political economy and its starting point. Therefore the workers are the rich and the non-workers (capitalists) the poor. On the contrary, however, the workers are the poor and the non-workers are actually the rich. Smith did not see any contradiction between his principle and his theoretical results and he describes the miserable situations of the working class. Faced with the misery of the workers, the French socialists support labour and give labour everything. 'Political economy starts from labour as the real soul of production; yet to labour it gives nothing, and to private property everything. Confronting this contradiction, Proudhon has decided in favour of labour against private property.' (MEC 3, p. 280)

Proudhon's *What is Private Property?* (1841) and *Philosophy of Misery* (1846) represent his critique of political economy. He criticises economic categories from his standpoint of 'equality' and tries to show that all products would be exchanged according to an equal 'value'. For him economic categories are not scientific reflections of capitalistic production relations. He thinks that he can change the situation only by replacing the present mode of exchange with 'equal' exchange, without the abolition of the capitalist mode of production itself.

Political economy is not directly responsible for the misery of the workers. It is a necessary result of the alienation of their labour-power, the only source of all wealth, to the capitalists. What political economists did was to analyse the real movement of capital (production and consumption) scientifically and formulate it as laws (MEC 3, pp. 270 and 280). Thus Marx criticises Proudhon by saying: 'We understand, however, that this apparent contradiction is the contradiction of estranged labour with itself, and that political economy has merely formulated the laws of estranged labour.' (MEC 3, p. 280)

From Marx's viewpoint, Proudhon does not understand the 'nature of capital' and its positive aspect at all. Without capital, neither modern civilisation nor the political emancipation of man is possible. Incidentally, Marx's critique of Proudhon's 'equality' is very interesting as well as important to understanding Marx's socialism. According to Marx, 'equality is man's consciousness of himself in the element of practice, i.e., man's consciousness of other men as his equals and man's attitude to other men as his equals'. (MEC 4, p. 39) Thus Proudhon is criticised by Marx in that 'Proudhon did not succeed in giving this thought appropriate development'. (MEC 4, p. 43) On the other hand, Marx characterised the communistic movement of production and consumption as 'social = human' in so-called 'Private Property and Communism' in 'Third Manuscript' of EPM. *The Holy Family* (1845) explains the concept as follows:

> Equality is the French expression for the unity of human essence, for man's consciousness of his species and his attitude towards his species, for the practical identity of man with man, i.e., for the social or human relation of man to man. (MEC 4, p. 39)

Marx's socialism as humanism is human intercourse in which men relate equally and to each other with products as an essential bond. It is the kind of social intercourse in which man realises his species-being.

Three Forms of Communism

Consequently Marx considers Proudhon to represent the first and crudest form of communism. The second form of communism is that which is 'still political in nature democratic or despotic; with the abolition of the state, yet still incomplete, and being still affected by private property'. (MEC 3, p. 296) Marx criticised this communism in that 'it has grasped its [private property's] concept, but not its nature'. (MEC 3, p. 296) This seems to be 'a communist society ... as it emerges from capitalist society'[24] as far as it is mediated through the negation of private property. Nevertheless the meaning of this criticism is clear for us by now, as we have already examined both the 'concept of private property' and its 'nature'. It is not enough merely to abolish the private property rights of capitalists. A new stage of society, i.e., the positive abolition of modern capitalist relations of production, must be the abolition of 'estranged labour'. Thus Marx formulates his communism as 'communism as the real appropriation of the human essence by and for man' (MEC 3, p. 296) or 'socialism as socialism', (MEC 3, p. 306) which does not require a negation (such as despotic inroads into the right of private property) any longer.

The Nature of Capital and Marx's Critique of Political Economy

The Limit of Classical Political Economy and Marx's Task

Political economy is not directly responsible for the misery of the worker. Its theoretical results could not be more cynical, the more it analyses the movement of present relations. 'There is a disproportionate growth in the cynicism of political economy from Smith through Say to Ricardo, Mill, etc'., because 'their science develops more consistently and truthfully'. (MEC 3, p. 291) However, readers must understand that Marx does not agree with political economy completely, or rather, he shows us the limits of political economy here. I will do my best to illustrate Marx' critique of political economy in EPM.

Economic Laws as the Laws of Estranged Labour

Political economy derived its laws through an analysis of the movement of capital. It is, without any doubt, an aspect of scientism. It does not and cannot, however, 'comprehend these laws, i.e., it does not demonstrate how they arise from the very nature of private property'. (MEC 3, p. 271) It cannot, because it does not grasp the 'nature of private property' fully. It is good at grasping 'labour (in general)' as the nature of capital. It sees wage-labour as the only 'natural', consequently, eternal form of labour, not as an historical form. This means that it cannot grasp the historical features of wage-labour, but only as the source of profit of capital. Just as Luther 'superseded external religiosity by making religiosity the inner substance of man', Smith superseded the 'external, mindless objectivity of wealth' (gold and silver of the mercantile system). As a result, however, just as 'man is brought within the orbit of religion' by Luther, man is brought within the orbit of wage-labour by Smith. It is no wonder that political economy is 'under the semblance of recognising man, the political economy whose principle is labour rather carries to its logical conclusion the denial of man'. (MEC 3, p. 291) This is the necessary result of its insufficiency in grasping the nature of capital. Marx writes:

> Because they make private property in its active form the subject, thus simultaneously turning man into the nature and at the same time turning man as non-natural into the nature the contradiction of reality corresponds completely to the contradictory being which they accept as their principle. (MEC 3, pp. 291f)

Marx can easily explain that 'the apparent contradiction is the contradiction of estranged labour with itself, and political economy has merely formulated the laws of estranged labour' by grasping the nature of capital as 'estranged labour', a non-natural form of human labour. A similar statement appears in the *Manuscripts of 1861–63* in the same context. Though lengthy I would like to quote his remark here to show that Marx is consistent from EPM to *Capital.*

> In this contradiction, political economy merely expressed the nature of capitalist production or, if you like, of wage-labour, of labour alienated from itself, which stands confronted by the wealth it has created as alien wealth, by its own productive power as the productive power of its product, by its enrichment as its own impoverishment and by its social power as the power of society.[25]

The main conclusion here is that Marx's starting point is where political economy ends its analysis, that is, its limit. Although Marx could not complete his comprehension of economic laws as the laws of estranged labour, one thing is clear: he is at the right starting point in EPM by grasping estranged labour as the 'nature of capital'.

The Nature of Capital and Marx's Critique of German Philosophy

A Critique of Hegel's Dialectics

'In the three years 1842–45 more was cleared away in Germany than at other times in three centuries.' (MEC 5, p. 27) Feuerbach, in particular is 'the only one who has at least made some progress and whose works can be examined *de bonne foi*' (MEC 5, pp. 27f) in the field of critique of Hegelian dialectics. Marx counts three great achievements of Feuerbach, including:

1. 'The establishment of true materialism and of real science, by making the social relationship of "man to man" the basic principle of the theory';
2. 'His opposing to the negation of the negation, which claims to be the absolute positive, ... positively based on itself'. (MEC 3, p. 328)

As a matter of fact, the only social relationship Feuerbach knows and recognises is at most friendship and relationships between men; consequently he does not criticise social relations in the Germany of his day. Marx reads in Feuerbach that 'sense-perception must be the basis of all science' (MEC 3, p. 303) and human history must be understood as starting from 'sense-perception in the twofold form of sensuous consciousness and sensuous need'. (MEC 3, p. 303) Actually Marx sees the 'open book of man's essential powers' (MEC 3, p. 302) in the history of industry.[26]

Thus Marx's critique of political economy should not be understood as his political economy. It includes so-called political economy, but it is wider ranging than that. He expected it to be the complete human science unifying natural and social sciences. Material production and consumption are observed as the manifestation of human life and 'appropriation for and by man of the human nature'. (MEC 3, p. 299) Private property is understood by Marx as 'only the perceptible expression of the fact that man becomes objective for himself and at the same time becomes to himself a strange and inhuman object'. If capital is civilisation itself, what workers are losing is not the products but civilisation. The positive negation of private property should not be conceived in the sense of immediate enjoyment but also of the complete emancipation of all human senses and qualities, in short the formation of 'a whole man'. (MEC 3, p. 299)

Marx's Answer to 'The Two-fold Proof'

Feuerbach, on the other hand, fails to match the outstanding achievement of Hegel's dialectic of negation: Hegel 'conceives the self-creation of man as a process'. (MEC 3, p. 332) In Hegelian philosophy objectification, estrangement and appropriation, in short everything, happens in pure thought. For example, when wealth and state power are understood by Hegel as entities estranged from the human being, this only happens in their form as thoughts. Consequently, the appropriation of man's essential powers, which have become objects, indeed alien objects, is in the first place only an appropriation occurring in consciousness, in pure thought.[27] Marx examines Hegel here: 'Hegel ... conceives objectification as loss of the object, as alienation and as transcendence of this alienation; that he thus grasps the nature of labour and comprehends objective man true, because real man as the outcome of man's own labour.' (MEC 3, pp. 332f)

Marx presents Hegel's speculative dialectic of negation as 'the two-fold proof' of private property. Let us investigate the matter for a while. Both 'division of labour and exchange', as Smith says, are specifically human activities. Animals are unable to combine differences in their attributes in the same species but not in different breeds. In this sense, division of labour and exchange show that human beings are community-beings and that each of them is the species-being. 'Division of labour' is 'the mutual completion and exchange of the activity itself', (MEC 3, p. 220) and 'exchange' is the mutual completion of the products. Division of labour and exchange reveal the social character of human labour or the social labour. However, 'the unity of human labour' appears as 'division of labour', because its 'social nature only comes into existence as its opposite, in the form of estrangement'.

(MEC 3, pp. 220f) The social character of labour does not appear directly and is not under the control of the individuals. The development of the division of labour and exchange represent the development of human social powers in estranged form. When they are carried out as the conscious activities of the members under their control, they are worth calling 'social' and 'human' activities.

Exchange, both of human activity within production itself and of human products against one another, is equivalent to species-activity and species-enjoyment,[28] the real, conscious and true mode of existence of which is social activity and social enjoyment. (MEC 3, pp. 216f)

The division of labour is the economic expression of the social character of labour within the estrangement. Or rather, 'since labour is only an expression of human activity within alienation, ... the division of labour, too, is therefore nothing but the estranged, alienated position of human activity as ... activity of man as a species-being'. (MEC 3, p. 317) Division of labour and exchange are 'perceptibly alienated expressions of human activity and essential power as a species activity and species of power'. (MEC 3, p. 321) These human activities can be realised as social powers of individuals and be reorganised as their own conscious activities only when they are universally produced by their own life activity. Truly social and human movement in production and consumption not only produces men and nature as social men and social nature but also requires social men and social nature as a starting point. In this very point lies the two-fold proof of private property. Human beings needed it to develop their social powers, and now it should be put under the control of their conscious association.

Likewise, ... both the material of labour and man as the subject, are the point of departure as well as the result of the movement (and precisely in this fact, that they must constitute the point of departure, lies the historical necessity of private property). Thus the social character is the general character of the whole movement. (MEC 3, p. 298)

Precisely in the fact that division of labour and exchange are aspects of private property lies the twofold proof, on the one hand that human life required private property for its realisation, and on the other hand that it now requires the supersession of private property. (MEC 3, p. 321)

Marx can see this result through his analysis of the 'nature of capital' (estranged labour). Thus it is natural that Soviet Marxism and its followers who deny EPM cannot see that. They have nothing to do with Marx in *Grundrisse*, in *Notes on James Mill* and in EPM.

Equally certain is it that individuals cannot gain mastery over their own social interconnections before they have created them. But it is an insipid notion to conceive of this merely objective bond as a spontaneous, natural attribute inherent in individuals and inseparable from their nature (in antithesis to their conscious knowing and willing). This bond is their product. It is a historical product. It belongs to a specific phase of their development. (G, pp. 161f)

'Universally developed individuals, whose social relations, as their own communal (*gemeinschaftlich*) relations, are hence also subordinated to their own communal control' (G, p. 162) and are the product of social production and social consumption. Communism as the negation of the negation is nothing more than the basis for this movement.

> Communism is the position as the negation of the negation, and is hence the actual phase necessary for the next stage of historical development in the process of human emancipation and rehabilitation. Communism is the necessary form and the dynamic principle of the immediate future, but communism as such is not the goal of human development, the form of human society. (MEC 3, p. 306)

CONCLUSIONS

We started our investigation of Marx's communism with dissimilarities between AD and *Capital*, i.e., the concepts of 'individual property', 'social property', the 'realm of necessity' and the 'realm of freedom'. When we examined the sources of those dissimilarities, we uncovered dissimilarities in the concepts 'appropriation' and thus 'appropriation of productive forces'.

Marx means by 'appropriation' the relationship of labour to its natural conditions, or production. As productive forces lie only in the relations of individuals, he means by 'appropriation of productive forces' the reorganisation of the social intercourse of men into conscious activity as human beings. 'Social = human' is used as the real existence of species-beings. Engels, on the other hand, understands by 'appropriation' taking over products as means of production or consumption. Thus he interprets the 'appropriation of productive forces' as taking over the means of production. Consequently, his communism is 'community of property' and lacks the content in terms of co-operation and free intercourse amongst workers, which is the basis of the universal development of individuals. In his concept of 'social property' the popularisation and the vulgarisation of Marx's communism is openly declared.

So-called existing socialism is the vulgarisation of Engels' communism, that is, 'crude communism' or the 'state capitalism' in EPM. It is not the proletariat who appropriate political power and control over production, but the Communist Party. The concept 'private property' advanced by some reformists during Perestroika, for example, by Pavel Bunichy, is more like Marx's 'common property' than 'capitalist private property', but less like 'individual property'. This also means that even the best and the brightest of Soviet Marxists cannot understand Marx's 'individual and social property' at all. They might have grasped and done away with the 'concept of private property' but cannot grasp the 'nature of private property', not to mention its abolition. Estranged labour must have been at its zenith there. The collapse of existing socialism proves its theoretical deficiencies and those of its followers in Western countries. However, Marx's communism, in his own words, still indicates the way to more human social relations. What is needed in existing socialism is not only liberalisation of capital and of its economy, but of the mode of workers' co-operation in the production process and in their social intercourse.

In modern capitalist society, on the other hand, what is needed is an understanding that the immense productive power of capital is our own social power and that we are producing the basis of universal individuality by producing the civilising power of capital. The problem is that very few understand the connection of Marx's theories to the 'nature of capital'.

Appendices

APPENDIX I
THE EDITING PROBLEMS OF *THE GERMAN IDEOLOGY*

All editions of *The German Ideology* hitherto available are almost apocryphal. Wataru Hiromatsu stated this scientifically in 1965,[1] causing a sensation among Japanese specialists.

'I Feuerbach' (hereafter GI) of *The German Ideology*, written by Marx and Engels[2] in 1845–46, is one of their most important works and is known as the birthplace of the so-called 'materialist interpretation of history'. However, GI was left unfinished, in Marx's phrase 'abandoned ... to the gnawing criticism of the mice all the more willingly as we have achieved our main purpose: self-clarification'.[3] For Japanese specialists it was not until Hiromatsu's work[4] appeared in 1974 that a scientific edition of GI became accessible. *Karl Marx-Frederick Engels Collected Works*, Vol.5 (Progress Publishers, 1976) and *The German Ideology* (Students' Edition) edited by C.J. Arthur (Lawrence & Wishart, 1974) give English-speaking readers access to GI.

However, both of them have editing problems and are not scientific enough. The latter, as it is a 'Students' Edition', is not intended to be scholarly. Paragraphs are often deleted and moved. The longest omission in the text is nearly two pages long.[5] This edition is a scissors-and-paste job. The former edition, on the other hand, is based on the new Russian edition and its arrangement of manuscripts is reliable. It contains the original sheet and page numbers. Although the arrangement of manuscripts is one of the main problems in editing GI, this is not all. GI is a result of the co-operation of Marx with Engels and the component manuscripts were written at different times. Consequently, a scientific edition must clearly reproduce the original text by specifying the text, insertions, notes, corrections, handwriting, etc. The reproduction of the text in the 1976 edition is still unsatisfactory. Consequently, a really scientific edition of GI is still unavailable in English.

A BIBLIOGRAPHICAL STUDY OF 'I FEUERBACH'

GI consists of the following three component manuscripts: 1. the so-called 'large volume', 2. the so-called 'small volume' and 3. half a sheet found by S.Bahne in 1962 (hereafter {B}). In the following, I will examine them one by one. Each sheet of the manuscripts is divided into four pages (hereafter cited as a to d) and carries two kinds of numbers: a sheet number in Engels' hand and a page number in Marx's. Hereafter, the sheet numbers are shown in { } and the page numbers in [ ] respectively.

The 'Large Volume'

The 'large volume' consists of the following two groups which may be divided into three blocks:

1. The First Group
   I. The First Block: {6}a=[8] to {11}c=[29]
   II. The Second Block: {20}b=[30] to {21}d=[35]
2. Second Group: The Third Block: {84}a=[40] to {92}a=[72]

The Meaning of Marginal Notes and Sheet Numbers

The pages [8],[9], [10] ({6}), [24] ({10}) and [28] ({11}) carry 'Feuerbach', and [28] ({11}) carries 'Bauer' in the margin. The crossed out paragraphs in the 'large volume' appear in the text of other parts of *The German Ideology*, i.e., 'II Saint Bruno' or 'III Saint Max'.[6] This implies the following:

1. To begin with, Marx and Engels did not have a plan for GI and wrote 'II' and 'III'.
2. Later, the authors changed their minds and planned GI.
3. Thus for GI they selected the sheets on Feuerbach in the manuscripts of 'II' and 'III' by making the marginal notes.

The sheet numbers of the 'large volume' are the numbers for 'II Saint Bruno' and 'III Saint Max' and the 'large volume', so the main body of GI is merely a selection from the manuscripts of 'II' and 'III'. Consequently, the missing sheet numbers do not indicate that the manuscripts are missing.

The Meaning of the Unnumbered Pages

On the other hand, some pages, e.g., {11}d and {20}a, were not numbered by Marx and the whole texts are crossed out. This implies that Marx did not use those pages for GI. These sheets were later paged by Marx for GI. Thus we generally follow page numbers but not sheet numbers when looking at the editing problems of GI.

The Number of Missing Pages

According to the sheet numbers, not to speak of the numbers after {92}, {1} to {5}, {12} to {19}, and {22} to {83} are missing. However, according to the page numbers, the number of missing pages is at most 11: [1] to [7] and [36] to [39]. It is not clear that the manuscripts began with page [1], unless we take the 'small volume' into account.

The 'Small Volume'

The 'small volume' consists of five numbered ({1}[7] to {5}) and two unnumbered sheets. None of them has any page number. {3} and {5} were numbered by Engels but others ({1}, {2} and {4}) by E. Bernstein. In form and in substance, {4} succeeds {3}. Thus, although Engels did not number {4}, it is clear that he took {3}, {4} and {5} as a series.

As far as the two unnumbered sheets (hereafter cited as {1?} and {2?} after V. Adoratskij's example) are concerned, {1?}a-b is obviously the draft of {1}. However, {2} is not a fair copy of {1}c-d & {2?} but a completely new addition. As I mentioned above, Marx numbered none of them. This might relate to the nature of the sheets. For example, {1}, half a sheet, is the Introduction to GI.

{B}

In 1962 S. Bahne discovered two and a half sheets of *The German Ideology* at IISG (The International Institute for Social History) in Amsterdam. Two of them are thought to belong to GI: 1) the one with a number in Marx's hand, i.e., [29]. In form and in substance, there is no doubt about its position in GI; 2) the other is {B}. {B} is half a sheet consisting of two (c and d) pages with numbers 1 and 2 – deciphered 'probably in Marx's hand' – and a marginal note 'Feuerbach'. Thus in recent editions of GI,[8] these numbers are thought to be for GI, i.e., [1] and [2]. But there is a problem. As Hiromatsu asserts, the crossed-out paragraphs in these pages appear on the first two pages of 'II Saint Bruno'. Thus there is a possibility that the page numbers are for 'II Saint Bruno' from which they were extracted. Later we will re-examine this problem.

The Core of the Editing Problems

The core of the editing problems is where we should arrange the 'small volume' and {B} in relation to the 'large volume'. If the sheet and page numbers of the three component manuscripts – 'large volume', 'small volume' and {B} – were consistent, there would not be any serious problems in editing GI, but they were numbered by different people at different times. When we are looking at the editing problems, we should note:

1. The page numbers of {B} and sheet numbers of the 'small volume' are not consistent, e.g., {1} and {2} were numbered by E. Bernstein.
2. Engels thought {3}-{4}-{5} were a series, but what Marx thought of them is not clear, because he did not number them. In *Ludwig Feuerbach and The End of German Classical Philosophy* (1888) Engels says that he had read GI again before going to print with the work.[9] Consequently {3} to {5} could have been numbered then.
3. As I have already mentioned, the 'large volume' is a bunch of extracts and is not a completed draft at all. Thus, arranging the 'small volume' and {B} in relation to the 'large volume' does not constitute the final format of GI. Topics are repeated from place to place, tempting editors into a scissors-and-paste job, but we should resist this temptation.

4. Thus, even if the page numbers of {B} (1 and 2) were [1] and [2], i.e., the first two pages of the 'large volume', it would mean that they were only additions to the first group of the 'large volume'.
5. Marx changed his way of numbering pages on the last page of sheet {6}. To begin with, using Engels' sheet numbers, Marx numbered sheet {6} with [6b] to [6e] – not with [6a] to [6d] – and the first pages of {7} and {8} with [7a] and [8a]. Then he changed his mind. He renumbered [6b]~[6e] which became [8]~[11] and paged the following sheets with [12] and after. Why? What is the implication of this change? In the next section, I will answer these questions by investigating the 'small volume' and the 'large volume'.

THE 'SMALL VOLUME'

The Relationship between {1?} & {2?} and {1} & {2}

In form and in substance, {1} is a fair copy of {1?}a-b, but {2} is not that of {1?}c-d & {2?}. {1?}c-d & {2?} does not appear in the fair copies {1} or {2}. Actually, {1?}c-d & {2?} is one page long and shares the theme with [6e] (=[11]), i.e., 'the first premise' of 'any interpretation of history'. However, the term 'the mode of production' appears here for the first time, and thus to eliminate this text is unacceptable.

{2} is a completely new addition on the nature of the German ideologists which was announced beforehand in the crossed-out paragraph on {1?}b-c:

> We preface therefore the specific criticism of individual representatives of this movement with a few general observations, elucidating the ideological premises common to all of them .... We immediately direct the remarks at Feuerbach because he is the only person who has at least made real progress and whose works can be examined *de bonne foi*.

Consequently, it is safe to say, {1?} & {2?} were written earlier than {1} & {2}.

MEGA2 places {2} before {1}, but this is incorrect. The contents of {2} can be summarised in the proposition that 'German criticism has, right up to its latest efforts, never quitted the realm of philosophy'. This corresponds to the closing words of {1}:

> If we wish to rate at its true value this philosophic charlatanry, which awakens even in the breast of the honest German citizen a glow of national pride, ... we must look at the whole spectacle from a standpoint beyond the frontiers of Germany.

Consequently, {1} should be placed before {2}.

The Relationship between {3} & {4} and {5}

In form and in substance, {4} follows {3}. The last sentence of {3} is completed in {4}. On the other hand, {5}a opens with the following sentence: 'The fact is, therefore, that definite individuals who are productively active in a definite way enter into these definite social and political relations.' This connection is expounded in {3} and {4} in the case of the so-called 'formations which precede the capitalist mode of production'. For example:

1. ' ... the whole internal structure of the nation itself depends on the stage of development reached in its production and its internal and external intercourse'. ({3}a)
2. 'The social structure is, therefore, limited to an extension of family ...'. ({3}b)
3. 'For this reason the whole structure of society is based on this communal ownership ...'. ({3}c)
4. 'The hierarchical structure of landownership, and the armed bodies of retainers associated with it, gave the nobility power over the serfs.' ({3}d)

Thus {5} should be understood as the concluding part of {3} and {4}. However, Hiromatsu thinks that {3} and {4} have nothing to do with {5}, and places them separately in his edition.

The Relationship between {1?}-{2?} and {3}-{4}-{5}

{3}-{4}-{5} are supposed to follow {1?}-{2?}, because the content of {3} and {4} corresponds to the closing words of {2?}. Compare the following quotations:

> The nature of individuals thus depends on the material conditions determining their production .... The form of this intercourse is again determined by production. ({2?})

> But not only the relation of one nation to others, but also the whole internal structure of the nation itself depends on the stage of development reached by its production and its internal and external intercourse. ({3})

Consequently, the order in the 'small volume' is thought to be {1?}-{2?}-{3}-{4}-{5}. However, {2} is not necessarily intended to be followed by {3} to {5}. We return to this problem later.

THE 'LARGE VOLUME'

The First Block: {6} to {11} ([8] to [29])

Here the concepts of the German ideologists, such as 'substance' and 'self-consciousness' of the Old Hegelians, and 'species', 'the Unique' and 'Man' of the Young Hegelians, are revealed to be mere abstractions of the historical development of the real individuals.

{6} to {8} ([8] to [19])

Here the idealist interpretation of history, which descends 'from heaven to earth' ([5]), is criticised. Marx and Engels ascend 'from earth to heaven' by investigating the production of life, i.e., the co-operation of real individuals. Production consists of the following five 'elements' or 'aspects':

1. 'The first historical fact is thus the production of the means to satisfy these needs, the production of material life itself.' ([11])

2. 'The second point is that the satisfaction of the first need ... leads to new needs'. ([12])
3. The production of other men. ([12])
4. A 'double relationship' of the production of life. ([13]) The production of life appears as a natural and as a social relationship. By social, the co-operation of several individuals is understood. 'It follows from this that a certain mode of production is always combined with a certain mode of cooperation, or social stage, and this mode of co-operation is itself a "productive force".' ([13])
5. 'Man also possesses "consciousness".' ([13])

{9} to {11} ([20] to [29])

Marx and Engels understand history as 'the succession of the separate generations'. Each generation exploits the materials, the capital funds, the productive forces handed down to it by all preceding generations, and thus, on the one hand, continues traditional activity in completely changed circumstances and, on the other, modifies old circumstances with a completely changed activity ([20]). The reproduction process becomes a dialectical process.

Consequently, the authors aim to 'give the writing of history a materialistic basis' ([11]) by observing 'this fundamental fact in all its significance and all its implications' and by according 'it its due importance' ([11]). On the one hand, they aim to analyse the whole material production and intercourse of individuals (civil society) at each stage as a definite mode of production and intercourse corresponding to a definite stage in the development of productive forces. On the other, they plan to see how real individuals change the mode of production.

The second Block: {20}b and {21}d ([30] to [35])

This is in fact an appendix to the first block and the materialist basis of the ideas of the ruling class is clarified.

TheThird Block: {84} to {92} ([40] to [72])

{84} to {90} ([40] to [67])

Here the development of private property since 'estate capital' ([43]) and the necessity of communism are investigated as the development of the division of labour,[10] or of productive forces and social intercourse. 'Empirical observation' brings out 'the connection of the social and political structure with production' ({5}) without any mystification and speculation.

{91} to {92} ([68] to [72])

This is an appendix to {84} – {90} and the statements that the relationship of forms of states and legal relations have their roots in the material conditions of life.

The Order of the 'Small Volume' and the 'Large Volume'

The Meaning of Marx's Change in Numbering

As we have already seen, to begin with Marx numbered the sheets [6b] to [6e] using Engels' sheet numbers. Then he changed the numbers of the pages to [8], [9], [10] and [11]. This implies:

1. that there were five sheets preceding [6b], or, he did not need to use the sheet number. Moreover, there was another page preceding [6b], i.e., [6a], because he began numbering pages with [6b]. The number of these missing manuscripts happened to be the same as that of the 'small volume' which actually consists of {1},{2},{3},{4},{5} and a page long draft, i.e., {1?}c~d & {2?};
2. that there were seven preceding pages, or he did not change [6b] into [8]. In other words, the five sheets and the page preceding {6}b were seven pages long in all. To be accurate, we are talking only about the main body of the text and are hereby excluding the number of pages of the Preface and Introduction. The volume is almost the same as {3}-{4}-{5};
3. that Marx found his original plan of numbering no longer worked, or, he did not need to give it up. For example, [6e] covered the same content as that of the preceding page. In this case, the preceding page was given up, because Marx changed [6e] into [11], meaning to use it for GI.

The Order of the 'Small Volume' and the 'Large Volume'

From all the observations above we can say that the 'small volume' consisted of {1?}, {2?}, {3}, {4}, {5}. Then Marx made the fair copy of {1?}a-c ({1}) and added {2}, but did not make a fair copy of {1?}c-d & {2?}. At this point, Marx expected that the order of the drafts was going to be {1}-{2}-{3}-{4}-{5} followed by the examination of Feuerbach's works ({1?}c-d & {2?} and the 'large volume'). Soon after, when Marx numbered {6}d and after from [6e], he found the content of {1?}c-d & {2?} was also covered there. Thus {1?}c-d & {2?} became useless, and {6} was renumbered.

If we assume that [6a] is {1?}c-d & {2?}, we can explain the change in numbering. In quantity, {1?}c-d & {2?} are actually one page long and share their theme with [6e](=[11]). In quantity, {3}, {4} and {5} are actually seven pages long. {1} and {2} have not been numbered by Marx from the start, probably because {1} is the Preface and {2} belongs to another chapter.

On the other hand, if we presume that the page numbers of {B} (1 and 2) are the page numbers for GI ([1] and [2]), the number of missing sheets and pages are four and five ([3] to [7]). As we have already seen, 1 and 2 are not likely to be [1] and [2]. Also it is not likely that only five out of 20 pages (four sheets) were to be used. In the 'large volume', for example, 25 out of 32 pages (eight sheets) are used. Moreover, this cannot explain the change in numbering.

Even if we assume that all seven pages preceding [8] are missing, the following points cannot be explained: 1. why do the seven missing pages happen to consist of five sheets? 2.why does Marx suddenly change his numbering in {6}e?

From all the observations above, we can say that: at the point when Marx extracted the 'large volume', and wrote {1?} and {2?}, there were five sheets preceding {6}, but at the point when he wrote {1} and {2}, there were five sheets ({1} to {5}) and 1 page ({1?}c-d & {2?}). Marx started his numbering {6} and after from [6b], with a plan to use {1?}c~d & {2?} as [6a], but when he reached [6e] he found {1?}c~d & {2?} were no longer needed. Only five sheets were supposed to precede {6}. Thus his new plan seemed to be {1} to {5} then {6}({1?}c-d & {2?}) then {7} to {21}. {1} and {2} were not paged because they did not belong to the main body of text for GI, as we shall see in the next section. However, we should also note that even this arrangement does not constitute the final format of GI, because the 'large volume' is incomplete.

The Chapters of 'I Feuerbach'

In GI similar chapter titles can be found on {1?}c and {2}a: '1 The Ideology in General, especially the German Philosophy' and 'A The Ideology in General, especially in German'; as I have already mentioned, {2} is a completely new addition and has no direct connection with {1?}c. Let us investigate this problem.

Both '1'and 'A' imply that originally GI was to consist of more than two chapters. The first chapter is, without doubt, 'A The Ideology in General, especially in German'. The question is the title of chapter 'B', and where it starts and ends. We can say with reasonable certainty that the title of chapter 'B' is 'Feuerbach', because this section of *The German Ideology* is 'I Feuerbach'.

On the other hand, as I have already quoted above, the crossed-out paragraph on {1?}b~c says that the critical observations on the German philosophy in general, i.e., chapter 'A', is brief and is immediately followed by a criticism of Feuerbach, i.e., chapter 'B Feuerbach'. Thus chapter 'A' seems to consist of {2} only. Consequently, {6} and that which follows (including {1?}c-d & {2?}) makes up 'B Feuerbach'[11] which is merely a collection of extractions from 'II Saint Bruno' and 'III Saint Max'. Thus it contains criticisms of the works of Bruno Bauer and Max Stirner, and others.

THE MISSING PAGES ([36] TO [39])

According to Marx's page numbers, four pages (one sheet) are missing: [36] to [39]. They seem to belong to the third block rather than the second, because page [35] is complete, but page [40] opens with an incomplete sentence on the 'difference between natural instruments of production and those created by civilisation'. Obviously, the page number indicates that Marx planned to use almost all the sentences in future. Naturally, therefore, he had intended to use the preceding pages about the development of the division of labour, i.e., of property relations.

Hiromatsu presumes that the missing pages [36] to [39] might be {3} and {4}, i.e., that only one page is missing, and that {5} is a variation of [12] to [16] ({7}b to {8}a). He asserts that the description of the historical development of the division of labour in {84} to {92} will be completed by placing {3}-{4} before them. But this requires some explanation.

First, Marx did not number the pages [36] to [38].

Second, although {2} is not necessarily followed by {3} & {4}, {3} & {4} are inseparable.

Third, {5} cannot be a variation of [12] to [16]. {5} was written after [12] to [16]. If the latter was a fair copy of {5}, a fair copy of {6} had been made beforehand.

Fourth, {3} & {4} is a little inconsistent with the text in {84} to {92} ([40] to [72]). Page [40] opens with the statement that 'Our investigation hitherto started from the instruments of production', but the investigations in {3} & {4} and in {84}c ([42]) to {87}b ([53]) do not start 'from the instruments of production'. This does not mean that the instruments of production do not play an important role in [42] to [53], but that they are not always consistent with each other. This indicates slightly different views between Marx and Engels.

THE POSITION OF {B}

The position of {B} is hard to determine, because the pages after [8] are still incomplete. Let us examine this problem here by investigating its numbers and content.

C.J. Arthur's 'Students' Edition' and the Japanese version (1976) of the *Karl Marx-Friedrich Engels Werke* (Bd.3, 1958), place {B} after page [29], which was also found by Bahne in 1962. In substance, {B} succeeds [29]. But the page numbers of {B} are 1 and 2, not [30] and [31].

Other recent editions of GI place {B} in front of {6} as if they were the first two pages of the 'large volume'. However, as I have already mentioned, the page numbers of {B} are likely ones for the draft 'II Saint Bruno'.

Furthermore, this arrangement distorts the structure of the 'large volume'. The contents of sheets {6} to {11} fall into the following two categories:

1) {6}a=[8] to {8}d=[19]: 'the premise of all human existence, and therefore, of all history' ([11]) = 'processing the nature through human labour' ([18]) = analysis of the co-operation and the social intercourse of real individuals
2) {9}a=[20] to {11}c=[29]: 'history as the succession of the separate generations' = 'the revision of human beings by human labour' ([18])

On the other hand, {B} deals with 'philosophical' and 'real' emancipation. Thus placing {B} before {6} does not clarify the difference between the two categories but rather obscures them. I do not think it is correct to place {B} just before {6}. Consequently, as in Hiromatsu's edition, {B} should be contained as an Appendix.

CONCLUSIONS

The present editions can be schematised as follows:

MEGA2: Preface-{2}-{1} ({1?}a~c)*-{1?}c~d & {2?} -{3}~{5}~{B}-[8]~[35]-[40]~[72]

(* Contained in theApparatus Volume)

Bagaturija (MEC): Preface-{1}-{2} ({1?}c~d & {2?})*-{3}~{5}- {B}-[8]~[35]-[40]~[72]

(* Contained in a footnote.)

Hiromatsu: Preface-{1}({1?}a~c)*-{2}-[8]~[12]({1?}c~d & {2?})-[13]~[16]({5})-[29]~[35]- {3}-{4}-[40]~[72]-Appendix={B}

(* Contained as a variation.)

However, from all the observations above, I propose the following:

1) Preface-{1} ({1?}a-c)*-{2}-{1?}c-d & {2?}-{3}~{5}- [8]~[29]-[30]~[35]-[40]~[72]-Appendix={B}

(* Contained as a variation.)

2) Preface-{1} ({1?}a-c)*-{2}- {3}~{5}- [8]~[11] ({1?}c-d & {2?})*-[12]~[16]-[17]~[35]-[40]~[72]-Appendix={B}.

(* Contained as a variation.)

1) is very orthodox and may be more widely acceptable than 2) because of the position of ({1?}c-d & {2?}). But 2) clarifies the structure of GI more than 1).

Bagaturija's and *Marx-Engels Collected Works'* editions are quite persuasive, except for the position of {B}. However, the editions do not distinguish insertions from the main text, nor Marx's hand from Engels'. On the other hand, the edition in the MEGA2 *Probeband* has a 'Scientific Apparatus' which gives us vital information about the manuscripts, but its circulation is very limited and it is awkward to consult the 'Scientific Apparatus' while reading the texts. The best edition seems to be Hiromatsu's. It is useful even for those who do not agree with his edition. The best use of it can only be made by Japanese readers, because its explanatory notes on typefaces and abbreviations are in Japanese. However, the two English editions are not yet scientific enough. Thus a scientific edition in English is required before any specialised discussion on GI and Marx's interpretation of history can reasonably be expected to take place.

APPENDIX II
AN ASPECT OF MARX'S CRITIQUE OF POLITICAL ECONOMY: THE CYNICISM OF POLITICAL ECONOMY

Marx's lifework, from 1843[1] until his death in 1883, is termed 'a critique of political economy'. 'Political economy' in the title means, without doubt, classical political economists·[2] including Smith and Ricardo, especially economic categories used by them. The 'critique', on the other hand, means proposing a new totality by analysing both grounds of the formation of the economic categories and their limitations. Thus, Marx's system is his new presentation of economic categories in which the scientific adequacy and inadequacy of the economic categories of Smith and Ricardo are clarified. So far there is no problem.

Strangely, however, problems occur as soon as I say that the Ricardian concept of 'value' is not an exception. Smith's and Ricardo's determinations of 'value' are criticised by Marx as being a confusion between 'value' and 'price'[3] and are re-cast in Chapter 1 of *Capital*, Volume 1. However, it has been asserted:

1. that, as far as the 'substance of value' is concerned, there is no difference between political economists and Marx; and
2. that the only difference between them is whether they have the theory of 'the value-form' or not, as if there were no intrinsic connection between the social substance of value and the value-form. Studies made in the last few decades asserted so, whether they are conscious or not, by schematising the formation of Marx's value theory as: a conversion from the negation in the early 1840s to the acceptation of the Ricardian value theory in the late 1840s.[4] Even if the conversion had been real and Marx had become a Ricardian, Marx in the late 1840s would not have been Marx yet and the 1840s had belonged to pre-history in the formation of Marx's value theory.

However, this presumes that the whole history has been shown. This indicates that Marx's critique of economic categories, thus his critique of the scientific inadequacy of political economy, has not been fully understood yet. Thus in this chapter I throw a new light on the scientific inadequacy of political economists, by investigating Marx's concept 'the cynicism of political economy' in his EPM and POP.[5] Sections 2 and 3 investigate the meaning and causes of the 'cynicism' of political economy. Section 4 attempts to illustrate Marx's critique of the cynicism.

THE MEANING OF THE CYNICISM OF POLITICAL ECONOMY

Political Economists, Socialists and Marx

The thoughts and theories of English political economists and Marx are not and cannot be similar. Smith and Ricardo, on the one hand, understood the capitalist mode of production as natural and eternal, confusing two kinds of private property: as founded on the labour of its producer, and on the labour of other man. Marx, on the other hand, began to study political economy to analyse an 'essential contradiction' in modern civil society underlying the separation of civil society and political State.

However, the relation between political economists and Marx is not a simple 'opposition' but a 'critique'. It is not Marx but socialists who oppose political economists. Like Proudhon, Marx attempts to 'criticise' or 'transcend' the opposition between them. For Marx, political economists and socialists respectively represent wealth and poverty in capitalist society, and neither of them is scientific enough. Both of them are one-sided and neither of them grasps wealth and poverty as necessary aspects, or moments, of capitalist mode of production. Marx, on the other hand, expounds that capitalist relations of production and commerce consist of both moments, i.e., the relations contain the contradiction between wealth and poverty in themselves.

The Meaning of the Cynicism of Political Economy

By 'political economists represent wealth' Marx does not mean that they did not know the misery of working class but that they did not comprehend it from the 'essence (*Wesen*) of capital'. Smith opens his *Wealth of Nations* with the statement:

> The annual labour of every nation is the fund which originally supplies it with all the necessaries and conveniences of life which it annually consumes, and which consist always either in the immediate produce of labour, or in what is purchased with that produce from other nations.

Labour is the origin of wealth. This is the principle of the system of Adam Smith. This proposition and 'capital is accumulated labour' are the basis of his labour theory of value. If so, as a result of this principle, it should have followed that labourers are the richest and non-labourers are the poorest. On the other hand, the work of Smith, being 'the scientific reflection of state of national economy in England',[1] describes the miserable conditions of labourers more precisely than anyone else, which Marx named 'the cynicism of political economy' in EPM.[7]

The problem is not that he describes the miserable conditions but that he does not comprehend (*begreifen*) how the misery occurs from his principle. He does not realise any contradiction between his principle and its result. He does not comprehend that the labour which produces wealth on capitalist's side produces poverty on labourer's, nor that it is neither natural nor eternal but an historical form of labour, i.e., estranged labour, under the command of another man. Consequently, the term the 'cynicism of political economy' means that political economists are scientific on the one hand, insofar as they represent the real economic conditions in England, but, on the other hand, they are not scientific enough, insofar as they do not comprehend the conditions from the essence of capital, as Marx states:

> But then, as it [political economy] continues to develop, it is forced to cast off its *hypocrisy* and step forth *in all its cynicism*. This it does, without troubling its head for one moment about all the apparent contradictions to which this doctrine leads, by developing in a more one-sided way, and thus more sharply and more logically, the idea of *labour* as the sole *essence of wealth*, by showing that the conclusions of this doctrine, unlike the original conception, are *anti-human* and finally by delivering the death-blow to *ground rent* – that last *individual and natural* form of private property and source of wealth independent of the movement of labour, that expression of feudal property which has already become entirely economic and is therefore incapable of putting up any resistance to political economy. (MEC 3, p. 291; EW, pp. 342f: italics original)

CYNICISM AND THE THEORIES OF VALUE AND SURPLUS VALUE

The understanding of the essence of wealth concerns theories of value and surplus value. Thus Marx's criticism of the cynicism of political economy concerns the one-sidedness of those theories of political economists. Here we deal with the problem.

Marx criticises that classical political economy as being cynical but not the monetary or mercantile systems, and that 'political economists become increasingly cynical from Smith through Say to Ricardo, James Mill, etc'. (MEC 3, p. 291; EW, p. 343) For the monetary and mercantile systems, wealth is a condition external to man, i.e., precious metal. The agricultural system partly transformed the essence of wealth from a condition external to man into man by recognising only agricultural products as wealth.[8]

Smith completed the transformation by asserting 'labour in general' is the essence of wealth. By the proposition 'labour is the sole source of wealth', Smith meant 'the labour of worker is the sole source of capitalist's profit'. He investigates labour only as the source and does not care that the labour is the source of poverty of the worker, and that labour is his life-activity through which he becomes a man. Thus the more political economists complete their doctrine, the more they become cynical about the results of their doctrine.

> But this is only because their science develops more logically and more truly. Since they make private property in its active form the subject, thereby making man as non-being [*Unwesen*] the essence [*Wesen*], the contradiction in reality corresponds entirely

to the contradictory essence which they have accepted as their principle. (MEC 3, p. 292; EW, p. 343)

In short, only political economists recognise labour as the subjective essence of wealth, and observe estranged labour as a natural and eternal form of human labour. On the other hand, none of them investigates the meaning of 'abstract' and 'estranged' labour in the development of history.

This means, on the one hand, that they understand capital as accumulated labour, but, on the other, they do not grasp it as 'command' over the labour of other man. On the contrary, the understanding of capital leads them to confusing 'capitalist private property' with 'private property, as founded on the labour of its producer'. In the next section, let us examine the point further.

THE CAUSES OF CYNICISM

The Scientific Adequacy of Political Economists

The capitalist relations of production and commerce produce wealth, on the one hand, and poverty, on the other. Thus it shows only the scientific aspect of them that political economists cynically describes the misery of workers. Marx's criticism of the cynicism is not a moral one, as Marx supports Ricardo against Chevalier: 'Thus M. Chevalier accuses Ricardo of abstracting from morality. But Ricardo allows political economy to speak its own language. If the language is not that of moral, it is not the fault of Ricardo.' (MEC 3, pp. 310f; EW, pp. 362f)

Everywhere in EPM, Marx admits that the economic categories and laws of political economists are nothing but scientific reflections of the real movement – production and consumption – of capital, as he writes in the opening paragraph of 'FM: LP' (the so-called part 'Estranged Labour'): 'We have started out from the premises of political economy. We have accepted its language and its laws ...'. (MEC 3, p. 270; EW, p. 322).[9]

Naturally, Marx keeps the same estimation of political economists in POP:

Ricardo establishes the truth of his formula by deriving it from all economic relations, and by explaining in this way all phenomena, even those like rent, accumulation of capital and the relations of wages to profits, which at first sight seem to contradict it; it is precisely that which makes his doctrine a scientific system: ... (MEC 6, p. 124)

This scientific aspect of political economists can be summarised in their labour theory of value based on reducing commodities into labour, and capital into accumulated labour. In this sense, the cynicism of them is the result of their scientific character.

The Scientific Inadequacy of Political Economists

However, the cynicism is essentially the result of the scientific inadequacy of their theories of value and surplus value, because they understand capitalist relations of production one-sidedly. They do not comprehend how the misery of the labourer is necessary under capitalist relations, i.e., the antagonistic character of capitalist relation of production.

'Capitalist private property'[10] is a sort of private property 'which rests on the exploitation of the alien labour', but not 'individual private property, as founded on the labour of its proprietor'.[11] But political economists mistook the former as the latter by overlooking the exploitation[12] of labour in the process of capitalist production. They do not show the historical conditions which transform labour into the substance of value, accumulated labour into capital. In this sense, the cynicism of political economists is a necessary result of their scientific inadequacy. This is the starting-point for Marx's scientific system, as he writes:

> Political economy proceeds from the fact of the right of private property. It does not explain it. It grasps the material process of private property, the process through which it actually passes, in general and abstract formula which it then takes as laws. It does not comprehend these laws, i.e., it does not show how they arise from the essence of private property .... We now have to grasp the essential connection between the right of private property, greed, the separation of labour [wage], capital [profit] and landed property [rent], exchange and competition, value and the devaluation of man, monopoly and competition, etc. – the connection between this entire system of estrangement and the money system. (MEC 3, pp. 270f; EW, pp. 322f)

As in the abridged sentences in the quotation above, Marx criticises political economists for not explaining the origin of profit. He is going to comprehend the intrinsic connections between economic categories, or the origin of economic categories. Naturally, Marx keeps the same criticism of the inadequacy of political economists in POP. 'Economists explain how production takes place in the above-mentioned relations, but what they do not explain is how these relations themselves are produced, i.e., the historical movement which gave them birth'. (MEC 6, p. 162)

In short, neither Smith nor Ricardo understand the origin of economic categories and both understand them unhistorically, that is, as natural and eternal. Although the material of political economists is the activities of real man, they do not grasp the historical conditions and the intrinsic connections between them. They comprehend neither the historical character nor the antagonistic character of economic categories. Marx transcends these scientific inadequacies of political economists by extracting the essence of capital[13] and expounding the economic laws as necessary laws of capital.

MARX'S CRITIQUE OF THE CYNICISM

We have seen that the cynicism of political economists emerges from their scientific adequacy and from the inadequacy of their theories of value and surplus value. Now it is time to investigate Marx's own theories.

Marx claims that Smith has revealed the subjective essence of wealth only 'within the realm of private property', (MEC 3, p. 290; EW, p. 342) i.e., ahistorically. The only form of labour Smith knows and recognises is wage-labour and he does not grasp it in historical context. However, Marx grasps it as 'estranged labour', the labour under the command of other man[14] through a two-fold analysis of the process of capitalist production, the zenith in the development of private property. The logic of EPM, his first system, can be summarised as follows:

1. Private property develops from landed property to capital. The reasons why capital is the zenith of private property can be comprehensible from the subjective and objective essences of it, i.e., labour in general and value, in which all social meanings are lost and they have reached the peak of abstraction.
2. As the essence of capital includes that of any sorts of private property, the historical development of landed property to capital is necessary. Or the 'civilised victory of movable capital' is contained in the concept of capital.
3. The development of economic systems, from the mercantile through Quesnay to Smith, can be understood as a necessary result of the development in private property.
4. As the relation of private property consists of capital and labour, which presuppose and exclude each other, it 'constitutes private property in its developed relation of contradiction: a vigorous relation, therefore, driving towards resolution'. (MEC 3, p. 294; EW, p. 345)
5. Logically, the right of private property is a result of estranged labour. Estranged labour is the 'essence' of private property and the right of private property is the 'concept' of private property.[15] Estranged labour, the essence of private property, reveals that capital is the power to command the labour of other man, that capital is self-increasing value, and that the misery of the labourer is a necessary result of estranged labour. For Marx, 'political economy has merely formulated the laws of estranged labour'.

To sum up, the subjective essence of capital, i.e., estranged labour, enables Marx to comprehend economic laws of political economists as necessary laws of capital, to comprehend history hitherto as prehistory of human society and to formulate the future social relations as the abolition of estranged labour. Reducing commodities into labour, and capital into accumulated labour, represents the scientific adequacy and inadequacy of political economists.

CONCLUSIONS

The Ricardian labour theory of value is the best of all classical labour theory of value. But it is not an exception to Marx's critique of economic categories, that is, of political economy. It has scientific adequacy and inadequacy due to his analytical method. On the one hand, Ricardo revealed the subjective essence of wealth by reducing commodities to labour and capital to accumulated labour. But, on the other, he abstracted all the historical conditions which give them historical forms: which make labour 'commodities' and accumulated labour 'capital'. Because of this methodological inadequacy, political economists cannot comprehend that wealth and poverty are the two necessary elements of capitalists' relations of production, nor recognise the contradiction between his principle and a result of it: that labour is the sole source of wealth and the labourer suffers most under capitalist conditions.

Marx characterised the two contradicting sides of political economists as 'the cynicism of political economy' in EPM and attempts to transcend it. To begin with, Marx extracts 'estranged labour' as 'the essence of private property in general' through a two-fold analysis of the process of capitalist production. The essence serves as the basis of comprehending economic laws as the necessary laws of capital, as the laws of 'estranged labour'. 'Estranged labour' (the labour under the command of another man) explains easily that the labour which produces wealth for capitalist produces poverty for the labourer, and that accumulated labour increases itself in the process of production through commanding the labour of another man.

Moreover, 'estranged labour' enables Marx to comprehend the necessity for the development of private property, of economic systems. 'Estranged labour' is the core which unites three elements of Marxism: a critique of political economy, socialism and philosophy. Marx's critique of the cynicism of political economy is the key to his critique of political economy which concerns the theories of value and surplus value. Current interpretations of Marx's theories of value and surplus value should be re-examined from this point of view.

NOTES

FOREWORD

1. In T. Carver (ed.), *The Cambridge Companion to Marx* (Cambridge & New York, 1991), pp. 23–54.
2. See T. Carver, *Engels* (Oxford: Oxford University Press, 1981 and repr.), ch. 7.
3. S. Collini (ed.), *On Liberty and other Writings: with The Subjection of Women and Chapters on Socialism* (Cambridge: Cambridge University Press, 1989).
4. W. Hiromatsu (ed.), *Die deutsche Ideologie* (Tokyo: Kawadeshobo, 1974).
5. John Plamenatz, *Man and Society*, vol. 2: *A Critical Examination of Some Important Social and Political Theories from Machiavelli to Marx* (London: Longmans, 1963); David McLellan, *Marx before Marxism* (London: Macmillan, 1970).
6. István Mészáros, *Marx's Theory of Alienation* (London: Merlin, 1970).
7. For a new translation of the classic text, see Karl Marx, 'Preface' to 'A Contribution to the Critique of Political Economy', in *Later Political Writings* (trans. and ed. Terrell Carver) (Cambridge: Cambridge University Press, 1996 and repr.), pp. 158–62; for a classic assessment and reading of this text, see G.A. Cohen, *Karl Marx's Theory of History: A Defence* (Oxford: Oxford University Press, 1978).
8. See, for example, T. Carver, 'Reading Marx: Life and Works', in Carver (ed.), *Cambridge Companion to Marx*, p. 15; C.J. Arthur, *Dialectics of Labour: Marx and his Relation to Hegel* (Oxford: Blackwell, 1986), pp. 141–6.
9. Frederick Engels, 'Speech at the Graveside of Karl Marx', in Karl Marx and Frederick Engels, *Selected Works* in one volume (London: Lawrence & Wishart, 1968 and repr.), pp. 429–30; for a discussion of Engels and Aveling on the Marx–Darwin relationship, see T. Carver, *Marx and Engels: The Intellectual Relationship* (Brighton: Harvester/Wheatsheaf, 1983), pp. 135–6.
10. See T. Carver, *The Postmodern Marx* (Manchester: Manchester University Press, 1998), ch. 9, 'Philosophy and Politics: Marx's Hegel', pp. 181–205.
11. See Christopher J. Arthur, 'Engels as Interpreter of Marx's Economics', in Christopher J. Arthur (ed.), *Engels Today: A Centenary Appreciation* (Basingstoke: Macmillan, 1996), pp. 173–209; Christopher J. Arthur, 'The Myth of "Simple Commodity Production"', *MEGA-Studien*, 1997/2, p. 191.
12. Carver, *Engels*, Chapter 6.

PREFACE

1. See MEC, 3, p. 355.
2. See CAP 1, p. 100. It is surprising that only a very few commentators have investigated the meaning of this phrase.
3. See CAP 1, p. 103.
4. See chapter 7 of this book. In my understanding EPM becomes fully understandable only when readers understand the 'general essence of private property' and the 'concept of private property'.
5. G, p. 105.

CHAPTER 1

1. 'Communism and the Augsburg Allgemeine Zeitung' by Karl Marx, *Rheinische Zeitung*, 16 October 1842, in MEC 1, p. 220.
2. Ibid.
3. MEC 3, p. 321.
4. MEC 1, p. 215.
5. MEC 1, p. 219.
6. Marx's letter to Ruge in September 1843.
7. MEC 3, p. 321.
8. *Grundrisse*, Penguin Books, p. 105.
9. MEC 3, p. 179.
10. MEC 3, p. 180.
11. Marx's letter to Ruge in September 1843.
12. MEC 3, p. 179.
13. MEC 3, p. 180.
14. Ibid.
15. MEC 3, p. 181.
16. MEC 3, p. 181.
17. Ibid.
18. MEC 3, p. 180f.
19. MEC 3, p. 181.
20. MEC 3, p. 220.
21. For detail see Chapter 6 of this book. Marx uses 'social' as equivalent to 'human', e.g., 'social = human'. This is very important in understanding Marx's view of socialism and of 'social property' in *Capital*, Vol. 1. Here, however, we should note that it was not French socialism but Hegel's *Philosophy of Right* with which Marx started his critical study.
22. MEC 3, p. 179.
23. MEC 3, p. 166.
24. MEC 3, p. 165.
25. MEC 3, p. 172.
26. MEC 3, p. 226.
27. MEC 3, p. 181.
28. Marx's Letter to Arnold Ruge in September 1843.
29. Thesis IV in 'Theses on Feuerbach' (1845).
30. Marx's letter to J. B. Schweitzer dated 24 January 1865, in *Karl Marx – Frederick Engels Selected Works in three volumes* (Progress Publishers, 1977), Vol. 2, p. 26.
31. MEC 1, p. 220.
32. MEC 3, p. 168.

CHAPTER 2

1. See Appendix I.
2. The terms 'formation', 'epoch' and 'progressive' are technical terms of geology and are to be understood as such. 'Progressive' does not mean the line of development is the necessary and the only one.
3. SW, p. 390.
4. In the strict sense, the antagonism between country and town begins in feudal property, although {3}c says 'We already find the antagonism of town and country' in the ancient mode of property.
5. In order to comprehend the antagonism between country and town, the essence of private property is to be grasped as 'commanding power over labour of other men', or, the advantages of capital over landed property cannot be comprehended. If Marx thought that civilisation begins only with the ancient mode of production, there might

not be any great difference between Marx and Engels on this point, but I do not think it likely.

6. See MEC 3, p. 247 or EW, p. 295.
7. See Chapter 10 of this book.
8. MEC 38, p. 96.
9. G, p. 706 or MEGA2, II-1, Teil 2, p. 582.
10. Engels had never used the term 'estrangement', but shared a similar view with Marx on capitalist production. For example:

> What are we to think of a law [of competition] which can only assert itself through periodic upheavals? It is certainly a natural law based on the unconsciousness of the participants ... . Carry on production consciously as human beings – not as dispersed atoms without consciousness of your species – and you have overcome all these artificial and untenable antitheses. (MEC 3, pp. 433f)

11. For example, see Chapter 9 of this book.
12. G. Bagaturija, 'The Structure and the Contents of the First Chapter of *The German Ideology* by K. Marx and F. Engels' in *Problems in Philosophy*, October-November, 1965.
13. F. Engels, 'Book Review: Marx's *Contribution to A Critique of Political Economy'* (1859). (MEC 16, p. 470)
14. See Part III, Chapter II of his *Anti-Dühring* in MEC 25, p. 254 or Chapter III of his *Socialism: Utopian and Scientific* in: *Marx/Engels Selected Works in one volume*, Progress Publishers, p. 411.
15. CAP 1, p. 102 .
16. SW, p. 389f.
17. CAP 1, p. 103.
18. MEC 3, p. 299 or EW, p. 351.
19. Ibid.
20. Marx also writes in the Preface to *A Critique of Political Economy* that GI was abandoned 'to the gnawing criticism of mice all the more willingly as we had achieved our main purpose – self-clarification'. This 'self-clarification' has been used by the Soviet Marxists to negate Marx's works preceding GI , especially EPM, in order to make Soviet society an exception to the criticism of 'crude communism' there. This has been successful so long as it found wider support among Western followers, but it is a crude understanding of the passage. In the context, it does not support their views at all.

CHAPTER 3

1. SW, p. 390.
2. For a detailed examination, see Chapters 4, 5 and 9 of this book.
3. In his letter to J. B. Schweitzer (dated January 24, 1865) , Marx writes:

> 'During my stay in Paris in 1844 I came into personal contact with Proudhon ... . In the course of lengthy debates, often lasting all night, I infected him to his great injury with Hegelianism, which, owing to his lack of German, he could not study properly. After my expulsion from Paris Herr *Karl Grün* continued what I had begun. As a teacher of German philosophy he had, besides, the advantage over me that he understood nothing about it himself.' (Karl Marx-Friedrich Engels *Selected Works in three volumes*, Progress Publishers, Moscow, 1977, Volume Two, p. 26).

4. Shigeyuki Sato, *Studies on Proudhon*, Bokutakusha, Tokyo, 1975, p. 367.
5. See Chapters 4 and 5 of this book.
6. Sato, op. cit., p. 88.
7. See MEC 6, p. 169. However, readers must note that this criticism does not mean Marx's categories have life in themselves, but that Proudhon is ranked lower than Hegel. Proudhon shares the speculative character of Hegelian dialectics, but his

category does not have life in it. Thus, 'The sequence of categories has become a sort of *scaffolding*.' (MEC 6, p. 169)

8. Marx's letter to J. B. Schweitzer dated January 24, 1865. See Karl Marx-Friedrich Engels *Selected Works in three volumes*, Volume Two, (Progress Publishers, Moscow, 1977), p. 26.
9. See MEC 6, p. 162. The importance of this point has been little noticed. This implies that Marx, Proudhon and political economists have not been fully understood yet.
10. Marx's letter to J. B. Schweitzer dated January 24, 1865, op. cit., p. 26.
11. Ibid.
12. See Chapters 3 and 4 of this book.
13. Shigeyuki Sato, *Studies on Proudhon*, Bokutakusha, Tokyo, 1975, p. 81.
14. Ibid, p. 84.
15. Ibid, p. 100.
16. Ibid, p. 133.
17. Pierre Ansart, *Sociologie de Proudhon*, Presses Universitaires de France, Paris, 1967, p. 43.
18. Ibid, chapter 2 § 2.
19. Keiichi Sakamoto, *Marxism and Utopia*, Kinokuniya, Tokyo, 1970, p. 118.
20. Sato, op. cit., p. 203.
21. 'First Observation' in Chapter Two of POP deals with the difference between 'analysis' and 'abstraction'. See, in particular, MEC 6, p. 163.
22. Sato, op. cit., p. 149.
23. Sato, op. cit., pp. 133, 148. Sato asserts: 'In Proudhon's *System of Economic Contradictions* the necessity for the continual realisation of justice and evil are corroborated simultaneously. Thus, it is clear that the necessity for the final victory of justice is not clarified in his book.' (Sato, op. cit., p. 161)
24. Sato, op. cit., p. 149.
25. MEGA2, II-3, Teil 4, p. 1449. Karl Marx, *Theories of Surplus Value*, Part III, Progress Publishers, 1971, p. 500.
26. Note the profound problem behind this confusion by Smith. Ricardo's criticism of Smith has both strong points and weaknesses. See Chapters 4 and 5 of this book.
27. See Chapter 4 of this book.
28. Here 'historical' does not mean history qua history, but historical conditions which each category expresses.
29. See Marx's criticism of political economists in *Economic and Philosophical Manuscripts of 1844* (MEC 3, p. 271). See also Chapter 4 of this book.
30. Editor's note 'b' in MEC 6, p. 198.
31. Note this with regard to his value theory in EPM. See Chapter 4, first section, of this book.
32. Proudhon gives 'property' an independent chapter: Chapter Eleven says 'Eighth Phase Property'.
33. See MEC 6, p. 179.
34. MEC 3, p. 303. For further detail, see Chapter 10 of this book.

CHAPTER 4

1. 'On Proudhon' (Marx's letter to J. B. Schweitzer dated 24 January 1865), *Karl Marx-Friedrich Engels Selected Works in three volumes*, Vol. 2 (Progress Publishers: Moscow, 1977), p. 26.
2. 'Preface' to *A Contribution to the Critique of Political Economy* (1859), in SW, p. 390.
3. In POP, Marx contrasts Ricardo, Bray and Hegel with Proudhon. This is neither to defend them from Proudhon's attacks nor to criticise Proudhon by using their theories. It is to illustrate that Proudhon has not transcended Ricardo the economist or Bray the Ricardian socialist. It is expressed best in the following quotation:

> He [Proudhon] wants to be the synthesis.... He wants to soar as the man of science above the bourgeois and the proletarians; he is merely the petty bourgeois, continually tossed back and forth between capital and labour, political economy and communism. (MEC 6, p. 178)

Stressing the scientific aspect of the Ricardian value theory in Chapter One and the methodological critique of him in Chapter Two of POP, albeit indirectly, is not a contradiction. On the contrary, a careful investigation of Chapter One reveals that the Ricardian value theory opposed to Proudhon is not his but the one re-read by Marx. Surprisingly few studies have clarified this. They have analysed the two chapters of POP separately. As a result, Marx's methodological and theoretical critique of Ricardo's 'cost of production' has been completely overlooked. The interpretation follows that in POP Marx 'accepted' or 'affirmed' the Ricardian value theory. I would like to argue against this undialectical interpretation of Marx's formation process in Chapter 8 of this book. The point is that Chapter One of POP is to be understood with regard to his methodological critique of Ricardo in Chapter Two.

Similarly, Bray is contrasted with Proudhon in order to show that Proudhon has no originality as a utopian interpreter of the Ricardian value theory. Likewise, Hegel is opposed to Proudhon, albeit his dialectics has nothing to do with Hegel's, in order to rail against methodological confusion. Marx illustrates on the one hand that Proudhon's dialectics have the same speculative structure as Hegel's, i.e., he understands economic categories as eternal by inverting the relationship between categories and real relations; on the other, that Proudhon's dialectics are doomed as speculative dialectics. Since his categories have no life in themselves, they need help for development from outside.

4. MEGA2, II-3, Teil 4, p. 1499. *Theories of Surplus Value*, Part III (Progress Publishers: Moscow 1971), p. 500.
5. See Marx's letter to J.B. Schweitzer dated 24 January 1865, in Karl Marx-Friedrich Engels *Selected Works in three volumes*, Vol. 2 (Progress Publishers, Moscow, 1977), p. 26. Marx came into personal contact with Proudhon in 1844 in Paris and 'infected him to his great injury with Hegelianism'. Both Marx and Proudhon attempt to criticise private property in the form of a critique of political economy by using a dialectical method. However, since Proudhon does not pursue the real movement of capitalist production, his dialectics have to be speculative just like the Hegelian. In other words, his critique of political economy is not a critique of economic categories.
6. MEGA2, II-3, Teil 4, p. 1499. *Theories of Surplus Value*, Part III (Progress Publishers: Moscow, 1971), p. 500.
7. See Part Three of this book. To ignore this fact is to misunderstand the whole of Marx's formation process.
8. As to this concept, see Chapter 10 of this book.
9. MEGA2, II-3, Teil 4, p. 1389. *Theories of Surplus Value*, Part III, pp. 258f.
10. CAP 1, pp. 102f. As Marx asserts in the 'First Observation', this is a necessary result of not pursuing the historical movement of production relations (MEC 6, p. 162).
11. G, p. 101.
12. Ibid.
13. MEGA2, II-3, Teil 3, p. 816. *Theories of Surplus Value*, Part III, p. 164. See also Footnotes 33, 34 and 35 of CAP 1, pp.173–6.
14. This brings us to the point I would like to make in the next chapter: Marx's critique of Ricardo's value theory in POP. What we should notice here, with regard to this, is Marx's following remark: 'There is no ready-constituted proportional relation' [of supply to demand], but only a constituting movement.' (MEC 6, p. 134)
15. See Editor's Note b in MEC 6, p. 198. As to how Proudhon explains the genesis of economic categories, see MEC 6, pp. 112 and 198f.

16. See Preface to the *Second Edition* of CAP 1, p. 103.
17. See, for example, MEC 6, pp. 111 and 162.
18. See G, p. 100f.
19. See, for example, EPM (MEC 3, pp. 281 and 289) and *Notes on James Mill* (MEC 3, p. 221f).
20. G, p. 102.
21. This brings us to another point which is going to be examined in Chapter 5 of this book: Marx's critique of the Ricardian concept 'cost of production' in Chapter One of POP.

CHAPTER 5

1. 'On Proudhon' (Marx's letter to J. B. Schweitzer dated 24 January 1865), in Karl Marx-Friedrich Engels *Selected Works in three volumes*, Vol. 2, p. 26.
2. The Preface to *A Critique of Political Economy* (1859), in SW, p. 390.
3. Assertions concerning the formation of Marx's value theory fall into the following four types:

   a) *Continuity Type*: Marx retained his critical views on Ricardo's value theory from beginning to end:
   i) the early Marx's 'estranged labour' is not an economic theory as such but the basic philosophy which produced his theories later: see Shiro Sugihara, *Mill and Marx* (Kyoto, 1973);
   ii) the early Marx's 'estranged labour' is the 'general essence (*Wesen*) of private property' obtained through a two-fold reductive analysis of the immediate process of capitalist production, from which other economic categories are developed or explained: see Chapter 10.
   b) *Rupture Type*: Marx changed his views on Ricardo's labour theory of value in his intellectual development: Soviet Marxists and their Western followers assert that the early Marx 'denied' or 'negated' the labour theory of value in 1844, but 'accepted' or 'affirmed' it in later works, e.g., *The German Ideology* (1845) or POP.
   iii) Marx 'accepted' or 'affirmed' the Ricardian theory of value in POP, but no more and no less than that: this type, e.g., Ernest Mandel, in 'The Formation of the Economic Thought of Karl Marx' (*Monthly Review Press*, 1971), asserts that Marx became a Ricardian in POP (p. 49). In other words, Marx was not Marx yet, and the work belongs to the prehistory in his intellectual development. However, Mandel thinks that he has clarified Marx's development as such.
   iv) Marx not only 'accepted' or 'affirmed' Ricardo's value theory but also criticised it on some points in POP, because of 'the materialist conception of history': e.g., D.I. Rosenberg, *Die Entwicklung der ökonomischen Lehre von Marx und Engels in den vierziger Jahren des 19. Jahrhunderts* (Dietz, 1958).

   Evidently type iv) is superior to type iii) insofar as it refers to Marx's criticism of Ricardo in POP; but neither of these commentators grasps the purpose of POP. It is not Proudhon but Ricardo whom Marx is really criticising. Added to this, neither of them clarifies the interconnection between 'the materialist conception of history' and the affirmation of Ricardo's labour theory of value. They prove nothing in fact.

   The basis of types iii) and iv) has already been thoroughly criticised in my 'Ricardo's Method Re-examined', which clarifies Marx's methodological critique of Ricardo in POP. The point here is the *differentia specifica* of Marx's value theory. Marx's dialectical method, thus his whole system, has been poorly understood by commentators.
4. MEGA2, II-3, Teil 3, p. 816. *Theories of Surplus Value*, Part II, p. 165. See also Footnotes 33, 34 and 35 of CAP 1, pp. 173–6.
5. Marx's *Notes on Adolph Wagner*, in T. Carver, *Karl Marx: Texts on Method* (Basil Blackwell, 1975), p. 198. It was not until *Grundrisse* (1857–58) that Marx began his

presentation of economic categories with 'the commodity'. Before then, he planned to begin with 'Value' (See MEGA2, II-1, Teil 2, p. 740. G, p. 881). It should be noted, however, that this 'value' was not value as 'exchange-value' but rather the unity of use-value and exchange-value (See MEGA2, II-1,Teil 1, p. 190. G, p. 267).

6. *Works of David Ricardo*, Volume 1 (new edition, London: John Murray 1888), Chapter 1 § 4.
7. See Ricardo's 'Absolute Value and Exchangeable Value', in: *Works of David Ricardo*, Vol. 4, pp. 358–412. Marx criticises Ricardo's vain attempt as a necessary result of the methodological inadequacy of his analysis. According to Marx, Ricardo's 'relative value' has a two-fold meaning: 'exchangeable value as determined by labour time' and 'exchangeable value of a commodity in terms of the use-value of another'. Ricardo's 'absolute value' is nothing but 'relative value' in the first sense. The inadequacy of Ricardo's analysis is that 'he does not examine the form of value – the particular form which labour assumes as the (social) substance of value' (MEGA2, II-3, Teil 3, pp. 815f. *Theories of Surplus Value*, Part II, p. 164). See also n. 22 below.
8. Marx's *Notes on Adolph Wagner*, op. cit., p. 183.
9. Ibid, p. 183.
10. *Works of David Ricardo*, Volume 1, p. 88.
11. Ibid, p. 88.
12. Ibid, p. 47.
13. Ibid, p. 12.
14. Ibid, p. 36.
15. *Works of David Ricardo*, Vol. 2, p. 34.
16. *Works of David Ricardo*, Vol. 1, p. 38. Ricardo agrees to the following remark by Smith: 'The real price of every thing, what every thing really costs to the man who wants to acquire it, is the toil and trouble of acquiring it.' (*Wealth of Nations*, Modern Library, p. 30. *Works of David Ricardo*, Vol. 4, p. 397)
17. G, p. 101.
18. Ibid, p. 103.
19. Ibid, pp. 136f.
20. Ibid, p. 306.
21. CAP 1, p. 198. The translator's note on this term is incorrect and should be moved to page 133.
22. See Marx's *Notes on Adolph Wagner*, op. cit., p. 207. In *Capital*, Vol. 1, Marx writes:

    > Since the producers do not come into social contact until they exchange the products of their labour, the specific social characteristics of their private labours appear only within this exchange. In other words, the labour of the private individual manifests itself as an element of the total labour of society only through the relations which the act of exchange establishes between the products, and, through their mediation, between the producers (p. 165, see also p. 129).

    For the early Marx's conception of metabolism and exchange-value, see especially MEC 3, pp. 216f, 298f.
23. Marx's *Grundrisse* is well-known for 'Marx's theory of history', such as 'formations which precede the capitalist mode of production' (Pelican edition, pp. 161f). What is important is that Marx's theory of history is grounded in his critical analysis of capitalist relations, or economic categories, e.g., the commodity, money and capital. On the other hand, Marx does not deal with future society in any independent chapter. This is a necessary result of his method. Since society or property relations is nothing more than the sum total of the relations of production and commerce, as illustrated in Marx's critique of Proudhon's analysis of 'property' (e.g., MEC 38, pp. 99f and MEC 6, p. 197), it is wrong to give future society an independent *chapter*. This is the reason why Marx writes that Chapter 32 of *Capital*, Vol. 1, 'itself is nothing else but a general summary of long expositions previously given in the chapters on capitalist production'

(Marx's letter to Mikhailovsky in 1877, in SW, p. 571). To put it the other way round, his views on future society are developed in each section of his analysis of the economic categories.

24. *Notes on James Mill*, in MEC 3, p. 217.
25. Ibid.
26. 'Cost' used by political economists falls into the following three categories in Marx's terminology in *Capital*, Vol. 3:

    1) value determined by the quantity of labour bestowed on production;
    2) 'cost price', consisting of raw materials and wages, i.e., the original cost for producers; and
    3) 'production cost', consisting of the average wage and profit – the average 'price'.

    See n. 31 below.

27. *Works of David Ricardo*, Vol. 2, pp. 102f.
28. This is not Marx's misunderstanding but his way of re-casting Ricardo's value theory. From the scientific point of view or from the genetic presentation of economic categories, it is in this way that Ricardo's value theory should be interpreted if it is to have a scientific validity.
29. Comparing the slave and the wage labourer, Hegel writes that the latter sells his labour in terms of time (see his *Philosophy of Right*, §67). It seems obvious that Marx uses labour-time with Hegel in mind when he states: 'Thus relative value, measured by labour-time, is inevitably the formula of the modern enslavement of the worker, instead of being, as M. Proudhon would have it, the 'revolutionary theory' of the emancipation of the proletariat.' (MEC 6, p. 125)
30. *Works of David Ricardo*, Vol. 1, p. 30.
31. Ibid, p. 36.
32. Approaches to the 'transformation problem' in the English speaking world seem to me neo-Ricardian (M. C. Howard and J. E. King, *The Political Economy of Marx* (Longman, second edition, 1985, Chapter 8) and has little to do with Marx's dialectical method, i.e., the genetic presentation of economic categories.
33. Marx writes in the *Results of the Immediate Process of Production* that the value of a commodity as the result of capital cannot be measured, because 'The labour expended on each commodity can no longer be calculated – except as an average, i.e., an ideal estimate .... This labour, then, is reckoned ideally as an aliquot part of the total labour expended on it' (see Appendix to *Capital*, Vol.1, pp. 953, 954, 955, 966 and 969). Similarly, 'the labour-time ... socially necessary' in Chapter 1 of *Capital* cannot be measured because the exact 'socially necessary' time is not clear before the process of exchange. In Marx's phrase in *A Contribution to the Critique of Political Economy* (1859), 'it exists only potentially in commodities' or is 'an emerging result (*werdendes Resultat*).' (MEW 13, pp. 31f)

    This concept is the determination of the individual commodity 'only as an average sample of its kind'. (CAP 1, p. 130) It is only the starting-point in his presentation and is demonstrated through his analysis of the value form, or exchange-value. As Marx's warns in its Introduction, in his 'theoretical method too, the subject, society, must always be kept in mind as the presupposition'. (CAP 1, p. 102) The nub is to grasp the capitalist relations of production and commerce as an historical form of metabolism between man and nature, and between men. What Marx clarifies is the specific social character of the products of the labour of private individuals who work independently of each other. With regard to his concept 'value', it is merely the *Anfang* in order to avoid tautology. Engels' view on value expounded in the Appendix to *Capital*, Vol. 3 is quite wrong as an explanation of Marx's value theory. Marx's *A Contribution to the Critique of Political Economy* (1859) should be more frequently referred to, because 'points worked out fully there are only touched upon [in Chapter 1 of *Capital*]'. (CAP 1, p. 89)

34. Marx's critique of Ricardo's value theory in the 1840s consists of the following two aspects: 1) Ricardo's determination of exchange-value by 'cost, including profits' and 2) his abstraction away from competition in the determination of exchange-value.

As to 1): political economists employed 'cost of production' in the following three ways using Marx's terminology in *Capital*: 'value', 'cost price' and 'production price'. Ricardo's 'cost, including profits' is 'production cost', which consists of the average wage and profit. Thus his determination of value by 'cost', not by 'labour', should be criticised for making his presentation of economic categories a tautology. This is the point which Marx had been making since his first encounter with Ricardo in 1844, noting the inversion of 'value' and 'price' in the political economists (see Engels' *Outlines of A Critique of Political Economy*, 1843 in MEC 3, p. 427).

As to 2): Ricardo did not take account of the fluctuation in the elements of exchange-value when he said that the 'variations of the ... market price of commodities from ... natural price' are only 'accidental and temporary'. But, as Marx argues in POP, it is these variations which determine exchange-value by labour time. Thus, it is quite right for the early Marx to criticise Ricardo for making the law of value an abstract formula (see MEC 3, pp. 270f), i.e., not a necessary law of capital (see *Notes on James Mill*, in MEC 3, p. 211), as Marx emphasises in his *Wage Labour and Capital* (1849):

> This determination of price by cost of production is not to be understood in the sense of the economists. The economists say that the average price of commodities is equal to the cost of production; that this is a law. The anarchical movement, in which rise is compensated by fall and fall by rise, is regarded by them as chance .... But it is solely ... in the course of these fluctuations that prices are determined by the cost of production. (MEC 9, p. 208; see also MEC 6, p. 415)

The point is that this is the cause of the difference between Ricardo's 'the quantity of labour bestowed on production' and Marx's 'the labour time ... socially necessary' and is closely connected with the social character of labour which sets the context of the value of the commodity. The latter has to be derived from the process of exchange. This has been understood, however, as the negation of Ricardo's labour theory of value by commentators, e.g., by Mandel (see pages 41f of his *The Formation of the Economic Thought of Karl Marx: 1843 to Capital* (New York: Monthly Review Press, 1971).

This comes from their misunderstanding of value and exchange-value in *Capital* and of the texts of the early Marx. It seems very likely that they have never read Hegel, Proudhon or Say, because they do not understand Marx's phrase 'abstract law' or his comments on Proudhon and Say, let alone his 'critique'. The following passage from Marx's *Notes on James Mill* is only meaningful for those who really understand the confusing of value with price in classical political economy:

> '*How this value* is more precisely determined must be described elsewhere, as also how it *becomes price*.' (MEC 3, p. 219; italics added)

35. On Marx's proposition 'The natural price of labour is no other than the minimum wage' (MEC 6, p. 125), Engels notes in the German edition of POP (1885) that: 'In *Capital*, Marx has put the above thesis right'. However, this seems to be incorrect. 'Natural price', in contrast with market price, is the 'average' but also the 'lowest which can be taken ... for any considerable time together' (Smith's *Wealth of Nations*, Modern Library, p. 61).
36. CAP 1, p. 129. It is only in *Capital*, Vol. 3, that the social use-value of commodities is realised and the quantitatively specific social need for each particular kind of product is satisfied. (CAP 1, pp. 773f)
37. *Works of David Ricardo*, Volume 1, p. 11.

CHAPTER 6

1. First of all, EPM is the first result of Marx's studies of political economy , as Marx states in its Preface: 'It is hardly necessary to assure the reader who is familiar with political economy that I arrived at my conclusion through an entirely empirical analysis based on an exhaustive critical study of political economy.' (MEC 3, p. 231; EW, p. 281)

   Furthermore, readers may nominate *Wage-Labour and Capital* or *The Poverty of Philosophy* as the representative of his writings in the 1840s. However, compared with EPM, *Wage-Labour and Capital* is limited to his economic theories and in *The Poverty of Philosophy* 'the decisive points of our view' are indicated but not expounded. On the other hand, EPM represents his first system, a trinity of a critique of political economy, socialism and philosophy. See n. 2.
2. As EPM is the first result of his studies of political economy, Marx's concept 'estranged labour' is to be understood in the context of not only his critique of Hegelian philosophy but also of political economy and socialism. It is the core principle by which the conflict between political economy and socialism is transcended, i.e., the means of comprehending economic laws as necessary laws of capital. For detail, see next section.
3. I. Mészáros, *Marx's Theories of Alienation* (Merlin Press, 1970) is a brilliant and eye-opening exception.
4. Usually, Marx's extracts and notes on Hegel's *Phenomenology* is counted as the 'Fourth Manuscript' of EPM, but here I do not, because it differs from the other three manuscripts of EPM in character.
5. For detail, see next chapter.
6. N.I. Lapin, 'A Comparative Analysis of Three Origins of Income in the Economic Philosophical Manuscript by Marx', in *Deutsche Zeitschrift für Philosophy*, Heft 2, 17 Jahrgang, 1969.
7. See, for example, T. Carver, *Marx and Engels* (Wheatsheaf Books, 1983), pp. xi–xii.
8. The writing order of the 'Paris Manuscript' assumed by N.I. Lapin and the editor of MEGA2, I-2 (I. Taubert) can be schematised as follows:

   1) *Notes on Say*, *Notes on Smith*, then the 'First Manuscript', then *Notes on Ricardo*, *Notes on James Mill*, then the 'Second Manuscript', the 'Third Manuscript'.
   2) *Notes on Say*, *Notes on Smith*, then EPM, and then *Notes on Ricardo*, *Notes on James Mill*.

   In his report 'The Case of the So-Called *Economic Philosophical Manuscripts of 1844*' at Linz in 1983, J. Rojahn agrees with Lapin's ordering. MEGA2, IV-2, seems confused in suggesting that, on the one hand, *Notes on Ricardo*, *Notes on James Mill* followed by the 'Second Manuscript', the 'Third Manuscript', and that, on the other hand, EPM followed by *Notes on Ricardo*, *Notes on James Mill*.
9. The 'devaluation of man' means the transformation of the slave into a free-worker, i.e., wage-labourer. See G, p. 289.
10. See the third paragraph of Chapter 5 of *The Wealth of Nations*, The Modern Library, New York, 1937.
11. Ibid.
12. *The Wealth of Nations*, op.cit., p. 48. *Works of David Ricardo*, Volume IV, pp. 365f.
13. See, for example, MEW, Bd. 4, Berlin, 1959, p. 337.
14. Profit is often explained from the abuse of human rights. However, Marx does not agree with that. See, for example, quotations from Pecqueur's *Théorie sociale* in MEC 3, p. 255; EW, p. 305.
15. This rent theory is in the Ricardian but not in the Smithian. Although Ricardo is not directly referred in the 'FM: FP', Marx is a Ricardian rather than a Smithian.
16. Later (in Appendix II), I will explore this point. There are no reasonable grounds for the assertion that Marx 'negated' or 'rejected' the classical labour theory of value. If

readers examine all of Marx's quotations from *The Wealth of Nations*, they will find that all of them are based on the 'dissolving' value theory.

17. It is careless and simplistic to comment that the first and second stages are not consistent or that Marx changed his original plan here.
18. *The Wealth of Nations*, op.cit., p. 61.
19. Here Marx is closer to Ricardo than to Smith. This also indicates that Marx had already read Ricardo's *Principle of Political Economy and Taxation* before he wrote the 'FM: FP'.
20. This is the core of Marx's view on 'competition', which enables him to comprehend the intrinsic connection between 'capital' and 'competition'. Almost the same view can be seen in his *Notes on Ricardo*.
21. See also n. 20 above. This is very important when we examine Marx's views on the classical labour theory of value in 1844. Marx is very consistent in his theories and each theory has an intrinsic connection with others. See also Marx's critique of political economists' views on 'competition' in the 'FM: LP'. (MEC 3, p. 271; EW, p. 323)
22. From this point of view, Marx says 'competition' is the 'driving force' of the laws of capital. See also nn. 20 and 21 above.
23. See also MEC 3, pp. 293f; EW, p. 345.
24. None of them seems to understand the philosophic term 'abstraction'.
25. Both grounds are concerned with *Notes on Ricardo* in 1844 but not with EPM. See, for example, Chapter 4 of W. Tuchscheerer, *Bevor 'Das Kapital' entstand*, Akademie-Verlag, Berlin, 1968.
26. *The Wealth of Nations*, op. cit., p. 60.
27. Ibid, p. 268.
28. Kyuzo Asobe, 'The Early Marx and Smith' – no English translation, in *The Formation of the Wealth of Nations* (Tokyo: Iwanami-shoten, 1976), p. 329. (Edited and published by the Japanese Association for the History of Economic Theories.)
29. Shigeji Wada, *The System of Adam Smith's 'The Wealth of Nations'*, Mineruba-shobo (Kyoto, 1978), p. 308.
30. The weak point of Engels' critique of classical labour theory of value is that he is not as consistent as Marx in understanding the economic categories as the theoretical expression of historical relations of production. See Chapter 9.

CHAPTER 7

1. Kenji Mizutani, *Alienation of Labour and Marx's Economics* (Tokyo, 1974), p. 39.
2. The translation is my own.
3. Fumio Hattori, *The Formation of Marxism* (Tokyo, 1987), p. 177.
4. The translation is my own. This is a determination of the 'relation of the non-worker to the worker and to the product of his labour'. This is well connected with the third consideration at the end of the 'FM: LP': 'Thirdly, the non-worker does every thing against the worker which the worker does against himself; but he does not do against himself what he does against the worker.' (MEC 3, p. 282; EW, p. 334)
5. Some Japanese economists criticise Marx for not distinguishing 'private property' from 'capital'. This is because they misunderstand the meaning of 'private property' here. And what is more, they do not understand that 'capital' should be explained from the appropriation of labour of the worker in the production process. 'Capital is a command over alien labour' in the production process. This is the first concept of capital by Marx, which is commonly found in private property in general. See the opening words of the 'Profit of Capital' column in the 'FM: FP':

> What is the basis of capital, that is, of private property in the products of other men's labour ... How does one become a proprietor of productive stock? How does one become owner of the products created by means of a large fortune, for instance, ...

> Capital is thus the power to command labour and its products. (MEC 3, pp. 246f; EW, p. 295)

> This latent slavery in the family, though still crude, is the first form of property, but even at this stage it corresponds perfectly to the definition of modern economists, who call it the power of disposing of the labour power of others. (MEC 5, p. 46)

> In the first case, therefore, property (landed property) appears as direct natural domination, in the second, as domination of labour, particularly of accumulated labour, capital. (MEC 5, p. 63)

6. The appropriation of alien labour by capital means the self-realisation of capital. Capital realises itself only through the self-estrangement of the worker. Marx writes:

   > Thus [in political economy] capital does not originally realize itself – precisely because the appropriation of alien labour (*fremde Arbeit*) is not itself included in its concept. Capital appears only afterwards, after already having been presupposed as capital – a vicious circle – as command over alien labour. Thus, according to A. Smith, labour should actually have its own product for wages, wages should be to the product, hence labour should not be wage labour and capital not capital. (G, p. 330)

7. See MEC 3, pp. 241–6; EW, pp. 288–95.
8. *Tableau Économique* (London: Macmillan, 1972), originally published 1766.

CHAPTER 8

1. Seiji Mochizuki sees a rupture between the two manuscripts and asserts that Marx gave up his original plan after writing the 'Second Manuscript'. Here I will argue against Mochizuki through all my investigations of the 'Third Manuscript'.
2. In my opinion, I. Mészáros, *Marx's Theory of Alienation* (4th edition, London: Merlin Press, 1975) is the only work which really understands EPM. See his investigation of the Preface to EPM. Usually Marx's notes on Hegel's *Phenomenology* are contained as the 'Fourth Manuscript', but this is not right, not only because the character of it differs from others but also because Marx calls the 'Critique of Hegel's Dialectic and Philosophy in General' the 'concluding chapter of the present work'. (MEC 3, p. 232; EW, p. 281)
3. The first part of the 'Critique of Hegel's Philosophy and Philosophy in General' – MEC 3, pp. 326–31 (line 7 from the bottom) – was written between the 'Private Property and Communism' and the 'Needs, Production and Division of Labour'. The second part of it – MEC 3, pp. 331–2, line 4 from the bottom – belongs to MEC 3, p. 312, line 6. The remaining part goes to MEC 3, p. 316, line 4 from the bottom.
4. See MEC 3, p. 291; EW, p. 342. This implies that Marx regards the English political economy as 'the scientific reflection of the state of the economy in England' (EW, p. 406). He regards the principle of political economy as that of modern civil society (capitalist society), the cynicism of political economists is that of capitalist society itself and that capitalist society is the mere political emancipation of man but not 'universal human emancipation'. (EW, p. 253) This is very important in understanding Marx's system and its purpose (see *Critique of Hegel's Philosophy of Right: Introduction*).
5. *Grundrisse*, Pelican edition, p. 414.
6. An insertion in Marx's hand on page 18 of *The German Ideology*.
7. See Norman Geras, *Marx & Human Nature* (New Left Books (NLB), 1983).
8. The distinction between the 'essence (or nature) of private property' and the 'concept of private property' is crucial for a full understanding of Marx's system. For more imformation, see Chapter 10.

9. See *Notes on James Mill*, EW, pp. 274–8. Marx's concept of 'absolute poverty' (MEC 3, p. 300; EW, p. 352) is to be understood in this context.
10. See MEC 3, pp. 304 and 337; EW, pp. 355 and 391 and GI (MEC 5, pp. 87f). In the Preface to the first edition of *Capital*, Volume 1, Marx writes that 'his standpoint' views 'the development of the economic formation of society' as 'a process of natural history' (CAP 1, p. 92). 'Natural history' there should be understood in the sense here as in EPM. (MEC 3, pp. 303f and 337; EW, pp. 355 and 391).

    Furthermore, it is also noteworthy that here Marx refers to 'the science of geogeny (*Geognosie*), i.e., the science which depicts the formation of the earth, its coming into being, as a process of self-generation'. (MEC 3, p. 305; EW, p. 356). Key terms in the 'guiding thread' for Marx's works in the Preface to *A Contribution to the Critique of Political Economy* (1859), such as 'formation', 'progressive epochs', are technical terms in geology and show that hitherto the 'thread' has been misunderstood. See Chapter 10.
11. The title of this section should be 'Production and Consumption in Socialism'. See the summary of this section in the opening paragraph of the 'Needs, Production and Division of Labour'. (MEC 3, p. 306; EW, p. 358)
12. For a full understanding of the meaning of 'abstract', see the 'Second Manuscript', especially MEC 3, pp. 285f; EW, pp. 335ff.
13. See MEC 3, p. 312; EW, p. 364 and *A Contribution to the Critique of Political Economy* (MEW 13, pp. 40f).
14. The text used to be read as 'species-spirit' but is officially corrected to 'species-enjoyment' as pointed out by Suguru Hosomi. See the following sentence in the quotation and other similar sentences (MEC 3, pp. 298 and 333; EW, pp. 350 and 386).
15. The modes of the division of labour are the modes of private property, and vice versa. See GI, especially MEC 5, pp. 32, 46, 74 and 86. For detail see Chapter 2.
16. In Marxian economics 'exploitation' is distinguished from 'plundering' which is not mediated by equal exchange.
17. The Preface to *A Contribution to the Critique of Political Economy* (1859), in SW, p. 390. This sort of proposition is unhelpful unless we understand it with regard to Marx's theoretical system.
18. MEGA2, I-2, assumes that *Notes on Ricardo* and *Notes on James Mill* were written after 'Money'. One of the reasons is that the editor , I. Taubert, thinks that Marx's views on money are sharper in *Notes on James Mill* than in 'Money' (Inge Taubert, 'Probleme und Fragen zur Datierung der "Ökonomisch-politischen Manuscripte" von Karl Marx', in *Beiträge zur Marx-Engels-Forschung*, 3, Berlin, 1978). She overlooks the authorial purposes of the two works.

CHAPTER 9

1. SW, p. 390.
2. Ibid.
3. For detail see n. 4 in Chapter 5. T. Carver, 'Marx and Engels's "Outlines of a critique of Political Economy"', in *History of Political Thought*, Vol. IV, No.2, 1983.
4. *Theories of Surplus Value*, Part III (Progress Publishers, 1972), p. 500.
5. Marx's letter to Kugelman dated 11 July, 1868.
6. J.R. McCulloch, *The Principles of Political Economy* (London, 1830).
7. Engels sees the highest pitch of the immorality of the economists in Malthus. See MEC 3, pp. 437f.
8. For more information on the concepts 'estranged labour' and 'command', see n.5 in Chapter 6.
9. *Theories of Surplus Value*, Part III, op.cit., p. 259.
10. For more information on the concepts 'estranged labour' and 'command', see n.5 in Chapter 6.

11. *Theories of Surplus Value*, Part III, op.cit., p. 259.
12. Ibid.
13. See Chapter 10.
14. G, p. 105.
15. See MEC 3, p. 288; EW, p. 340. *Grundrisse* is famous for its concept 'the civilizing tendencies of capital', but it is not in *Grundrisse* that Marx formulated the concept for the first time. That which we should notice is that this concept is based on the 'essence of capital'.
16. The last few decades saw some assumptions on the writing order of Marx's *Notes on Ricardo, Notes on James Mill*, EPM. Irrespective of the order, EPM is not just a collection of notes such as *Notes on Ricardo, Notes on James Mill*. Each section of EPM is intrinsically connected. EPM is really worthy of being called 'manuscripts'. However, *The German Ideology* is a mere collection of notes. See Appendix I.
17. Thus there is no wonder that Soviet Marxists have made all efforts to separate the parts of EPM and to deny the concept 'estranged labour'. EPM is more instructive and critical in understanding Marx's system of political economy, philosophy and socialism (including Soviet socialism) than any other works.
18. See, for example, MEC 3, pp. 216f and his criticism of 'crude communism' in MEC 3, pp. 294ff.
19. MEC 3, pp. 221 and 312; EW, pp. 270 and 364.
20. Marx agreed publication with Leske of his two volumes of *A Critique of Politics and Political Economy*, on 1 February 1845. In the first half of October 1844, in his letter to Marx, Engels urged Marx to finish the work as soon as possible. However, Marx did not follow this suggestion. This indicates the difference in thoroughness between them.
21. See Marx's concept 'abstraction' below.
22. On the production in future relations Engels writes: 'Carry on production consciously as human beings – not as dispersed atoms without consciousness of your species – and you have overcome all these artificial and untenable antitheses.' (MEC 3, p. 434)
23. Marx's brief summary of OCPE is contained in MEGA2, IV-2, pp. 485–8.
24. In the manuscript 'value' has been written above 'price'. This does not mean that Marx confused the two concepts. On the contrary, this is a good example that he distinguished 'value' from 'price' at this stage of his study.
25. See Chapter 5.
26. 'Labour time' can be found in Engels' OCPE. The origin of this term is in Hegel's *Philosophy of Right*.
27. MEGA2, IV-2, p. 404.

CHAPTER 10

1. I need not remind readers that this chapter suggests indirectly what should be done away with in modern capitalism and 'existing socialism' in China, another daughter of Soviet Marxism.
2. In his *Critique of the Gotha Programme* (1875) Marx distinguished 'a communist society ... just as it emerges from capitalist society' (MEC 24, p. 85) from 'a communist society ... as it has developed on its own foundations' (ibid.). Lenin termed these 'socialism' and 'communism'.

   Although these are widely accepted, I do not follow this terminology here, but rather Marx's in EPM where 'socialism as socialism' is taken to be higher than 'communism' which requires the negation of private property.

   Engels called himself a communist to distinguish himself from the French reformists known as 'socialists' in the 1840s. However, as far as Marx is concerned, communism and socialism as used here have the same meaning.

3. Also Marx's *Secret Diplomatic History of the Eighteenth Century* and *The Story of the Life of Lord Palmerston* (edited and with introduction and notes by Lester Hutchinson, Lawrence & Wishart, London, 1969) is included.
4. Engels adds 'trust' to these in his *Socialism: Utopian and Scientific* (1891). See MEC.
5. Engels uses the term 'in the hands of the producers working together'once in the present version of AD. (MEC 25, p. 267) This is a supplement to the fourth edition of his *Socialism: Utopian and Scientific*. To be fair, Marx actually writes 'in the hands of the State' in *The Communist Manifesto*. However, the 'State' here is equivalent to the 'individuals', because he explains it as 'i.e., of the proletariat organised as the ruling class'. (MEC 6, p. 504)
6. Marx wrote the first and second German edition and the French version of *Capital*. The reason why I quote the second German edition of *Capital* here is that the underlined sentences are modified in the present German and the English editions.
7. CAP 1, p. 283.
8. Ibid, p. 284.
9. Ibid, p. 285.
10. Ibid, p. 290.
11. See also MEC 3, pp. 276f.
12. CAP 1, p. 447.
13. Ibid, p. 424.
14. Kunihiko Uemura asserts that Marx's concepts 'association', 'individual property', etc., were pioneered by Adolf Schulz. In Schulz, however, 'individual property' is based on the very low stage of German industries in the 1840s and an 'association' of workers is not the positive abolition of 'the nature of capital' at all. On the other hand, Marx's 'association' is to be based on the co-operation was which developed to the extreme by capital and is equivalent to the positive abolition of 'the nature of capital'. In this sense, for Marx, Shulz is an utopian socialist rather than a pioneer. Marx writes in EPM: 'Association, applied to land, shares the economic advantage of large-scale landed property, and first brings to realisation the original tendency inherent in [land] division, namely, equality.' (MEC 3, p. 268)
15. CAP 1, p. 171.
16. Ibid, p. 166.
17. See Marx's critique of the 'community of women' (MEC 3, p. 294 and MEC 6, p. 502).
18. MEGA2, II-2, p .54. See also MEC 3, pp. 298 and 312f.
19. Equality between the sexes and between the labours are the basis for this. See the section '[C] VIII Positive Aspect of Wage Labour' of *Wages* (1847):

    > Secondly: the halo of sanctity is entirely gone from all relationships of the old society, since they have been resolved into pure money relationships. Likewise, all so-called higher kinds of labour, intellectual, artistic, etc., have been turned into articles of commerce and have thereby lost their old sanctity. (MEC 6, p. 436. See also MEC 3, pp. 285–8)

    Marx's communism, as the reorganisation of man's relation to nature and to other men, is a critique of Christianity.
20. See 'two questions'. (MEC 3, p. 241) These two questions are answered 'on the basis of the above exposition, which has been presented almost in the words of the political economists' in the quotations which follow. See 'two other problems'. (MEC 3, p. 281) The way in which the 'First Manuscript' ends does suggest that Marx tries to solve those problems through an analysis of the 'property relation of capitalist' in the 'Second Manuscript'. See the 'distinction between ... immovable and movable private property' (MEC 3, pp. 285–9) which shows the 'necessary victory of the capitalists over the landowners'. (MEC 3, p. 288) See 'the movement through which these constituents [labour and capital] have to pass'. (MEC 3, p. 289). See 'the antithesis

between lack of property and property'. (MEC 3, pp. 293f). See also the 'examination of division of labour and exchange'. (MEC 3, p. 321)

21. Compare Marx's notes in *Notes on Say* with Say's original text (MEGA2, IV-2, pp. 316–9). Marx's 'private property' is Say's 'right of private property'. In other words, Marx is explaining the genesis of the 'right of private property'.
22. The following section '3. The Rule of Capital over Labour and the Motives of the Capitalist' has nothing but quotations from Smith and Say. However, we can understand Marx's intention in the section through the quotations, i.e., 'the plans and speculations of the employers of capital regulates and direct all the most important operations of labour, and profit is the end proposed by all those plans and projects.' (MEC 3, p. 250)
23. MEGA2, II-3, p. 1433. *Theories of Surplus Value*, Vol. III, Progress Publishers, pp. 297 and 306.
24. SW, p. 568.
25. MEGA2, II-3, p. 1389. *Theories of Surplus Value*, III, Progress Publishers, p. 259.
26. Engels misleadingly named this the 'materialist interpretation' of history. Marx himself, on the other hand, calls this in the Preface to *A Contribution to the Critique of Political Economy* (1859) 'the general result at which I arrived and which, once won, served as a guiding thread for my study'. I would like to examine this dissimilarity in the near future. The point is in re-reading it as Marx's method of his system (a critique of political economy).
27. Marx writes that 'Hegel's standpoint is that of modern political economy'. (MEC 3, p. 333) Because the only labour Hegel knows and recognises is the present form of labour (wage labour) and he does not see it as estranged labour. Unless the estranged labour is abolished Hegel's real man does not come out through human labour.
28. The text used to be read as 'species-spirit' but is officially corrected as 'species-enjoyment' as pointed out by Suguru Hosomi. See the following sentence in the quotation and other similar sentences (MEC 3, pp. 298 and 333).

APPENDIX I

1. Wataru Hiromatsu, 'The Editing Problem of *The German Ideology*', in *The Formation of Marxism* (Shiseisha: Tokyo, 1974).
2. To be accurate, *The German Ideology* was not written solely by Marx and Engels. 'Doctor Georg Kuhlmann of Holstein' or The Prophecies of True Socialism' is in J. Weydemeyer's hand and 'M. Hess' is written at the end. See Footnote 143 of MEC 5, p. 606.
3. 'Preface' to *A Contribution to the Critique of Political Economy* (1859), in SW, p. 390.
4. Hiromatsu's *The German Ideology* (Kodansha-shinsha, Tokyo, 1974) reproduces the original texts of GI both in German and in Japanese, but notes are in Japanese only. Although G.A. Bagaturija's new Russian edition and a Japanese edition derived from it were published in 1965 and 1966 respectively, they are still not scientific enough. Hiromatsu's edition clarifies insertions and handwriting by using different typefaces.
5. This edition completely omits page [27] of the original. Compare op.cit., p. 60 with MEC 5, pp. 55ff.
6. See the second paragraph of 'II Saint Bruno'. (Saint Bruno: Bruno Bauer; Saint Max: Max Stirner.)
7. In fact, {1} is half a sheet.
8. See Probeband (1972) of MEGA2 and G.A. Bagaturija's new Russian edition (in: *Problems of Philosophy*, October-November of 1965), place {B} before {6}. The latter arranges the manuscripts as: {1}-{2}-{1?}c~d-{2?}-{3}-{4}-{5}-{B}-{6}- {7}-{8}-{9}-{10}-{11}-{20}-{21}-{84}-{85}-{86}-{87}-{88}-{89}-{90}-{91}-{92}. This arrangement is persuasive, except the position of {B}.

   MEC 5 (1976), also places {B} before {6} (see p. 38).
9. MEW 2, p. 254.

10. This part differs a great deal from {3} and {4} which is almost the same as the so-called 'formations which precede capitalist mode of production' in *Grundrisse*, Marx's manuscripts of 1857–1858. Thus I believe this part was written by Engels. C. Arthur's 'Student Edition' places [41] after [64] (see, op.cit., p. 91).
11. Hiromatsu completely misunderstands the structure of GI. According to him, the main body of chapter 'B' is 'the description of the history of the division of labour, or of the forms of property' (*The Formation of Marxism*, op.cit., p. 188). For him, the second chapter of GI has nothing to do with Feuerbach, and there is no chapter on Feuerbach in GI.

APPENDIX II

1. There are two assumptions on dating Marx's start of studying political economy: in the autumn of 1843 and in the spring of 1844. Judging from Marx's interest in political economy, I think it was in the year of 1843.
2. By the term 'classical political economy', commentators often understand Smith through Ricardo to James Mill, but here is a diversion from Marx. He states in *A Contribution to the Critique of Political Economy* (1859):

   > Analysing commodities into two forms of labour, use-value into real and properly carried labour, and exchange-value into labour-time or equal social labour, is the last product of critical examination of one and half centuries long classical political economy, which starts with William Petty in England, with Boisguillebert in France, and ends with Ricardo in England and with Sismondi in France. (MEW 13, p. 37)

3. See, for example, Chapter X of *Theories of Surplus Value*, Part III (Progress Publishers: Moscow, 1968).
4. See, for example, E. Mandel, 'The formation of Economic Thought of Karl Marx', *Monthly Review Press*, 1971.
5. Here I take up EPM and POP not only because the term can be found there but also because both works show the continuity of the early and late Marx in method, thought and theories.
6. See MEC 3, p. 193; EW, p. 406; MEW 1, p. 396.
7. See MEC 3, p. 291; EW, p. 342. With regard to this, Smith is termed 'the Luther of political economy', because he transcended a condition external to man and transformed the essence of private property into man, i.e., labour.
8. See n.7 above.
9. In fact, this is the opening paragraph of the 'FM: LP' (the so-called part 'Estranged Labour'). Because this is only a summary of the 'FM: FP', we can conclude with a reasonable certainty that Marx thinks so anywhere in EPM.
10. CAP 1, p. 928.
11. CAP 1, p. 929.
12. In Marx's terminology, 'exploitation' is distinguished from 'usurpation' which is not mediated by equal exchange.
13. For detail, see Chapter 7 of this book.
14. See Chapter 7 of this book.
15. See the third section of Chapter 10 of this book.

INDEX

Works by Marx and Engels are listed by title.

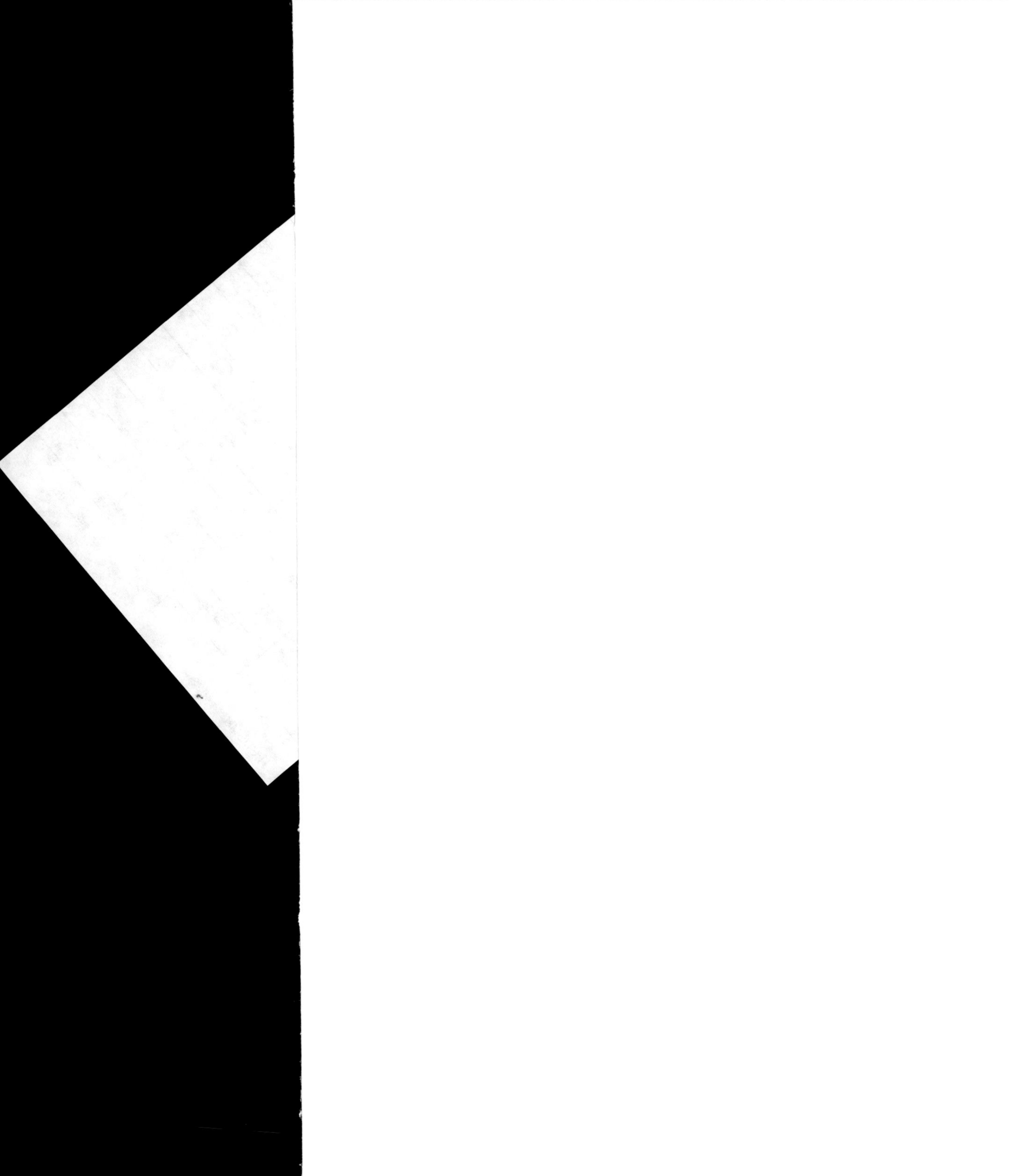

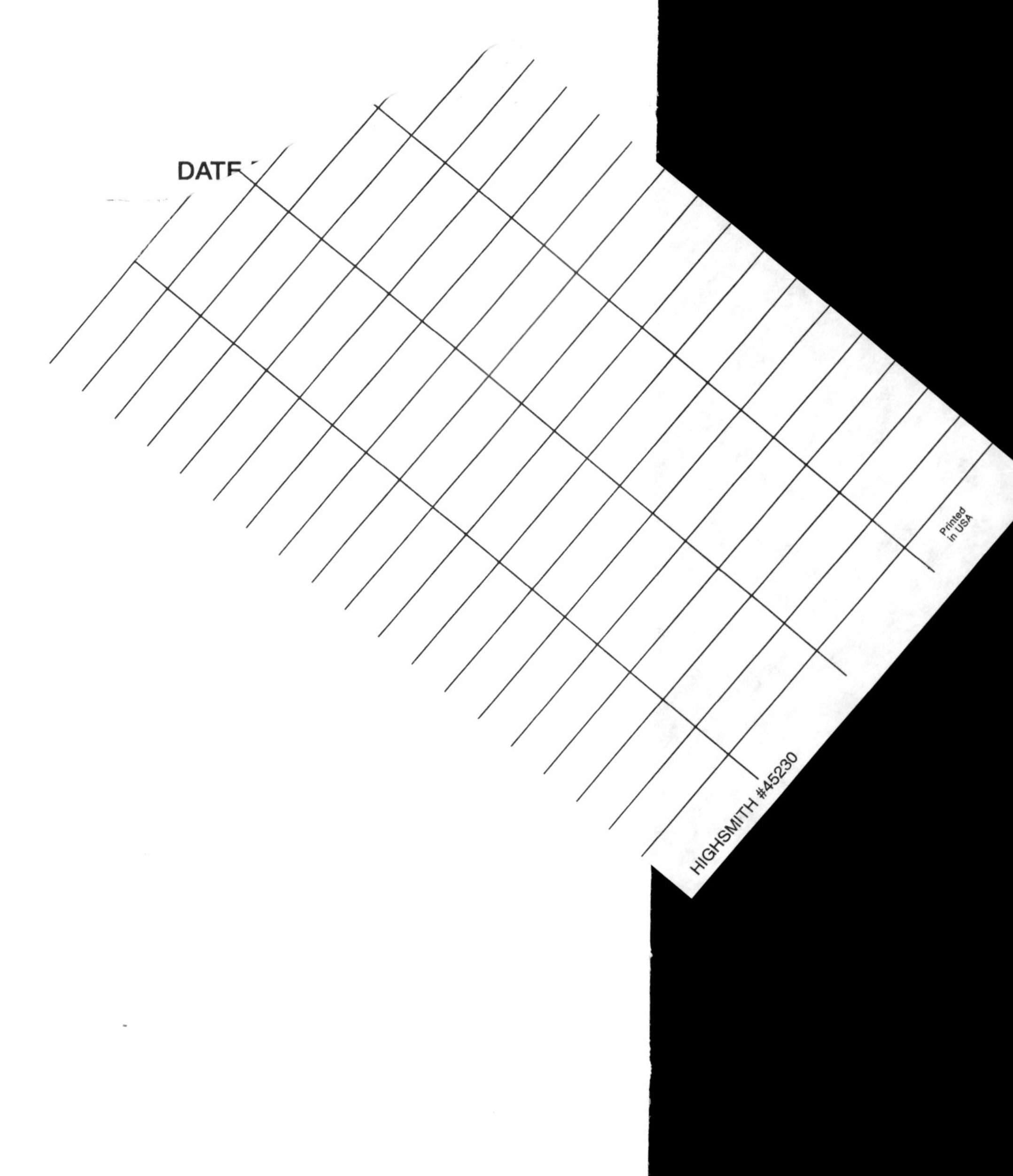
HIGHSMITH #45230
Printed in USA